Handbook of E-Tourism

Handbook of E-Tourism

Jayant Choksi
Meenakshi S

2026

Agri Horti Press
New Delhi-110 084

ISBN: 978-93-49690-64-6 (Hardbound)

Published By
Agri Horti Press
New Delhi
E-mail: agrihortipress@gmail.com
Digitally Printed at : Replika Press Pvt. Ltd.

Preface

Handbook of E-Tourism explores the dynamic intersection of digital technologies and the tourism industry, offering a comprehensive examination of how electronic platforms, tools, and systems are transforming travel behavior, tourism marketing, destination management, and service delivery. Designed for students, scholars, industry professionals, and policymakers, this volume provides both foundational knowledge and critical insights into the evolving landscape of e-tourism.

As global connectivity continues to grow, tourism has increasingly integrated digital innovations to enhance efficiency, accessibility, and user experience. From online travel agencies and booking systems to virtual tours, AI-driven customer service, and personalized travel planning through big data analytics, the shift to e-tourism has redefined the way destinations are promoted and how tourists interact with them. This transformation has been accelerated further by changing consumer expectations and the necessity of digital adaptation in response to global challenges such as the COVID-19 pandemic.

This handbook is structured to address key components and emerging trends within e-tourism. Initial chapters focus on the conceptual foundations of e-tourism, including the evolution of tourism technologies, digital consumer behavior, and the theoretical frameworks underpinning electronic service adoption in the travel sector. These chapters provide the context for understanding the broader impacts of digitization on the tourism value chain.

Subsequent sections explore specific technological applications such as destination management systems (DMS), geographic information systems (GIS), mobile applications, social media platforms, and blockchain-based transaction systems. Special emphasis is placed on digital marketing strategies, user-generated content, and reputation management, all of which have become central to influencing travel decisions and enhancing destination visibility.

The book also investigates the role of data in e-tourism, covering topics such as data analytics, personalization algorithms, privacy concerns, and ethical considerations in data-driven service provision. By presenting case studies from around the world, it illustrates how destinations leverage data to tailor experiences and make informed managerial decisions.

Attention is also given to virtual and augmented reality technologies, smart tourism infrastructure, and the integration of Internet of Things (IoT) in enhancing real-time services and sustainable practices. These developments are considered within the context of "smart destinations" and the broader shift toward responsible, inclusive, and technologically enabled tourism ecosystems.

The concluding chapters discuss the challenges and opportunities associated with e-tourism, including digital divides, cybersecurity, regulatory frameworks, and future innovations. These reflections are essential for understanding the balance between technological advancement and equitable access in a globally diverse tourism market.

Throughout this handbook, interdisciplinary perspectives are emphasized to highlight the interconnectedness of tourism, information systems, communication studies, economics, and sustainability. Each chapter draws on current research and practice, aiming to provide actionable insights as well as conceptual clarity.

We express our appreciation to the contributors, researchers, and professionals whose work has informed this volume. It is our aspiration that Handbook of E-Tourism serves as a valuable resource for those seeking to understand, implement, or innovate within the digital dimensions of tourism.

Jayant Choksi
Meenakshi S

Contents

1

Introduction

Tourism is travel for recreational, leisure, or business purposes. The World Tourism Organization defines tourists as people "traveling to and staying in places outside their usual environment for not more than one consecutive year for leisure, business and other purposes".

Tourism has become a popular global leisure activity. After slowly recovering from the contraction resulting from the late-2000s recession, where tourism suffered a strong slowdown from the second half of 2008 through the end of 2009, and the the outbreak of theH1N1 influenza virus, international tourist arrivals surpassed the milestone 1 billion tourist globally for first time in history in 2012. International tourism receipts (the travel item of the balance of payments) grew to US$1.03 trillion (€740 billion) in 2011, corresponding to an increase in real terms of 3.8% from 2010. In 2012, China became the largest spender in international tourism globally with US$102 billion, surpassing Germanyand United States. China and emerging markets significantly increase their spending over the past decade, with Russia and Brazil as noteworthy examples.

Tourism is important, and in some cases, vital for many countries. It was recognized in the Manila Declaration on World Tourism of 1980 as "an activity essential to the life of nations because of its direct effects on the social, cultural, educational, and economic sectors of national societies and on their international relations." Tourism brings in large amounts of income in payment for goods and services available, accounting for 30% of the world's exports of services, and 6% of overall exports of goods and services. It also creates opportunities for employment in the service sector of the economy, associated with tourism. These service industries includetransportation services, such as airlines, cruise ships, and taxicabs; hospitality services, such as accommodations, including hotelsand resorts; and entertainment venues, such as amusement parks, casinos, shopping malls, music venues, and theatres.

Theobald (1994) suggested that "etymologically, the word tour is derived from the Latin, 'tornare' and the Greek, 'tornos', meaning 'a lathe or circle; the movement around a central point or axis'. This meaning changed in modern English to represent 'one's turn'. The suffix -ism is defined as 'an action or process; typical behaviour or quality', while the suffix, -ist denotes 'one that performs a given action'. When the word tour and the suffixes -ism and -ist are combined, they suggest the action of movement around a circle.

One can argue that a circle represents a starting point, which ultimately returns back to its beginning. Therefore, like a circle, a tour represents a journey in that it is a round-trip, i.e., the act of leaving and then returning to the original starting point, and therefore, one who takes such a journey can be called a tourist."

In 1941, Hunziker and Krapf defined tourism as people who travel "the sum of the phenomena and relationships arising from the travel and stay of non-residents, insofar as they do not lead to permanent residence and are not connected with any earning activity."In 1976, the Tourism Society of England's definition was: "Tourism is the temporary, short-term movement of people to destinationoutside the places where they normally live and work and their activities during the stay at each destination. It includes movements for all purposes." In 1981, the International Association of Scientific Experts in Tourism defined tourism in terms of particular activities selected by choice and undertaken outside the home. In 1994, the United Nations classified three forms of tourism in itsRecommendations on Tourism Statistics:

- Domestic tourism, involving residents of the given country traveling only within this country.
- Inbound tourism, involving non-residents traveling in the given country.
- Outbound tourism, involving residents traveling in another country.

Today, three schools discuss on the roots of tourism. The French School, led by A. Houlot argued that the term tourism comes from the old Aramaic Tur, which was used for the trip, exploration and movement of people in the Bible. This word had been used, for the first time, when Moses begins his expedition to the lands of Canaán. Nevertheless, another school of thought - the Onomastic School - considers the origin of the concept not from a linguistic perspective but rather links it to the last name of the French aristocracy Della Tour.

According to this school, after Carlos V signs a treaty with England in 1516, in celebration of this event, the future king gives the Della Tour family exclusive rights to conduct commercial transport and related businesses. Last but not least, a third school focuses on the Anglo-saxon world, situating the Theobald´s development under the lens of scrutiny. Surmising that the roots of the word tourism comes from the Ancient Anglo-saxon term Torn, these scholars found evidence to think the term was coined in XIIth century which by farmers to denote those travels with intentions to return.

Over centuries, the meaning of the word has been shifted to be politically adopted. By the middle of the 18th century, the English noblemen used the term "turn" to refer to the trips undertaken for education, search and culture exploration. In reality, the purpose of the noblemen's trip to the different parts of Kingdom was to acquire knowledge that was later useful for governing.

E-TOURISM

Travel technology (also called tourism technology, and hospitality automation) is the application of Information Technology (IT) or Information and Communications Techno-logy (ICT) in the travel, tourism and hospitality industry. One form of travel technology is flight tracking.

Since travel implies locomotion, travel technology was originally associated with the computer reservations system (CRS) of the airlines industry, but now is used more inclusively, incorporating the broader tourism sector as well as its subset the hospitality industry. While travel technology includes the computer reservations system, it also represents a much broader range of applications, in fact increasingly so. Travel technology includes virtual tourism in the form of virtual tourtechnologies. Travel technology may also be referred to as *e-travel / etravel* or *e-tourism / etourism* (eTourism), in reference to "electronic travel" or "electronic tourism".

eTourism can be defined as the analysis, design, implemen-tation and application of IT and e-commerce solutions in the travel&tourism industry; as well as the analysis of the respective economic processes and market structures and customer relationship management.

From a communication science perspective, eTourism can be also defined as every application of Information and Communication Technologies (ICTs) within both the hospitality and tourism industry, as well as within the tourism experience. Travel technology is increasingly being used to describe systems for managing and monitoring travel, including travel tracking and flight tracking systems.

In other contexts, the term "travel technology" can refer to technology intended for use by travelers, such as light-weight laptop computers with universal power supplies or satellite Internet connections. That is not the sense in which it is used here.

Applications

Travel technology includes many processes such as dynamic packaging which provide useful new options for consumers. Today the tour guide can be a GPS tour guide, and the guidebook could be an audioguide, podguide or I-Tours, such asCity audio guides. The biometric passport may also be included as travel technology in the broad sense.

XML-based technologies have become increasingly important for the travel industry. XML can be used to support air reservation booking or to implement optional services and merchandising functions in the booking process. Another important application of XML is the establishing of direct connections between Airlines and Travel Agencies. In order to create a generally accepted XML-standard, the Open Axis Group was founded.

INFORMATION AND COMMUNICATIONS TECHNOLOGY

Information and communications technology (ICT) is often used as an extended synonym for information technology(IT), but is a more specific term that stresses the role of unified communications and the integration oftelecommunications (telephone lines and wireless signals), computers as well as necessary enterprise software, middleware, storage, and audio-visual systems, which enable users to access, store, transmit, and manipulate information.

The term *ICT* is also used to refer to the convergence of audio-visual and telephone networks with computer networksthrough a single cabling or link system. There are large economic incentives (huge cost savings due to elimination of the telephone network) to merge the telephone network with the computer network system using a single unified system of cabling, signal distribution and management.

Global Costs of IT

The money spent on IT worldwide has been most recently estimated as US $3. 5 trillion and is currently growing at 6% per year – doubling every 15 years. The 2014 IT budget of US federal government is nearly $82 billion. IT costs, as a percentage of corporate revenue, have grown 50% since 2002, putting a strain on IT budgets. When looking at current companies' IT budgets, 75% are recurrent costs, used to "keep the lights on" in the IT department, and 25% are cost of new initiatives for technology development.

The average IT budget has the following breakdown:

- 31% personnel costs (internal)
- 29% software costs (external/purchasing category)
- 26% hardware costs (external/purchasing category)
- 14% costs of external service providers (external/services).

ICT Development Index

The ICT Development Index compares the level of ICT use and access across the world.

The WSIS Process and ICT Development Goals

On 21 December 2001, the United Nations General Assembly approved Resolution 56/183, endorsing the holding of theWorld Summit on the Information Society (WSIS) to discuss the opportunities and challenges facing today's information society. According to this resolution, the General Assembly related the Summit to the United Nations Millennium Declaration's goal of implementing ICT to achieve Millennium Development Goals. It also emphasized a multi-stakeholder approach to achieve these goals, using all stakeholders including civil society and the private sector, in addition to governments.

ICT in Education

Information and Communication Technology (ICT) can contribute to universal access to education, equity in education, the delivery of quality learning and teaching, teachers' professional development and more efficient education management, governance and administration. That are used for visual And audio communication which will be easily understood by student Organizations like UNESCO takes a holistic and comprehensive approach to promoting ICT in education. Access, inclusion and quality are among the main challenges they can address. The Organization's Intersectoral Platform for ICT in education focuses on these issues through the joint work of three of its sectors: Communication & Information, Education and Science.

Electronic Data Processing

Electronic Data Processing (**EDP**) can refer to the use of automated methods to process commercial data. Typically, this uses relatively simple, repetitive activities to process large volumes of similar information. For example: stock updates applied to an inventory, banking transactions applied to account and customer master files, booking and ticketing transactions to an airline's reservation system, billing for utility services. The modifier "electronic" or "automatic" was used with "data processing" (DP), especially ca. 1960, to distinguish human clerical data processing from that done by computer. History

The first commercial business computer was developed in the United Kingdom in 1951, by the J. Lyons and Co. catering organization. This was known as the 'Lyons Electronic Office' - or LEO for short. It was developed further and used widely during the 1960s and early 1970s. (Joe Lyons formed a separate company to develop the LEO computers and this subsequently merged to form English Electric Leo Marconi and then International Computers Limited. By the end of the 1950s punched card manufacturers, Hollerith, Powers-Samas, IBM and others, were also marketing an array of computers. Early commercial systems were installed exclusively by large organizations. These could afford to invest the time and capital necessary to purchase hardware, hire specialist staff to developbespoke software and work through the consequent (and often unexpected) organizational and cultural changes.

At first, individual organizations developed their own software, including data management utilities, themselves. Different products might also have 'one-off' bespoke software. This fragmented approach led to duplicated effort and the production of management information needed manual effort.

High hardware costs and relatively slow processing speeds forced developers to use resources 'efficiently'. Data storageformats were heavily compacted, for example. A common example is the removal of the century from dates, which eventually led to the 'millennium bug'.

Data input required intermediate processing via punched paper tape or punched card and separate input to a repetitive, labor-intensive task, removed from user control and error-prone. Invalid or incorrect data needed correction and resubmission with consequences for data and account reconciliation.

Data storage was strictly serial on paper tape, and then later to magnetic tape: the use of data storage within readily accessible memory was not cost-effective. Significant developments took place in 1959 with IBM announcing the 1401 computer and in 1962 with ICT (International Computers & Tabulators) making delivery of the ICT 1301. Like all machines during this time the core processor together with the peripherals – magnetic tape decks, discs, drums, printers and card and paper tape input and output required considerable space in specially constructed air conditioned accommodation. Often parts of the punched card installation, in particular sorters, were retained to present the card input to the computer in a pre-sort form that reduced the processing time involved in sorting large amounts of data.

Data processing facilities became available to smaller organization in the form of the computer services bureau. These offered processing of specific applications e. g. payroll and were often a prelude to the purchase of customers own computer. Organizations used these facilities for testing programs while awaiting the arrival of their own machine.

These initial machines were delivered to customers with limited software. The design staff was divided into two groups. *Systems analysts* produced a systems specification and *programmers* translated the specification into machine language.

Literature on computers and EDP was sparse through articles appearing in accountancy publications and material supplied by the equipment manufacturers. The first issue of The Computer Journal published by The British Computer Societyappeared in mid 1958. The UK Accountancy Body now named The Association of Chartered Certified Accountants formed an Electronic Data Processing Committee in July 1958 with the purpose of informing its members of the opportunities created by the computer. The Committee produced its first booklet in 1959, An Introduction to Electronic Computers. Also in 1958 The Institute of Chartered Accountants in England and Wales produced a paper Accounting by Electronic Methods. The notes indicated what appears capable and the possible implications of using a computer.

Progressive organizations attempted to go beyond the straight systems transfer from punched card equipment and unit accounting machines to the computer, to producing accounts to the trial balance stage and integrated management information systems. New procedures redesigned the way paper flowed, changed organizational structures, called for a rethink of the way information was presented to management and challenged the internal control principles adopted by the designers of accounting systems. But the full realization of these benefits had to await the arrival of the next generation of computers

Today

As with other industrial processes commercial IT has moved in most cases from a custom-order, craft-based industry where the product was tailored to fit the customer; to multi-use components taken off the shelf to find the best-fit in any situation. Mass-production has greatly reduced costs and IT is available to the smallest organization.

LEO was hardware tailored for a single client. Today, Intel Pentium and compatible chips are standard and become parts of other components which are combined as needed. One individual change of note was the freeing of computers and removable storage from protected, air-filtered environments. Microsoft and IBM at various times have been influential enough to impose order on IT and the resultant standardizations allowed specialist software to flourish.

Software is available off the shelf: apart from products such as Microsoft Office and IBM Lotus, there are also specialist packages for payroll and personnel management, account maintenance and customer management, to name a few. These are highly specialized and intricate components of larger environments, but they rely upon common conventions and interfaces.

Data storage has also standardized. Relational databases are developed by different suppliers to common formats and conventions. Common file formats can be shared by large main-frames and desk-top personal computers, allowing online, real time input and validation.

In parallel, software development has fragmented. There are still specialist technicians, but these increasingly use standardized methodologies where outcomes are predictable and accessible. At the other end of the scale, any office manager can dabble in spreadsheets or databases and obtain acceptable results (but there are risks). Specialized software is software that is written for a specific task rather for a broad application area. These programs provide facilities specifically for the purpose for which they were designed.

INFORMATION TECHNOLOGY

Information technology (IT) is the application of computers

andtelecommunications equipment to store, retrieve, transmit and manipulate data, often in the context of a business or other enterprise.

The term is commonly used as a synonym for computers and computer networks, but it also encompasses other information distribution technologies such as television and telephones. Several industries are associated with information technology, including computer hardware, software, electronics, semiconductors, internet, telecom equipment, e-commerce and computer services. Humans have been storing, retrieving, manipulating and communicating information since the Sumerians in Mesopotamia developed writing in about 3000 BC, but the term *information technology* in its modern sense first appeared in a 1958 article published in the *Harvard Business Review*; authorsHarold J. Leavitt and Thomas L. Whisler commented that "the new technology does not yet have a single established name. We shall call it information technology (IT)." Their definition consists of three categories: techniques for processing, the application of statistical and mathematical methods to decision-making, and the simulation of higher-order thinking through computer programs.

Based on the storage and processing technologies employed, it is possible to distinguish four distinct phases of IT development: pre-mechanical (3000 BC–1450 AD), mechanical (1450–1840), electromechanical (1840–1940) and electronic (1940–present). This article focuses on the most recent period (electronic), which began in about 1940.

History of Computer Technology

Devices have been used to aid computation for thousands of years, probably initially in the form of a tally stick. TheAntikythera mechanism, dating from about the beginning of the first century BC, is generally considered to be the earliest known mechanical analog computer, and the earliest known geared mechanism. Comparable geared devices did not emerge in Europe until the 16th century, and it was not until 1645 that the first mechanical calculator capable of performing the four basic arithmetical operations was developed.

Electronic computers, using either relays or valves, began to appear in the early 1940s. The electromechanical Zuse Z3, completed in 1941, was the world's first programmable computer, and by modern standards one of the first machines that could be considered a complete computing machine. Colossus, developed during the Second World War to decryptGerman messages was the first electronic digital computer. Although it was programmable, it was not general-purpose, being designed to perform only a single task. It also lacked the ability to store its program in memory; programming was carried out using plugs and switches to alter the internal wiring. The first recognisably modern electronic digital stored-program computer was the Manchester Small-Scale Experimental Machine (SSEM), which ran its first program on 21 June 1948.

The development of transistors in the late 1940s at Bell Laboratories allowed a new generation of computers to be designed with greatly reduced power consumption. The first commercially available stored-program computer, the Ferranti Mark I, contained 4050 valves and had a power consumption of 25 kilowatts. By comparison the first transistorised computer, developed at the University of Manchester and operational by November 1953, consumed only 150 watts in its final version.

Data Storage

Early electronic computers such as Colossus made use of punched tape, a long strip of paper on which data was represented by a series of holes, a technology now obsolete. Electronic data storage, which is used in modern computers, dates from World War II, when a form of delay line memory was developed to remove the clutter from radarsignals, the first practical application of which was the mercury delay line. The first random-access digital storage device was the Williams tube, based on a standard cathode ray tube, but the information stored in it and delay line memory was volatile in that it had to be continuously refreshed, and thus was lost once power was removed. The earliest form of non-volatile computer storage was the magnetic drum, invented in 1932 and used in the Ferranti Mark 1, the world's first commercially available general-purpose electronic computer.

IBM introduced the first hard disk drive in 1956, as a component of their 305 RAMAC computer system. Most digital data today is still stored magnetically on hard disks, or optically on media such as CD-ROMs. Until 2002 most information was stored on analog devices, but that year digital storage capacity exceeded analog for the first time. As of 2007 almost 94% of the data stored worldwide was held digitally: 52% on hard disks, 28% on optical devices and 11% on digital magnetic tape. It has been estimated that the worldwide capacity to store information on electronic devices grew from less than 3exabytes in 1986 to 295 exabytes in 2007, doubling roughly every 3 years.

Databases

Database management systems emerged in the 1960s to address the problem of storing and retrieving large amounts of data accurately and quickly. One of the earliest such systems was IBM's Information Management System (IMS), which is still widely deployed more than 40 years later. IMS stores data hierarchically, but in the 1970s Ted Codd proposed an alternative relational storage model based on set theory and predicate logic and the familiar concepts of tables, rows and columns. The first commercially available relational database management system (RDBMS) was available from Oraclein 1980.

All database management systems consist of a number of components that together allow the data they store to be accessed simultaneously by many users while maintaining its integrity. A characteristic of all databases is that the structure of the data they contain is defined and stored separately from the data itself, in a database schema.

The extensible markup language (XML) has become a popular format for data representation in recent years. Although XML data can be stored in normal file systems, it is commonly held in relational databases to take advantage of their "robust implementation verified by years of both theoretical and practical effort". As an evolution of the Standard Generalized Markup Language (SGML), XML's text-based structure offers the advantage of being both machine and human-readable.

Data Retrieval

The relational database model introduced a programming-language independent Structured Query Language (SQL), based on relational algebra.

The terms "data" and "information" are not synonymous. Anything stored is data, but it only becomes information when it is organized and presented meaningfully. Most of the world's digital data is unstructured, and stored in a variety of different physical formats even within a single organization. Data warehouses began to be developed in the 1980s to integrate these disparate stores. They typically contain data extracted from various sources, including external sources such as the Internet, organized in such a way as to facilitate decision support systems (DSS).

Data Transmission

Data transmission has three aspects: transmission, propagation, and reception. It can be broadly categorized asbroadcasting, in which information is transmitted unidirectionally downstream, or telecommunications, with bidirectional upstream and downstream channels.

XML has been increasingly employed as a means of data interchange since the early 2000s, particularly for machine-oriented interactions such as those involved in web-oriented protocols such as SOAP, describing "data-in-transit rather than... data-at-rest". One of the challenges of such usage is converting data from relational databases into XMLDocument Object Model (DOM) structures.

Data Manipulation

Hilbert and Lopez identify the exponential pace of technological change (a kind of Moore's law): machines' application-specific capacity to compute information per capita roughly doubled every 14 months between 1986 and 2007; the per capita capacity of the world's general-purpose computers doubled every 18 months during the same two decades; the global telecommunication capacity per capita doubled every 34 months; the world's storage capacity per capita required roughly 40 months to double (every 3 years); and per capita broadcast information has doubled every 12. 3 years.

Massive amounts of data are stored worldwide every day, but unless it can be analysed and presented effectively it essentially resides in what have been called data tombs: "data archives that are seldom visited". To address that issue, the field of data mining – "the process of discovering interesting patterns and knowledge from large amounts of data" – emerged in the late 1980s.

Academic Perspective

In an academic context, the Association for Computing Machinery defines IT as "undergraduate degree programs that prepare students to meet the computer technology needs of business, government, healthcare, schools, and other kinds of organizations.... IT specialists assume responsibility for selecting hardware and software products appropriate for an organization, integrating those products with organizational needs and infrastructure, and installing, customizing, and maintaining those applications for the organization's computer users."

Commercial and Employment Perspective

In a business context, the Information Technology Association of America has defined information technology as "the study, design, development, application, implementation, support or management of computer-based information systems". The responsibilities of those working in the field include network administration, software development and installation, and the planning and management of an organization's technology life cycle, by which hardware and software are maintained, upgraded and replaced.

The business value of information technology lies in the automation of business processes, provision of information for decision making, connecting businesses with their customers, and the provision of productivity tools to increase efficiency.

WORLD TOURISM STATISTICS AND RANKINGS

Total volume of cross-border tourist travel

International tourist arrivals reached 1.035 billion in 2012, up from over 983 million in 2011, and 940 million in 2010. In 2011 and 2012, international travel demand continued to recover from the losses resulting from the late-2000s recession, where tourism suffered a strong slowdown from the second half of 2008 through the end of 2009. After a 5% increase in the first half of

2008, growth in international tourist arrivals moved into negative territory in the second half of 2008, and ended up only 2% for the year, compared to a 7% increase in 2007. The negative trend intensified during 2009, exacerbated in some countries due to the outbreak of the H1N1 influenza virus, resulting in a worldwide decline of 4.2% in 2009 to 880 million international tourists arrivals, and a 5.7% decline in international tourism receipts.

INTERNATIONAL TOURISM RECEIPTS

International tourism receipts grew to US$1.03 trillion (740 billion) in 2011, corresponding to an increase in real terms of 3.8% from 2010. The World Tourism Organization reports the following countries as the top ten tourism earners for the year 2011, with theUnited States by far the top earner.

History

Wealthy people have always travelled to distant parts of the world, to see great buildings, works of art, learn new languages, experience new cultures, and to taste different cuisines. Long ago, at the time of the Roman Republic, places such as Baiae were popular coastal resorts for the rich. The word tourist was used by 1772 and tourism by 1811.

The origins of modern tourism can be traced back to what was known as the Grand Tour which was a traditional trip of Europeundertaken by mainly upper-class European young men of means, mainly from England. The custom flourished from about 1660 until the advent of large-scale rail transit in the 1840s, and was associated with a standard itinerary. It served as an educational rite of passage. Though primarily associated with the British nobility and wealthy landed gentry, similar trips were made by wealthy young men of Protestant Northern European nations on the Continent, and from the second half of the 18th century some South American, U.S., and other overseas youth joined in. The tradition was extended to include more of the middle class after rail and steamship travel made the journey less of a burden, and Thomas Cook made the "Cook's Tour" a byword.

The New York Times recently described the Grand Tour in this way:

Three hundred years ago, wealthy young Englishmen began taking a post-Oxbridge trek through France and Italy in search of art, culture and the roots of Western civilization. With nearly unlimited funds, aristocratic connections and months (or years) to roam, they commissioned paintings, perfected their language skills and mingled with the upper crust of the Continent.

—Gross, Matt., "Lessons From the Frugal Grand Tour." New York Times 5 September 2008.

The primary value of the Grand Tour, it was believed, laid in the exposure both to the cultural legacy of classical antiquity and theRenaissance, and to the aristocratic and fashionably polite society of the European continent.

Emergence of Leisure travel

Leisure travel was associated with the Industrial Revolution in the United Kingdom - the first European country to promote leisure time to the increasing industrial population. Initially, this applied to the owners of the machinery of production, the economic oligarchy, the factory owners and the traders. These comprised the new middle class. Cox & Kingswas the first official travel company to be formed in 1758.

The British origin of this new industry is reflected in many place names. In Nice, France, one of the first and best-established holiday resorts on the French Riviera, the long esplanade along the seafront is known to this day as the Promenade des Anglais; in many other historic resorts in continental Europe, old, well-established palace hotels have names like the Hotel Bristol, Hotel Carlton, or Hotel Majestic - reflecting the dominance of Englishcustomers.

A pioneer of the travel agency, Thomas Cook's idea to offer excursions came to him while waiting for the stagecoach on the London Road at Kibworth. With the opening of the extended Midland Counties Railway, he arranged to take a group of 540 temperancecampaigners from Leicester Campbell Street station to a rally in Loughborough, eleven miles away. On 5 July 1841, Thomas Cook arranged for the rail company to charge oneshilling per person that included rail tickets and food for this train journey. Cook was paid a share of the fares actually charged to the passengers, as the railway tickets, being legal contracts between company and passenger, could not have been issued at his own price. This was the first privately chartered excursion train to be advertised to the general public; Cook himself acknowledging that there had been previous, unadvertised, private excursion trains. During the following three summers he planned and conducted outings for temperance societies and Sunday-school children. In 1844 the Midland Counties Railway Company agreed to make a permanent arrangement with him provided he found the passengers. This success led him to start his own business running rail excursions for pleasure, taking a percentage of the railway tickets.

Four years later, he planned his first excursion abroad, when he took a group from Leicester to Calais to coincide with the Paris Exhibition. The following year he started his 'grand circular tours' of Europe. During the 1860s he took parties to Switzerland, Italy, Egypt and United States. Cook established 'inclusive independent travel', whereby the traveller went independently but his agency charged for travel, food and accommodation for a fixed period over any chosen route. Such was his success that the Scottish railway companies withdrew their support between 1862 and 1863 to try the excursion business for themselves.

MODERN DAY TOURISM

Many leisure-oriented tourists travel to the tropics, both in the summer and winter. Places of such nature often visited are: Bali in Indonesia, Colombia, Brazil, Cuba, Grenada, theDominican Republic, Malaysia, Mexico the various Polynesian tropical islands, Queenslandin Australia, Thailand, Saint-Tropez and Cannes in France, Florida, Hawaii and Puerto Rico, in the United States, Saint Vincent and the Grenadines, Barbados, Trinidad and Tobago, Jamaica, St.Lucia, Sint Maarten, St. Martin's Island in Bangladesh, Saint Kitts and Nevis, The Bahamas, Anguilla, Antigua and Barbuda, Aruba, Turks and Caicos Islands, andBermuda.

In 1936, the League of Nations defined foreign tourist as "someone traveling abroad for at least twenty-four hours". Its successor, theUnited Nations, amended this definition in 1945, by including a maximum stay of six months.

Winter tourism

Although it is acknowledged that the Swiss were not the inventors of skiing, it is well documented that St. Moritz, Graubünden became the cradle of the developing winter tourism; since that year of 1865 in St. Moritz, when many daring hotel managers choose to risk opening their hotels in winter. It was, however, only in the 1970s when winter tourism took over the lead from summer tourism in many of the Swiss ski resorts. Even in winter, portions of up to one third of all guests (depending on the location) consist of non-skiers.

Major ski resorts are located mostly in the various European countries (e.g. Andorra, Austria, Bulgaria, Bosnia-Herzegovina, Czech Republic, Cyprus, Finland, France, Germany, Iceland, Italy, Norway, Latvia, Lithuania, Poland, Serbia, Sweden, Slovakia, Slovenia,Spain, Switzerland, Turkey), Canada, the United States (e.g. Colorado, California, Utah, Montana, Wyoming, New York, New Jersey, Michigan, Vermont, New Hampshire) New Zealand, Japan, South Korea, Chile, and Argentina.

Mass tourism

Mass tourism could only have developed with the improvements in technology, allowing thetransport of large numbers of people in a short space of time to places of leisure interest, so that greater numbers of people could begin to enjoy the benefits of leisure time.

In the United States, the first seaside resorts in the European style were at Atlantic City,New Jersey and Long Island, New York.

In Continental Europe, early resorts included: Ostend, popularised by the people ofBrussels; Boulogne-sur-Mer (Pas-de-Calais) and Deauville (Calvados) for the Parisians; andHeiligendamm, founded in 1793, as the first seaside resort on the Baltic Sea.

Adjectival tourism

Adjectival tourism refers to the numerous niche or specialty travel forms of tourism that have emerged over the years, each with its own adjective. Many of these have come into common use by the tourism industry and academics. Others are emerging concepts that may or may not gain popular usage.

Examples of the more common niche tourism markets include:

- Agritourism
- Birth tourism
- Culinary tourism
- Cultural tourism
- Extreme tourism
- Geotourism
- Heritage tourism
- LGBT tourism
- Medical tourism
- Nautical tourism
- Pop-culture tourism
- Religious tourism
- Sex tourism
- Slum tourism
- War tourism
- Wildlife tourism

Recent developments

There has been an up-trend in tourism over the last few decades, especially in Europe, where international travel for short breaks is common. Tourists have a wide range of budgets and tastes, and a wide variety of resorts and hotels have developed to cater for them. For example, some people prefer simple beach vacations, while others want more specialised holidays, quieter resorts, family-oriented holidays or niche market-targeted destination hotels.

The developments in technology and transport infrastructure, such as jumbo jets, low-cost airlines and more accessible airports have made many types of tourism more affordable. On 28 April 2009 The Guardian noted that "the WHO estimates that up to 500,000 people are on planes at any time." There have also been changes in lifestyle, for example some retirement-age people sustain year round tourism. This is facilitated by internet sales of tourist services. Some sites have now started to offer dynamic packaging, in which an inclusive price is quoted for a tailor-made package requested by the customer upon impulse.

There have been a few setbacks in tourism, such as the September 11 attacks and terrorist threats to tourist destinations, such as inBali and several European cities. Also, on 26 December 2004, a tsunami, caused by the 2004 Indian Ocean earthquake, hit the Asian countries on the Indian Ocean, including the Maldives. Thousands of lives were lost including many tourists. This, together with the vast clean-up operations, stopped or severely hampered tourism in the area for a time.

The terms tourism and travel are sometimes used interchangeably. In this context, travel has a similar definition to tourism, but implies a more purposeful journey. The terms tourism and tourist are sometimes used pejoratively, to imply a shallow interest in the cultures or locations visited by tourists.

Sustainable tourism

"Sustainable tourism is envisaged as leading to management of all resources in such a way that economic, social and aesthetic needs can be fulfilled while maintaining cultural integrity, essential ecological processes, biological diversity and life support systems." (World Tourism Organization) Sustainable development implies "meeting the needs of the present without compromising the ability of future generations to meet their own needs." (World Commission on Environment and Development, 1987)

Sustainable tourism can be seen as having regard to ecological and socio-cultural carrying capacities and includes involving the community of the destination in tourism development planning. It also involves integrating tourism to match current economic and growth policies so as to mitigate some of the negative economic and social impacts of 'mass tourism'. Murphy (1985) advocates the use of an 'ecological approach', to consider both 'plants' and 'people' when implementing the sustainable tourism development process. This is in contrast to the 'boosterism' and 'economic' approaches to tourism planning, neither of which consider the detrimental ecological or sociological impacts of tourism development to a destination.

However, Butler questions the exposition of the term 'sustainable' in the context of tourism, citing its ambiguity and stating that "the emerging sustainable development philosophy of the 1990s can be viewed as an extension of the broader realization that a preoccupation with economic growth without regard to its social and environmental consequences is self-defeating in the long term." Thus 'sustainable tourism development' is seldom considered as an autonomous function of economic regeneration as separate from general economic growth.

ECOTOURISM

Ecotourism, also known as ecological tourism, is responsible travel to fragile, pristine, and usually protected areas that strives to be low impact and (often) small scale. It helps educate the traveler; provides funds for conservation; directly benefits the economic development and political empowerment of local communities; and fosters respect for different cultures and for human rights.

Pro-poor tourism

Pro-poor tourism, which seeks to help the poorest people in developing countries, has been receiving increasing attention by those involved in development; the issue has been addressed through small-scale projects in local communities and through attempts by Ministries of Tourism to attract large numbers of tourists. Research by the Overseas Development Institute suggests that neither is the best way to encourage tourists' money to reach the poorest as only 25% or less (far less in some cases) ever reaches the poor; successful examples of money reaching the poor include mountain-climbing in Tanzaniaand cultural tourism in Luang Prabang, Laos.

Recession tourism

Recession tourism is a travel trend, which evolved by way of the world economic crisis. Identified by American entrepreneur Matt Landau (2007), recession tourism is defined by low-cost, high-value experiences taking place of once-popular generic retreats. Various recession tourism hotspots have seen business boom during the recession thanks to comparatively low costs of living and a slow world job market suggesting travelers are elongating trips where their money travels further.

Medical tourism

When there is a significant price difference between countries for a given medical procedure, particularly in Southeast Asia, India,Eastern Europe and where there are different regulatory regimes, in relation to particular medical procedures (e.g. dentistry), traveling to take advantage of the price or regulatory differences is often referred to as "medical tourism".

Educational tourism

Educational tourism developed, because of the growing popularity of teaching and learning of knowledge and the enhancing of technical competency outside of the classroom environment. In educational tourism, the main focus of the tour or leisure activity includes visiting another country to learn about the culture, such as in Student Exchange Programs and Study Tours, or to work and apply skills learned inside the classroom in a different environment, such as in the International Practicum Training Program.

Creative tourism

Creative tourism has existed as a form of cultural tourism, since the early beginnings of tourism itself. Its European roots date back to the time of the Grand Tour, which saw the sons of aristocratic families traveling for the purpose of mostly interactive, educational experiences. More recently, creative tourism has been given its own name by Crispin Raymond and Greg Richards, who as members of the Association for Tourism and Leisure Education (ATLAS), have directed a number of projects for the European Commission, including cultural and crafts tourism, known as sustainable tourism. They have defined "creative tourism" as tourism related to the active participation of travellers in the culture of the host community, through interactive workshops and informal learning experiences.

Meanwhile, the concept of creative tourism has been picked up by high-profile organizations such as UNESCO, who through the Creative Cities Network, have endorsed creative tourism as an engaged, authentic experience that promotes an active understanding of the specific cultural features of a place.

More recently, creative tourism has gained popularity as a form of cultural tourism, drawing on active participation by travelers in the culture of the host communities they visit. Several countries offer examples of this type of tourism development, including the United Kingdom, Austria, France, the Bahamas, Jamaica, Spain, Italy and New Zealand.

The growing interest of tourists in this new way to discover a culture regards particularly the operators and branding managers, attentive to the possibility of attracting a quality tourism, highlighting the intangible heritage (craft workshops, cooking classes, etc. .) and optimizing the use of existing infrastructure (for example, through the rent of halls and auditorium).

Dark tourism

One emerging area of special interest has been identified by Lennon and Foley (2000) as "dark" tourism. This type of tourism involves visits to "dark" sites, such as battlegrounds, scenes of horrific crimes or acts of genocide, for example: concentration camps. Dark tourism remains a small niche market, driven by varied motivations, such as mourning, remembrance, education, macabre curiosity or even entertainment. Its early origins are rooted in fairgrounds and medieval fairs.

Doom tourism

Also known as "Tourism of Doom," or "Last Chance Tourism" this emerging trend involves traveling to places that are environmentally or otherwise threatened (the ice caps of Mount Kilimanjaro, the melting glaciers of Patagonia, The coral of the Great Barrier Reef) before it is too late. Identified by travel trade magazine Travel Age West editor-in-chief Kenneth Shapiro in 2007 and later explored in The New York Times, this type of tourism is believed to be on the rise. Some see the trend as related to sustainable tourism orecotourism due to the fact that a number of these tourist destinations are considered threatened by environmental factors such as global warming, over population or climate change. Others worry that travel to many of these threatened locations increases an individual's carbon footprint and only hastens problems threatened locations are already facing.

GROWTH

The World Tourism Organization (UNWTO) forecasts that international tourism will continue growing at the average annual rate of 4%. With the advent of e-commerce, tourism products have become one of the most traded items on the internet.Tourism products and services have been made available through intermediaries, although tourism providers (hotels, airlines, etc.), including small-scale operators, can sell their services directly. This has put pressure on intermediaries from both on-line and traditional shops. It has been suggested there is a strong correlation between tourism expenditure per capita and the degree to which countries play in the global context. Not only as a result of the important economic contribution of the tourism industry, but also as an indicator of the degree of confidence with which global citizens leverage the resources of the globe for the benefit of their local economies. This is why any projections of growth in tourism may serve as an indication of the relative influence that each country will exercise in the future.

Space tourism is expected to "take off" in the first quarter of the 21st century, although compared with traditional destinations the number of tourists in orbit will remain low until technologies such as a space elevator make space travel cheap. Technological improvement is likely to make possible air-ship hotels, based either on solar-powered airplanes or largedirigibles. Underwater hotels, such as Hydropolis, expected to open in Dubai in 2009, will be built. On the ocean, tourists will be welcomed by ever larger cruise ships and perhaps floating cities.

Sports tourism

Since the late 1980s, sports tourism has become increasingly popular. Events such as rugby, Olympics, Commonwealth games, Asian Games and football World Cups have enabled specialist travel companies to gain official ticket allocation and then sell them in packages that include flights, hotels and excursions.

The focus on sport and spreading knowledge on the subject, especially more so recently, lead to the increase in the sport tourism. Most notably, the international event such as the Olympics caused a shift in focus in the audience who now realize the variety of sports that exist in the world. In the United States, one of the most popular sports that usually are focused on was Football. This popularity was increased through major events like the World Cups. In Asian countries, the numerous football events also increased the popularity of football. But, it was the Olympics that brought together the different sports that lead to the increase in sport tourism. The drastic interest increase in sports in general and not just one sport caught the attention of travel companies, who then began to sell flights in packages. Due to the low number of people who actually purchase these packages than predicted, the cost of these packages plummeted initially. As the number start to rise slightly the packages increased to regain the lost profits. With the certain economic state, the number of purchases decreased once again. The fluctuation in the number of packages sold was solely dependent on the economic situation, therefore, most travel companies were forced to set aside the plan to execute the marketing of any new package features.

Latest trends

As a result of the late-2000s recession, international arrivals suffered a strong slowdown beginning in June 2008. Growth from 2007 to 2008 was only 3.7% during the first eight months of 2008. This slowdown on international tourism demand was also reflected in the air transport industry, with a negative growth in September 2008 and a 3.3% growth in passenger traffic through September. The hotel industry also reported a slowdown, with room occupancy declining. In 2009 worldwide tourism arrivals decreased by 3.8%. By the first quarter of 2009, real travel demand in the United States had fallen 6% over six quarters. While this is considerably milder than what occurred after the 9/11 attacks, the decline was at twice the rate as real GDP has fallen.

However, evidence suggests that tourism as a global phenomena shows no signs of substantially abating in the long term. Much literature, especially that following the Mobilities paradigm, suggests that travel is necessary in order to maintain relationships, as social life is increasingly networked and conducted at a distance. For many vacations and travel are increasingly being viewed as a necessity rather than a luxury, and this is reflected in tourist numbers recovering some 6.6% globally over 2009, with growth up to 8% in emerging economies.Introduction to Tourism Marketing

Marketing is an integral part of any substantive tourism enterprise. As the market is expanding and consolidating, the role of marketing as a driving force in a business endeavor is also being recognized. With growing competition, organisations in tourism business have no option but to engage in organised and targeted marketing. A professional approach to marketing always helps, whether it is on the tour operator end or at destinations. Guides, escorts, restaurants, hotels, transporters, shops etc closely compete one another and have to outmarket one another to stay ahead. A proper tourism marketing strategy at national level calls for close cooperation between the government, tourism industry and the local population.

Marketing: Definition and Concepts

Concept of marketing extends broader than just selling or promotion of a product. It is related to an array of things like marketing research, needs assessment of the consumers, product development, pricing and distribution. As per the definition given by Philip Kotler:

"Marketing is the analysis, planning, implementation, and control of carefully formulated programs designed to bring about voluntary exchanges of values with target markets for the purpose of achieving organizational objectives. It relies heavily on designing the organisation's offering in terms of the target markets' needs and desires, and on using effective pricing, communication, and distribution to inform, motivate, and service the markets."

BRITISH INSTITUTE OF MARKETING DEFINES IT AS

"The management process responsible for identifying, anticipating and satisfying customer requirements profitably."

Evolution of Marketing

Marketing as a concept has developed in the last 30 years. Development of marketing and modern business practices has three distinct stages: Production Era, Sales Era and Marketing Era. Marketing era arrived when organizations began to produce what they could sell rather than trying to sell what they manufactured. While planning and designing a product, customers'needs, wants, tastes and satisfaction were considered. Growth of competition prompted organisations to develop marketing techniques.

Change in traveling trends also demanded a new approach. The emergence of long haul traveler created the need for marketing research which took into account market trends, consumer behavior and ascertained procedure to make products which satisfied the users of tourism products.

Gradual social and economic development resulted in segmentation of mass market into specialized target markets. Tackling these markets demanded new approach which was in tune with new times.

Selling and Marketing

Selling and Marketing are totally different concepts. The major difference is that selling focuses on the needs of the seller while marketing concentrates on the requirements of the buyer. A marketing oriented organisation focuses on customer needs and gains profits through customer satisfaction. Several organizations in tourism sector are product oriented. They emphasise on the available services of products but ignore consumers' needs or attitudes. A marketing oriented tourist organisation takes a completely different approach. They develop their services around the tourists' needs.

Business Philosophy

A marketing oriented business philosophy keeps consumer needs at the centre of all activities. An organisation could offer a quality tourism product but if it lacks supporting infrastructure, it would have no takers. A tourist organisation needs to take care of needs like accessibility, accommodation, leisure and entertainment facilities. Tourists have their own needs, preferences and tastes, and these have to be taken into account.

In modern tourism market place, marketing is the ideal approach for organising business. This approach is backed by market research which provides proper understanding of tourism, destination and business structure needed. Product development is based on consumer feedback. Thanks to this approach, a tourism business can satisfy customer needs and success of the products is ensured. This approach also brings for organisation a reputed market standing. However, for proper success, the philosophy has to be ingrained in the minds of the employees of the organisation.

Features of Tourism Marketing

Tourism is a service product rather than being a physical thing. Tourism organisations try to sell an experience. A tourism product has certain features:

- Any sample of a tourism product is not possible. Services can be used only at the given time.
- A tourist can only buy the experience. He/she cannot own the product.
- Tourism business is seasonal in nature. It could be off-color during off season.
- Product is amalgamation of several services.
- Several intermediaries are involved in designing and packaging of a tourism product. Efficiency of the product has to ensured at every level.

Tourism market is constantly changing. Specialised tourism has emerged, laying stress on consumer needs. Introduction of consumer protection laws has played a role in changing the scenario of tourism market.

2

E-Commerce

E-commerce (also written as *e-Commerce, e-Commerce* or similar variants), short for **electronic commerce**, is trading in products or services using computer networks, such as the Internet. Electronic commerce draws on technologies such as mobile commerce, electronic funds transfer, supply chain management, Internet marketing, online transaction processing, electronic data interchange (EDI), inventory management systems, and automated data collection systems. Modern electronic commerce typically uses the World Wide Web for at least one part of the transaction's life cycle, although it may also use other technologies such as e-mail. E-commerce businesses may employ some or all of the following:

- Online shopping web sites for retail sales direct to consumers
- Providing or participating in online marketplaces, which process third-party business-to-consumer or consumer-to-consumer sales
- Business-to-business buying and selling
- Gathering and using demographic data through web contacts and social media
- Business-to-business electronic data interchange
- Marketing to prospective and established customers by e-mail or fax (for example, with newsletters)
- Engaging in pretail for launching new products and services

TIMELINE

A timeline for the development of e-commerce:

- 1971 or 1972: The ARPANET is used to arrange a sale between students at the Stanford Artificial Intelligence Laboratory and the Massachusetts Institute of Technology, later described as "the seminal act of e-commerce" in John Markoff's book *What the Dormouse Said.*
- 1979: Michael Aldrich demonstrates the first online shopping system.
- 1981: Thomson Holidays UK is first business-to-business online shopping system to be installed.
- 1982: Minitel was introduced nationwide in France by France Télécom and used for online ordering.
- 1983: California State Assembly holds first hearing on "electronic commerce" in Volcano, California. Testifying are CPUC, MCI Mail, Prodigy, CompuServe, Volcano Telephone, and Pacific Telesis. (Not

permitted to testify is Quantum Technology, later to become AOL.)

- 1984: Gateshead SIS/Tesco is first B2C online shopping system and Mrs Snowball, 72, is the first online home shopper
- 1984: In April 1984, CompuServe launches the Electronic Mall in the USA and Canada. It is the first comprehensive electronic commerce service.
- 1984: California becomes first US state to enact an Electronic Commerce Act defining basic consumer rights online.
- 1990: Tim Berners-Lee writes the first web browser, WorldWideWeb, using a NeXT computer.
- 1992: Book Stacks Unlimited in Cleveland opens a commercial sales website (www. books. com) selling books online with credit card processing.
- 1992: St. Martin's Press publishes J. H. Snider and Terra Ziporyn's Future Shop: How New Technologies Will Change the Way We Shop and What We Buy.
- 1993: Paget Press releases edition No. 3 of the first AppStore, The Electronic AppWrapper
- 1994: Netscape releases the Navigator browser in October under the code name Mozilla. Netscape 1. 0 is introduced in late 1994 with SSL encryption that made transactions secure.
- 1994: Ipswitch IMail Server becomes the first software available online for sale and immediate download via a partnership between Ipswitch, Inc. and OpenMarket.
- 1994: "Ten Summoner's Tales" by Sting becomes the first secure online purchase.
- 1995: The US National Science Foundation lifts its former strict prohibition of commercial enterprise on the Internet.
- 1995: Thursday 27 April 1995, the purchase of a book by Paul Stanfield, Product Manager for CompuServe UK, from W H Smith's shop within CompuServe's UK Shopping Centre is the UK's first national online shopping service secure transaction. The shopping service at launch featured W H Smith, Tesco, Virgin Megastores/Our Price, Great Universal Stores (GUS), Interflora, Dixons Retail, Past Times, PC World (retailer) and Innovations.
- 1995: Jeff Bezos launches Amazon. com and the first commercial-free 24-hour, internet-only radio stations, Radio HK and NetRadio start broadcasting. Dell and Cisco begin to aggressively use Internet for commercial transactions. eBay is founded by computer programmer Pierre Omidyar as AuctionWeb.
- 1996: IndiaMART B2B marketplace established in India.
- 1996: ECPlaza B2B marketplace established in Korea.
- 1996: Sellerdeck, formerly Actinic, the UK's first PC/LAN e-commerce

platform established.

- 1998: Electronic postal stamps can be purchased and downloaded for printing from the Web.
- 1998: Cbazaar formerly chennaibazaar. com, India's first B2C eCommerce portal launched by Rajesh Nahar and Ritesh Katariya.
- 1999: Alibaba Group is established in China. Business. com sold for US $7. 5 million to eCompanies, which was purchased in 1997 for US $149, 000. The peer-to-peer filesharing software Napster launches. ATG Stores launches to sell decorative items for the home online.
- 2000: The dot-com bust.
- 2001: Alibaba. com achieved profitability in December 2001.
- 2002: eBay acquires PayPal for $1. 5 billion. Niche retail companies Wayfair and NetShops are founded with the concept of selling products through several targeted domains, rather than a central portal.
- 2003: Amazon. com posts first yearly profit.
- 2003: Bossgoo B2B marketplace established in China.
- 2004: DHgate. com, China's first online b2b transaction platform, is established, forcing other b2b sites to move away from the "yellow pages" model.
- 2007: Flipkart is established in India. Business. com acquired by R. H. Donnelley for. $345 million.
- 2009: Zappos. com acquired by Amazon. com for $928 million. Retail Convergence, operator of private sale website RueLaLa. com, acquired by GSI Commerce for $180 million, plus up to $170 million in earn-out payments based on performance through 2012.
- 2010: Groupon reportedly rejects a $6 billion offer from Google. Instead, the group buying websites went ahead with anIPO on 4 November 2011. It was the largest IPO since Google.
- 2011: Quidsi. com, parent company of Diapers. com, acquired by Amazon. com for $500 million in cash plus $45 million in debt and other obligations. GSI Commerce, a company specializing in creating, developing and running online shopping sites for brick and mortar businesses, acquired by eBay for $2. 4 billion.
- 2013: US eCommerce and Online Retail holiday sales reach $46. 5 billion, up 10 percent.
- 2014: Overstock. com processes over $1 million in Bitcoin sales. India's e-commerce industry is estimated to have grown more than 30% from 2012 to $12. 6 billion in 2013. US eCommerce and Online Retail sales projected to reach $294 billion, an increase of 12 percent over 2013 and 9% of all retail sales. Alibaba Group has the largest Initial public offering ever, worth $25 billion.

  Business applications

Some common applications related to electronic commerce are:

- Document automation in supply chain and logistics
- Domestic and international payment systems
- Enterprise content management
- Group buying
- Print on demand
- Automated online assistant
- Newsgroups
- Online shopping and order tracking
- Online banking
- Online office suites
- Shopping cart software
- Teleconferencing
- Electronic tickets
- Social networking
- Instant messaging
- Pretail

GOVERNMENTAL REGULATION

In the United States, some electronic commerce activities are regulated by the Federal Trade Commission (FTC). These activities include the use of commercial e-mails, online advertising and consumer privacy. The CAN-SPAM Act of 2003establishes national standards for direct marketing over e-mail. The Federal Trade Commission Act regulates all forms of advertising, including online advertising, and states that advertising must be truthful and non-deceptive. Using its authority under Section 5 of the FTC Act, which prohibits unfair or deceptive practices, the FTC has brought a number of cases to enforce the promises in corporate privacy statements, including promises about the security of consumers' personal information. As result, any corporate privacy policy related to e-commerce activity may be subject to enforcement by the FTC.

The Ryan Haight Online Pharmacy Consumer Protection Act of 2008, which came into law in 2008, amends the Controlled Substances Act to address online pharmacies.

There is also collaboration between Google and US federal authorities to block illegal online pharmacies from appearing in Google search results. Recently FedEx Corporation pleaded not guilty to charges made against it regarding dealing with illegal online pharmacies.

Conflict of laws in cyberspace is a major hurdle for harmonisation of legal framework for e-commerce around the world. In order to give a uniformity to e-commerce law around the world, many countries adopted the UNCITRAL Model Law on Electronic Commerce (1996)

Internationally there is the International Consumer Protection and Enforcement Network (ICPEN), which was formed in 1991 from an informal network of government customer fair trade organisations. The purpose was stated as being to find ways of co-operating on tackling consumer problems connected with cross-border transactions in both goods and services, and to help ensure exchanges of information among the participants for mutual benefit and understanding. From this came Econsumer. gov, an ICPEN initiative since April 2001. It is a portal to report complaints about online and related transactions with foreign companies.

There is also **Asia Pacific Economic Cooperation** (APEC) was established in 1989 with the vision of achieving stability, security and prosperity for the region through free and open trade and investment. APEC has an Electronic Commerce Steering Group as well as working on common privacy regulations throughout the APEC region.

In **Australia**, Trade is covered under Australian Treasury Guidelines for electronic commerce, and the Australian Competition and Consumer Commission regulates and offers advice on how to deal with businesses online, and offers specific advice on what happens if things go wrong.

In **the United Kingdom**, The Financial Services Authority (FSA) was formerly the regulating authority for most aspects of the EU's Payment Services Directive (PSD), until its replacement in 2013 by the Prudential Regulation Authority and theFinancial Conduct Authority. The UK implemented the PSD through the Payment Services Regulations 2009 (PSRs), which came into effect on 1 November 2009. The PSR affects firms providing payment services and their customers. These firms include banks, non-bank credit card issuers and non-bank merchant acquirers, e-money issuers, etc. The PSRs created a new class of regulated firms known as payment institutions (PIs), who are subject to prudential requirements. Article 87 of the PSD requires the European Commission to report on the implementation and impact of the PSD by 1 November 2012.

In **India**, the Information Technology Act 2000 governs the basic applicability of e-commerce. It is based upon UNCITRAL Model but is not a comprehensive legislation to deal with e-commerce related activities in India. Further, e-commerce laws and regulations in India are also supplemented by different laws of India as applicable to the field of e-commerce. For instance, e-commerce relating to pharmaceuticals, healthcare, traveling, etc. are governed by different laws though the information technology act, 2000 prescribes some common requirements for all these fields. The competition commission of India (CCI) regulates anti competition and anti trade practices in e-commerce fields in India. Some stakeholders have decided to approach courts and CCI against e-commerce websites to file complaint about unfair trade practices and predatory pricing by such e-commerce websites.

In **China**, the Telecommunications Regulations of the People's Republic of China (promulgated on 25 September 2000), stipulated the Ministry of Industry and Information Technology (MIIT) as the government department regulating all telecommunications related activities, including electronic commerce. On the same day, The Administrative Measures on Internet Information Services released, is the first administrative regulation to address profit-generating activities conducted through the Internet, and lay the foundation for future regulations governing e-commerce in China. In 28 August 2004, the eleventh session of the tenth NPC Standing Committee adopted The Electronic Signature Law, which regulates data message, electronic signature authentication and legal liability issues. It is considered the first law in China's e-commerce legislation. It was a milestone in the course of improving China's electronic commerce legislation, and also marks the entering of China's rapid development stage for electronic commerce legislation.

Forms

Contemporary electronic commerce involves everything from ordering "digital" content for immediate online consumption, to ordering conventional goods and services, to "meta" services to facilitate other types of electronic commerce.

On the institutional level, big corporations and financial institutions use the internet to exchange financial data to facilitate domestic and international business. Data integrity and security are pressing issues for electronic commerce.

Aside from traditional e-Commerce, m-Commerce (mobile commerce) as well as the nascent t-Commerce channels are often seen as the 2013 poster children of electronic I-Commerce.

Global Trends

In 2010, the United Kingdom had the biggest e-commerce market in the world when measured by the amount spent per capita. The Czech Republic is the European country where ecommerce delivers the biggest contribution to the enterprises´ total revenue. Almost a quarter (24%) of the country's total turnover is generated via the online channel.

Among emerging economies, China's e-commerce presence continues to expand every year. With 384 million internet users, China's online shopping sales rose to $36. 6 billion in 2009 and one of the reasons behind the huge growth has been the improved trust level for shoppers. The Chinese retailers have been able to help consumers feel more comfortable shopping online. China's cross-border e-commerce is also growing rapidly. E-commerce transactions between China and other countries increased 32% to 2. 3

trillion yuan ($375. 8 billion) in 2012 and accounted for 9. 6% of China's total international trade In 2013, Alibaba had an e-commerce market share of 80% in China.

Other BRIC countries are witnessing the accelerated growth of eCommerce as well. Brazil's eCommerce is growing quickly with retail eCommerce sales expected to grow at a healthy double-digit pace through 2014. By 2016, eMarketer expects retail ecommerce sales in Brazil to reach $17. 3 billion. India has an internet user base of about 243. 2 million as of January 2014. Despite being third largest userbase in world, the penetration of Internet is low compared to markets like the United States, United Kingdom or France but is growing at a much faster rate, adding around 6 million new entrants every month. The industry consensus is that growth is at an inflection point. In India, cash on delivery is the most preferred payment method, accumulating 75% of the e-retail activities.

E-Commerce has become an important tool for small and large businesses worldwide, not only to sell to customers, but also to engage them.

In 2012, ecommerce sales topped $1 trillion for the first time in history.

Mobile devices are playing an increasing role in the mix of eCommerce. Some estimates show that purchases made on mobile devices will make up 25% of the market by 2017. According to Cisco Visual Networking Index, in 2014 the amount of mobile devices will outnumber the number of world population.

In the past 10 years, e-commerce is in a period of rapid development. Cross-border e-commerce is called the Internet thinking along with traditional import and export trade. Cross-border e-commerce enables international trade towards more convenient and free open to cooperate between different countries in the world, incorporating developed and developing countries. In the short term, developing countries may be limited to IT, but in the long term, they would change the barrier to develop their IT facilities, and continuing to close to developed countries. The moment, developing countries like China and India are developing e-commerce very rapidly, such as China 's Alibaba, the financing capital (£15 billions) is the highest ever in e-commerce company. In addition, China is becoming the biggest e-commerce provider in the world. The number of Internet users in China which amounts to 600 millions, and which is doubled than USA users in total.

For traditional businesses, one research stated that information technology and cross-border e-commerce is a good opportunity for the rapid development and growth of enterprises. Many companies have invested enormous volume of investment in mobile applications. The DeLone and McLean Model stated that 3 perspectives are contributed to a successful e-business, including information system quality, service quality and users satisfaction. There is no limit of time and space, there are more opportunities to reach out to customers around the world, and to cut down unnecessary intermediate links, thereby reducing the cost price, and can benefit from one on one large customer data analysis, to achieve a high degree of personal customization strategic plan, in order to fully enhance the core competitiveness of the products in company

Impact on Markets and Retailers

Economists have theorized that e-commerce ought to lead to intensified price competition, as it increases consumers' ability to gather information about products and prices. Research by four economists at the University of Chicago has found that the growth of online shopping has also affected industry structure in two areas that have seen significant growth in e-commerce, bookshops and travel agencies. Generally, larger firms are able to use economies of scale and offer lower prices. The lone exception to this pattern has been the very smallest category of bookseller, shops with between one and four employees, which appear to have withstood the trend.

Individual or business involved in e-commerce whether buyers or sellers rely on Internet-based technology in order to accomplish their transactions. E-commerce is recognized for its ability to allow business to communicate and to form transaction anytime and anyplace. Whether an individual is in the US or overseas, business can be conducted through the internet. The power of e-commerce allows geophysical barriers to disappear, making all consumers and businesses on earth potential customers and suppliers. eBay is a good example of e-commerce business individuals and businesses are able to post their items and sell them around the Globe.

In e-commerce activities, supply chain and logistics are two most crucial factors need to be considered. Typically, cross-border logistics need about few weeks time round. Based on this low efficiency of the supply chain service, customer satisfaction will be greatly reduced. Some researcher stated that combining e-commerce competence and IT setup could well enhance company's overall business worth. Other researcher stated that e-commerce need to consider the establishment of warehouse centers in foreign countries, to create high efficiency of the logistics system, not only improve customers' satisfaction, but also can improve customers' loyalty.

Some researcher investigated that if a company want to enhance international customers' satisfaction, where cultural website need to be adapted in particular country, rather than solely depending on its local country. However, according to this research findings, the researcher found that German company had treated its international website as the same local model, such as in UK and US online marketing. A company could save money and make decision quickly via the identical strategy in different country. However, opportunity cost could be occurred, if the local strategy does not match to a new market, the company could lose its potential customer.

Impact on Supply Chain Management

For a long time, companies had been troubled by the gap between the benefits which supply chain technology has and the solutions to deliver those benefits. However, the emergence of e-commerce has provided a more practical and effective way of delivering the benefits of the new supply chain technologies.

E-commerce has the capability to integrate all inter-company and intra-company functions, meaning that the three flows (physical flow, financial flow and information flow) of the supply chain could be also affected by e-commerce. The affections on physical flows improved the way of product and inventory movement level for companies. For the information flows, e-commerce optimised the capacity of information processing than companies used to have, and for the financial flows, e-commerce allows companies to have more efficient payment and settlement solutions. In addition, e-commerce has a more sophisticated level of impact on supply chains: Firstly, the performance gap will be eliminated since companies can identify gaps between different levels of supply chains by electronic means of solutions; Secondly, as a result of e-commerce emergence, new capabilities such implementing ERP systems have helped companies to manage operations with customers and suppliers. Yet these new capabilities are still not fully exploited. Thirdly, technology companies would keep investing on new e-commerce software solutions as they are expecting investment return. Fourthly, e-commerce would help to solve many aspects of issues that companies may feel difficult to cope with, such as political barriers or cross-country changes. Finally, e-commerce provides companies a more efficient and effective way to collaborate with each other within the supply chain.

THE SOCIAL IMPACT OF E-COMMERCE

Along with the e-commerce and its unique charm that has appeared gradually, virtual enterprise, virtual bank, network marketing, online shopping, payment and advertising, such this new vocabulary which is unheard-of and now has become as familiar to people. This reflects that the e-commerce has huge impact on the economy and society from the other side. For instance, B2B is a rapidly growing business in the world that leads to lower cost and then improves the economic efficiency and also bring along the growth of employment.

To understand how the e-commerce has affected the society and economy, this article will mention three issues below:

1. The e-commerce has changed the relative importance of time, but as the pillars of indicator of the country's economic state that the importance of time should not be ignored.
2. The e-commerce offers the consumer or enterprise various information they need, making information into total transparency, will force enterprise no longer is able to use the mode of space or advertisement to raise their competitive edge. Moreover, in theory, perfect competition between the consumer sovereignty and industry will maximize social welfare.
3. In fact, during the economic activity in the past, large enterprise frequently has advantage of information resource, and thus at the expense of consumers. Nowadays, the transparent and real-time information protects the rights of consumers, because the consumers can use internet to pick out the portfolio to the benefit of themselves. The competitiveness of enterprises will be much more obvious than before, consequently, social welfare would be improved by the development of the e-commerce.
4. The new economy led by the e-commerce change humanistic spirit as well, but above all, is the employee loyalty. Due to the market with competition, the employee's level of professionalism becomes the crucial for enterprise in the niche market. The enterprises must pay attention to how to build up the enterprises inner culture and a set of interactive mechanisms and it is the prime problem for them. Furthermore, though the mode of e-commerce decrease the information cost and transaction cost, however, its development also makes human being are overly computer literate. In hence, emphasized more humanistic attitude to work is another project for enterprise to development. Life is the root of all and high technology are merely an assistive tool to support our quality of life.

The e-commerce is not a kind of new industry, but it is creating a new economic model. Most of people agree that the e-commerce indeed to be important and significant for economic society in the future, but actually that is a bit of clueless feeling at the beginning, this problem is exactly prove the e-commerce is a sort of incorporeal revolution. Generally speaking, as a type of business active procedure, the e-commerce is going to leading an unprecedented revolution in the world, the influence of this model far exceeded the commercial affair itself. Except the mentioned above, in the area of law, education, culture and also policy, the e-commerce will continue that rise in impact. The e-commerce is truly to take human beings into the information society.

Distribution Channels

E-commerce has grown in importance as companies have adopted pure-click and brick-and-click channel systems. We can distinguish pure-click and brick-and-click channel system adopted by companies.

- Pure-click or pure-play companies are those that have launched a website without any previous existence as a firm.
- Bricks-and-clicks companies are those existing companies that have added an online site for e-commerce.
- Click-to-brick online retailers that later open physical locations to supplement their online efforts.

Examples of new e-commerce systems

According to eMarketer research company, "by 2017, 65. 8 per cent of Britons will use smartphones" (cited by Williams, 2014).

Bringing online experience into the real world, also allows the development of the economy and the interaction between stores and customers. A great example of this new e-commerce system is what the Burberry store in London did in 2012. They refurbished the entire store with numerous big screens, photo-studios, and also provided a stage for live acts. Moreover, on the digital screens which are across the store, some fashion shows´ images and advertising campaigns are displayed (William, 2014). In this way, the experience of purchasing becomes more vivid and entertaining while the online and offline components are working together.

Another example is the Kiddicare smartphone app, in which consumers can compare prices. The app allows people to identify the location of sale products and to check whether the item they are looking for is in stock, or if it can be ordered online without going to the 'real´ store (William, 2014). In the United States, the Walmart app allows consumers to check product availability and prices both online and offline. Moreover, you can also add to your shopping list items by scanning them, see their details and information, and check purchasers´ ratings and reviews.

ELECTRONIC BUSINESS

Electronic business, or **e-business**, is the application of information and communication technologies (ICT) in support of all the activities of business. Commerce constitutes the exchange of products and services between businesses, groups and individuals and can be seen as one of the essential activities of any business. Electronic commerce focuses on the use of ICT to enable the external activities and relationships of the business with individuals, groups and other businesses or e business refers to business with help of internet i. e. doing business with the help of internet network. The term "e-business" was coined by IBM's marketing and Internet team in 1996. E-Business Strategy

The term electronic business (commonly referred to as E-business or e-business) is sometimes used interchangeably with e-commerce. In fact, e-business encompasses a broader definition that includes not only e-commerce, but customer relationship management (CRM), business partnerships, e-learning, and electronic transactions within an organization.

Electronic-business methods enable companies to link their internal and external data-processing systems more efficiently and flexibly, to work more closely with suppliers and partners, and to better satisfy the needs and expectations of customers. In practice, e-business is more than just e-commerce. While e-business refers to a strategic focus with an emphasis on the functions that occur using electronic capabilities, e-commerce is a subset of an overall e-business strategy.

E-Business Process

E-business involves business processes that span the entire value chain: electronic purchasing and supply-chain management, electronic order processing, customer service, and business partner collaboration. Special technical standards for e-business facilitate the exchange of data between companies. E-business software allows the integration of intrafirm and interfirm business processes. E-business can be conducted using the Internet, intranets, extranets, or some combination of these.

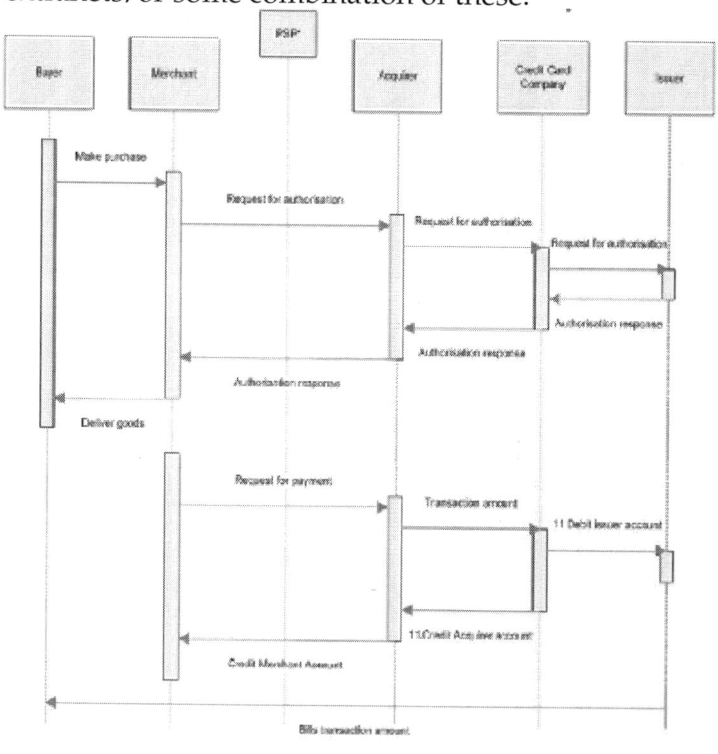

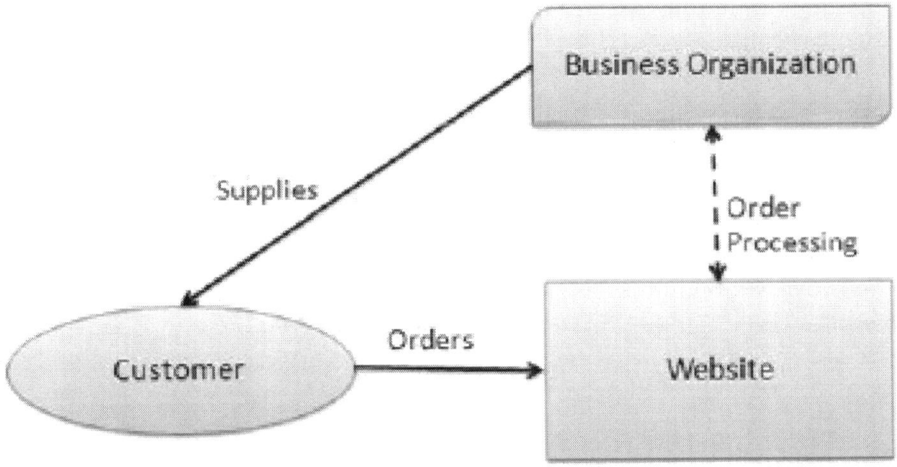

E-business/e-commerce transaction

This is an example of the electronic steps for a credit-card transaction.

In the emerging global economy, e-commerce and e-business have become increasingly necessary components of business strategy and strong catalysts for economic development. The integration of information and communications technology (ICT) in business has revolutionized relationships within organizations and those among organizations and individuals. Specifically, the use of ICT in business has enhanced productivity, encouraged greater customer participation, and enabled mass customization.

Advantages of E-Commerce

E-business enhances three primary processes:

1. *Production processes* including procurement, ordering and replenishment of stocks; processing of payments; electronic access to suppliers; and production control processes
2. *Customer-focused processes* including promotional and marketing efforts, Internet sales, customer purchase orders and payments, and customer support
3. *Internal management processes* including employee services, training, internal information-sharing, videoconferencing, and recruiting. Electronic applications enhance information flow between production and sales forces to improve sales-force productivity. ICT improves the efficiency of work-group communications and electronic publishing of internal business information.

E-business Strategic Planning

Developing an e-business requires extensive research and planning in order to be successful in cyberspace. This planning involves the development of a solid and concise business plan, and a focused marketing plan well before a website is created. An e-business plan must have clearly defined goals as it is difficult for any business organization to stay on track if there are no goals in place for guidance.

E-business Strategic Planningn recent years, the Internet has presented a wealth of opportunities for conducting commerce on a global scale. As a result, there has been a significant increase in both the number of start-up businesses in the e-commerce field, as well as the number of traditional "brick and mortar" businesses entering this "new economy." According to Forrester Research, an independent technology and market research company, US online retail sales will grow from $172 billion in 2005 to $329 billion in 2010. This increase translates to a steady 14% compound annual growth rate over the next 5 years. E-commerce will represent 13% of total US retail sales in 2010.

Developing an e-business requires extensive research and planning in order to be successful in cyberspace. This planning involves the development of a solid and concise business plan, and a focused marketing plan well before a website is created. An e-business plan must have clearly defined goals as it is difficult for any business organization to stay on track if there are no goals in place for guidance.

Strategic planning determines where an organization is headed over the next year or more, how it's going to get there and how it will know if the results are successful. There are a variety of perspectives, models and approaches used in strategic planning. The way that a strategic plan is developed is dependent on the nature of the organization's leadership, culture of the organization, size of the organization, complexity of the organization's environment and expertise of planners. Goals-based planning is perhaps the most common strategic planning model and begins with focus on the organization's mission and vision and strategies to achieve these goals.

Vision and Mission Statements

A successful organization understands that it takes more than a good plan to succeed in business. It takes an empowered organization with impassioned leadership, focused on realistic goals. It takes vision, consensus and a sense of purpose. According to Jack Welch, previous Chairman for General Electric, "Good business leaders create a vision, articulate the vision, passionately own the vision, and relentlessly drive it to completion." The vision statement describes what the leaders of an organization want it to look like in ideal terms in the future - the results they seek to achieve and characteristics needed to possess in order to achieve those results. The strategic vision statement provides direction and motivation for organizational goal setting.

A mission statement is an organization's declaration of its principles, purposes, and objectives that can be used to initiate, evaluate, and refine all life activities. It is an enduring statement of purpose for an organization that identifies the scope of its operations in product and market terms, and reflects its values and priorities. Every company no matter how big or small, needs a mission statement as a source of direction, a kind of compass, that lets its employees, its customers, and even its stockholders know what it stands for and where it's headed. A mission statement gives everyone the opportunity to know what the organization is about.

Environmental Analysis

Environmental analysis plays a central role in strategic management. For a company to gain or maintain a sustainable competitive advantage in the e-commerce marketplace, it must be ever attentive, watching and preparing for shifts in the business environment and must be prepared to alter its strategies and plans when the need arises. Companies conduct environmental analysis to identify market opportunities and threats and also to anticipate changes in highly complex and dynamic environments. By anticipating changes accurately, companies can gain competitive advantage through quick action. Environmental analysis assesses current environmental circumstances and projects, forecasts, and monitors their future situation. According to eSocrates. com, a knowledge, management and eLearning company, Environmental analysis also helps the firm to position itself in a continually evolving environment by matching its characteristics to the environment's demands.

Competitive Factors

In formulating an e-business strategy, a company must consider the strategies of their competitors. A competitive analysis allows them to identify the competition within the same market in order to analyze their strengths and weaknesses. This will help a company develop strategies that will provide them with a definite advantage and barriers that can be established in order to prevent competition from taking over the market. A competitive analysis can also identify any weaknesses that can be improved within the business development cycle.

Economic Factors

The economic environment consists of factors that affect consumer purchasing power and spending patterns. The environment in which an organization operates is very much determined by macro-economic factors. A recession can dramatically reduce total income and expenditure levels in the economy, in turn affecting consumer demand. Higher taxes, internet rates and inflation similarly serve as disincentives to consumer confidence (and therefore spending), while economic growth and prosperity can generate spending and an overall "feel-good factor." The importance of the economic environment - the broad trends in employment, inflation and growth that shape regions, nations and the world - to the growth of e-business in the U. S. should not be underestimated.

Social / Demographic Factors

Demography is the study of human populations in terms of size, density, location, age, ethnicity, income, occupation and other statistics, as well as those variables bringing about change in that population. The demographic environment consists of the customers who form the marketplace. These customers may be demographic environment shifts as customers enter the market, mature, and leave the market.

As the consumer's level of comfort with online functions such as e-mail and research continues to increase, so too will their level of participation in e-commerce. A growing online consumer base, increases in new product categories, and efforts by online retailers to optimize online shopping experiences will spark significant growth in e-commerce in years to come.

Long Term Objectives

One of the key purposes of a comprehensive planning process is to establish a set of long-term objectives and recommend a series of strategies and policies to ensure that these goals are attained in the most effective way. The established goals combined represent an organization's vision or desire for a future condition that will enhance its overall image and quality of life. It is important to understand that these objectives serve as the backbone of the strategic plan. That means that any planning element included in this plan should function as reinforcement to these objectives. The achievements of an organization are based on the combined efforts of each individual within the organization working toward common objectives. These objectives should be practical, should be clearly understood by everyone within the organization and should mirror the organization's basic personality and character.

Here are some steps that an organization can take to evolve the company culture toward e-business:

- In order to be successful, e-business requires that information flow freely within an organization. Business experts need to be designated in each major functional area to facilitate the free flow of information and connect people and processes throughout the enterprise.
- Recognize that an e-business is an inside-out proposition. In order to operate as a true e-business, your core processes must be predominantly

real-time, online, integrated and interactive.

- Remember that continual education and training is essential. Everyone within the organization must be knowledgeable of basic e-business concepts. For those who are accountable in areas that involve direct interaction with customers, more detailed training is needed.
- Instill a sense of urgency necessary to deliver the level of service that should help drive business decisions. Customers now expect immediate quality service, whether it is in person, on the phone or on the web.
- Recognize that the Internet and the realities of e-business have permanently changed the barriers to competition. Viable competitors can spring up almost overnight.

The completion of a written strategic plan document marks an important milestone in the planning process, but major benefits accrue to the organization only when the plan is put into operation. Achieving the established goals will require effort and attention from every part of the organization. Research must be conducted in order to determine all questions concerning success measurement. The questions "What do we want to achieve with this e-business website?" and "How do we know when the goal for the site is reached?" are of primary interest.

Continuous planning with feedback is a strategic planning necessity that involves company wide activity. Ongoing measurement and evaluation after completion is necessary to track success of the e-business plan and to determine if any further changes or modifications need to be made. Most importantly, one must constantly revisit their strategic plan to ensure that they are meeting the customer's needs and providing the highest level of customer service.

E Business Strategy -e commerce business strategies

With the advent of the Internet and plenty of web development technologies around the world, e-business is the new mantra of businesses in today's world. The Internet has in many ways facilitated the development of businesses worldwide that can reach out to a wider consumer base and advertises their products more effectively and efficiently. Corporate communications, interface designs, cutting edge applications are also found on the Internet. E business has been added as the latest domain in business and has become a must-have in the highly competitive technology driven open market. E Business Strategy can be summarized as the strategies governing E Businesses through calculated information dissemination.

Information dissemination has been widely regarded as the forte of ebusiness, which uses information technology in a most efficient manner. Not only has e-business has come to play an important role in the world trade scenario; there is no business without an accompanying e-business in today's world. E business gives a business the opportunity to open its portal to the global market and become a part of the global business community. The most important feature of e-business is that the helps businesses move on to the international scene at minimal cost but with maximum efficiency. E-business has achieved unprecedented levels of success as business models, which have not been enjoyed by any other business models. Some of the examples would be MRP (Material Requirements Planning), EDI (Electronic Data Interchange) or ERP (Enterprise Resource Planning). The essential features of e-business strategies are supply chain management and email marketing.

A state-of-the-art E Business Strategy would generally include:

Supply chain management: effective management of the supply chain can be handled with the help of e-business strategies, which will ensure better coordination between the wholesalers and the retailers of various products. Better integration of the supply chain right from the source till the final delivery of the product can be effectively implemented using e-business strategy. This also brings us to the point of e- commerce where a parallel network of buying and selling can be observed using dissemination of information over the Internet. Everything ranging from automobiles to electronic gizmos can be bought over the Internet in a hassle free manner under the aegis of sound supply chain management.

Customer service and customer relationship manage-ment: effective e-business strategies would involve better customer service and customer relationship management ensuring the highest level of consumer satisfaction. E business is targeted at providing the customer-friendly services, which would include the timely delivery of goods right at the doorstep of the consumer.

Inventory and service management integration: e business strategies can also help in better inventory and service management integration through formulating specific plans for inventory accumulation and purchasing machinery and equipment which will avoid unnecessary purchases which can lead to higher expenditures entailing different tax implications.

Tactical operations alignment: tactical operations directed towards short-term goals as opposed to strategic planning aimed at long term goals can be better coordinated implementing the e-business strategies.

E-business diverges from the traditional sphere of business by speeding up the business activities and giving a totally new dimension and definition to businesses worldwide be it whether partnerships, joint ventures or large corporations. The internet, intranet, cellular networks and other forms of digital technology have created a niche value chain among clients, employees, suppliers, stakeholders and traders coordinated in the world of web marketing. The tools and pillars of e-business strategies include acceptance of payments over the Internet, online advertising, on-line trading and auction deals over the Internet. E-business strategies will also differ for small and medium-sized businesses. Apart from regular sources, e-business strategies can generate revenue from maintenance of current channel integrity, revenue made from paid marketing alliances, revenues derived from franchisees and subscriptions.

E-COMMERCE IN TRAVEL AND TOURISM

E-commerce is bringing new business opportunities to the global travel and tourism industry. Tourism-related institutions and Internet companies are joining to tap the potential market created by e-commerce. This paper is an historical analysis of penetration of e-commerce in the travel and tourism industry. The analysis identifies a number of consistent customer experience across different channels, among airlines, and involving both international and domestic travel in emerging economies with limited internet access. It is argued, from this analysis, that there area number of emerging new technologies such as mobile devices and global positioning systems which need to be taken into account and effects systematically assessed. The paper concludes that a major challenge facing the industry is to assess the impact of these technologies on different aspects of the travel industry and to find out how much value-added services they actually provide to consumers.

Information technology has introduced e-commerce through the development of the Internet and the World Wide Web. These developments have impacted both consumer and industry behaviors in the areas of travel and tourism. Consumers have more options regarding vacation and budget planning. 95 per cent of web users have searched the Internet to gather travel related information. 93 per cent visited destination web sites and nearly one half used e-mail to gather travel-related information (Xinran, Dae- Young & Morrison, 2006). Almost three- fourths of online travel buyers used search engines prior to making their purchases. In addition to the Internet, technology gadgets such as GPS 's, mobile phones, smart phones and hand-held devices have improved consumers' tourism and travel experiences. Information accessibility regarding travel, destination, bookings, payments, hotels, attractions, and the quality of maps are areas for improvement.

Information and Communication Technologies (ICT) have affected the travel and tourism industry for at least 50 years, particularly in the areas of automation and networking of distribution channels. Local travel agents that used the global distribution system have adjusted marketing strategies and expanded services in order to realize increased competitive advantage. Local tourism business comprehension and utilization of the Internet has permitted increased visibility in additional market segments. Businesses have increased services globally by registering with online travel agents, online advertising agents, and inter-organizational reservation systems. In addition, many businesses have developed websites which offer planning, booking and payment services online for added consumer convenience. Businesses that have not made use of the Internet cannot compete and therefore they must grasp the opportunity before they are out-competed by those that have.

Information technology has played a central role in the growth and improvement of the travel and tourism industry. The lasting effects of technology are improved information accessibility, a higher level of competition, and a larger market of consumers and businesses around the globe.

Information Technology in the Tourism and Travel Industry

During the pre- computerized time, the role of the travel agent was to advise clients on travel destinations and to act as an intermediary in the complicated process of arranging travel bookings. Even as late as the early 1990's, consumers booked cruise travel and tourism through travel agents as many companies did not offer direct bookings. There were two waves of information technology that have had a major impact on the industry. The first of these is the development of the direct reservation systems, such as the American Airlines SABRE system. The second is the development of online sales channels via the Internet.

Literature review on "Impact of e-commerce in Travel and Tourism industry and challenges for adopting it."

E-commerce in travel and tourism is growing day by day which provide opportunity to this industry to groom and grow. Due to change in Information technology, e commerce is emerged in this industry and companies are now heading toward e-business through website, internet and different online software. Moving from traditional business way to e-commerce way is quite challenging and various factors are standing as a barrier for companies to adapt e-commerce. There several advantages and disadvantages of e-commerce in travel and tourism industry. To adapt e-commerce, this industry's main challenge is to transform traditional buyers to e-commerce buyers. The purpose of this literature review is to give short introduction on travel and tourism industry along with the impact on this industry after adaption of ecommerce. What will be benefits after adapting e-commerce and what are the barriers which stop firms to enter in e-business? A short description on consumer behaviour on e-commerce is also gazed on this review.

Tourism Industry is one of the back bones of economy in developed, developing and underdeveloped countries and one of the major sources of foreign exchequer. This industry is growing very rapidly and millions of people are directly and indirectly associated with this Industry. This industry represents accounts for 9. 9 percent of global GDP, 10. 9 percent of world exports, and 9. 4 percent of world investment. (World Economic Forum, 2009). The use of internet is rapidly growing day by day and as per International Telecommunication union (2009), around 2 billion people will be online by end of 2010. Hence, internet will be effective tool to promote and open up new opportunities for travel and tourism industry sector though e-commerce. "E-commerce is defined as the process of buying and selling or exchanging products, services and information via computer networks including the internet."(Turban et. al, 2000). There are various advantages of using internet in tourism as it is fast and easy to access destination, receive price, search popular destinations and get information about destination etc as well as it generates income for many people around the globe. However, it has some limitations as some information may not be correct, outdated, portrayed and we have seen several online fraud case too. In a nutshell, due to its various benefits rather than some limitations, it is essential for travel and tourism industry to adopt e-commerce for their growth and success.

With rise of internet usage on people's daily life, tourism industries are tapping business through e-commerce. E-commerce refers both financial and informational transaction through electronic media between on organization, between people or to third party (Chaffey et. al, 2006). Through e-commerce, these industries are trying to reach global population to enhance their business through different e-commerce tools and ad there will be more and more challenge to these sectors in coming days for adopting e-commerce.

Objectives

From the above little introduction, we can simply say that e-commerce is bringing various opportunities in travel and tourism sectors. Many industries on this field had already adopted e-commerce and some are on the way to adopt it to enhance their services and better facilitate their customers however these developments have certain impacts on the behaviour of customers as well in industry. (Mamaghaini, 2009)

My prime focus on this research paper is to find out the impact and challenge of e-commerce in travel and tourism industry and reviewing it through different academic journals. Through those journals I will be able to answer, how will be travel and tourism industry benefit if they adopt e-commerce, what are the customers' perceptions on travel and Tourism Company which adopts e-commerce and what are the benefits and limitations of e-commerce in travel and tourism. Further my main objectives of research are to find out following:-

- Overall impact of e-commerce in travel and tourism industry

- Customers' perceptions of e-commerce in travel and tourism industry
- Benefits and limitations of e-commerce in travel and tourism industry
- Major challenges in adopting e-commerce in travel and tourism industry

LITERATURE REVIEW

Many researchers or scholars have done various researches about e-commerce in travel and tourism industry. Many of them have pointed positive impact of e-commerce in travel and tourism and some have pointed challenges for adopting e-commerce and barriers of e-commerce in travel and tourism industry.

As per Werthner H. and Ricci F., e-commerce in travel and tourism industries are continuously increasing despite of tough economic problems. (Werthner H., Ricci F., 2004). As per them, this industry is adopting application of B2B (business to business) and B2C (business to consumer). This industry has changed the ways of do business for traditional ways to modern way, i. e. e-commerce via web and other online transaction software where as other industries are still adopting the traditional way. Web is changing the behaviour of consumers are well as they are becoming less loyal, take less time for choosing and consuming the tourism products. As this industry is service oriented business industry, companies are implementing various new techniques to satisfy consumer needs and providing information to them through web and different value generating strategies like value extraction, value capture, value addition value creation(Werthner H., Ricci F., 2004). Travel and tourism is information based service orientated business and the product is termed as "confidence good" (Werthner H., Ricci F., 2004) and prior comprehensive assessment of quality is impossible however due to use of e-commerce feeds backs from consumers can be obtained in short span of time and this services can be enhanced accordingly. Due to adoption of e-commerce in travel and tourism industry consumers are becoming more powerful players as they can choose their destination and sites in few minutes whereas travel agents, travel websites etc see diminishing power in sales however they are providing new market functionality using new technologies to attract more consumers. Many tour operator, travel agents, online travel agents are using these strategy to attract more consumers however using more high-tech technologies needs huge investments, need more high skill human resource etc.

There are various factors which are considered that travel and tourism will adapt ecommerce strategy. As per Kim (2004), there are main two factors for conducting successful e-commerce strategy which are security of the e-commerce system and user-friendly Web interface. Security means not only securing own system but also providing security assurance to users who are using the sites or online software. User friendly web interface give consumer trust and it's easy to convenience for customers. Beside these factors other factors are also essential to succeed which are top management support, IT infrastructure, and customer acceptance. Top management support plays vital role as per Kim as they are the decision makers and their support and decision will direct the company to use the strategy. Further, he also explained that without proper IT structure and skilled human resources, e-commerce strategy will fail. One of the factors he explained is customer acceptance; customer acceptance means the way customer accepts the web or online software of the company and it should have very rich contents and very easy to use. These factors will decide whether business will get more customers. Customers intend to use research website quality due to content richness and ease of use. (Law and Bai, 2008).

Law and Bai on their research paper mentioned there are two types of customers who use travel companies websites, those are buyers and browsers. Buyers are those people who actually intend to buy the services whereas browsers are those who intend to surf and get information only. Those browsers can be converted to buyers by improving the website contents, making it attractive, provided very rich in contents and very user friendly to use. As more and more travel companies are applying these strategies, the increase in percentage of website buyers and browsers are also increasing day by day. This is due to adaption of e-commerce technology in travel and tourism industry.

There are various benefits for small and medium sized tourism enterprise to use e-commerce. In journal of Kim (2004), he pointed few benefits of using e-commerce in tourism which are as follows; -

- Providing easy access to information on tourism products and services
- Providing better information on tourism products and services
- Providing convenience for customers
- Expanding choices by customers
- Creating new markets
- Establishing interactive relationship with customers
- Improving customer services
- Improving image and public recognition of the small & medium sized tourism enterprises
- Saving time for providing tourism services
- Providing customized & specialized tourism products & services
- Reducing operating cost
- Simplifying the process business
- Interacting with business partners
- Founding new business partners

(Kim, 2004)

Due to adopting of e-commerce by small and medium enterprises are beneficial in various aspects. In Kim research, he explained by adopting e-commerce companies can interact with customers frequently which will enhance their customer service and use of ecommerce also reduce their operating costs as lots of human resource is not needed and new opportunity of finding new agents, creating new markets etc. Due to use of ecommerce by small and medium enterprises they can save time as well.

E- Commerce is huge lap in travel and tourism industry moving from traditional way to technological way and there are various barriers for travel and tourism companies to adapt e-commerce in their business. As mentioned by Kim (2004), include 'limited knowledge of available technology,' 'lack of awareness,' 'cost of initial investment,' 'lack of confidence in the benefits of e-commerce,' and 'cost of system maintenance.' These barriers also include 'shortage of skilled human resources,' and 'resistance to adoption of e-commerce.' Further he mentioned 'insufficient e-commerce infrastructure,' and 'small e-commerce market size' might be barrier factors depending upon the market size (Kim, 2004).

Moving from traditional way to technological way is not easy so in order to adapt e-commerce huge investment on Information Technological (IT) have to done along with this staffs have to be trained accordingly. It is not always possible for small and medium size companies to invest huge amount and get skill human resource people. Some countries have different rules and regulation for e-commerce business rather than traditional ways. Government rules and regulation also plays a vital role for adapting e-commerce. Further, websites and software must be rich in contents very easy to use, updated time to time. If these factors are ignored than these factors will be barrier of e-commerce in tourism.

There are several challenges to adopt e-commerce in travel and tourism industry. As per Mamaghani (2009), the behaviour of customers is changing and due to e-commerce they swap agency in few minutes if they are not happy with them. Customers expect the same service, same treatment as offered by travel agencies through their outlet or through the web. Different customers have different ways of surfing internet as per their level of internet knowledge as well user friendly website and website's rich contents. To adapt e-commerce by company, they have to focus on their detailed of services, product availability, special offers, personalized information which are important factors consumers search on web for the product. He further mentioned that "Individual e-commerce customers have been known to be demanding and unforgiving". As such, regular maintenance, upgrade of technologies and continuous improvement of customer service are the core factors for enhancing business and attracting more customers. Consumers these days are far more demanding and want convenience, speed and a seamless buying experience. Main challenges as per Mamaghani is to create awareness among customers about product, make them loyal.

Due to drastic change in technology, Internet, mobile and handheld portals available, consumers access the Internet for travel planning and companies have to grasp these technologies and move as per the change in technology which of course is expensive and need skilled human resource manpower. Some countries have weak Information technology structure and people from these countries might have problems for using e-commerce. One of the main challenge as per Mamaghaini that adaptation of e-commerce in travel and tourism is to build trust of people in internet system so that they could choose e-commerce instead of tradition way.

To build the trust among people, companies can try to capture a part of the traditional travel agent client market by focusing on different advertisement, emphasizing online agents' knowledge. (Wolfe et. al, 2004). Wolfe et. al have mentioned that companies can lure their customers via providing personalized service through email, web texts customized web sites that are built "on the fly" based on users' specific profiles and needs. The main theme of writers is to gain customer confidence and trust toward the website. "The challenge is determining how a web site can exude trust and good service". To build customer trust, Wolfe et al have suggested online travel agencies have to give telephone numbers or e-mail contact information. This phone numbers and email address can be useful for customers who want proper information about destination, services and some specific questions. An e-mail reply or telephone call allows companies to respond more inquiries with politeness in a professional way which of course provide sense of postal mail. In this way a browser may be transformed to buyer.

Similarly, to attract more consumers, website should provide virtual tour of the destination. Virtual tour means description of the destination by through audio and visual mode by sharing videos, photo, destination details with pictures etc. (Cho et. al, 2002). Cho et. al have mentioned that virtual tour attracts customers as it give the picture of the destination, hotel details where they are suppose to go, stay and enjoy. Virtual tour enables tourists to become more confident about their trip, they can choose the destination which leads them more satisfaction rather than booking the product through tradition way. At least, they can picture destination, hotel, transportation system etc about the destination before their travel date.

BUSINESS MODEL

A **business model** is an "abstract representation of an organization, be it conceptual, textual, and/or graphical, of all core interrelated architectural, co-operational, and financial arrangements designed and developed by an organization presently and in the future, as well as all core products and/or services the organization offers, or will offer, based on these arrangements that are needed to achieve its strategic goals and objectives." This definition by Al-Debei and Avison (2008) indicates that value proposition, value architecture, value finance, and value network articulate the primary constructs or dimensions of business models.

A business model describes the rationale of how an organization creates, delivers, and captures value, in economic, social, cultural or other contexts. The process of business model construction is part of business strategy.

In theory and practice, the term *business model* is used for a broad range of informal and formal descriptions to represent core aspects of a business, including purpose, business process, target customers, offerings, strategies, infrastructure, organiza-tional structures, sourcing, trading practices, and operational processes and policies. The literature has provided very diverse interpretations and definitions of a business model. A systematic review and analysis of manager responses to a survey defines business models as the design of organizational structures to enact a commercial opportunity. Further extensions to this design logic emphasize the use of narrative or coherence in business model descriptions as mechanisms by which entrepreneurs create extraordinarily successful growth firms.

Business models are used to describe and classify businesses, especially in an entrepreneurial setting, but they are also used by managers inside companies to explore possibilities for future development. Well-known business models can operate as "recipes" for creative managers. Business models are also referred to in some instances within the context of accounting for purposes of public reporting.

History

Over the years, business models have become much more sophisticated. The *bait and hook* business model (also referred to as the "razor and blades business model" or the "tied products business model") was introduced in the early 20th century. This involves offering a basic product at a very low cost, often at a loss (the "bait"), then charging compensatory recurring amounts for refills or associated products or services (the "hook"). Examples include: razor (bait) and blades (hook); cell phones (bait) and air time (hook); computer printers (bait) and ink cartridge refills (hook); and cameras (bait) and prints (hook). A variant of this model is Adobe, a software developer that gives away its document reader free of charge but charges several hundred dollars for its document writer.

In the 1950s, new business models came from McDonald's Restaurants and Toyota. In the 1960s, the innovators wereWal-Mart and Hypermarkets. The 1970s saw new business models from FedEx and Toys R Us; the 1980s fromBlockbuster, Home Depot, Intel, and Dell Computer; the 1990s from Southwest Airlines, Netflix, eBay, Amazon. com, andStarbucks.

Today, the type of business models might depend on how technology is used. For example, entrepreneurs on the internet have also created entirely new models that depend entirely on existing or emergent technology. Using technology, businesses can reach a large number of customers with minimal costs. In addition, the rise of outsourcing and globalization has meant that business models must also account for strategic sourcing, complex supply chains and moves to collaborative, relational contracting structures.

Theoretical and empirical insights to business models

Design logic and narrative coherence

Design logic views the business model as an outcome of creating new organizational structures or changing existing structures to pursue a new opportunity. Gerry George and Adam Bock (2011) conducted a comprehensive literature review and surveyed managers to understand how they perceived the components of a business model. In that analysis these authors show that there is a design logic behind how entrepreneurs and managers perceive and explain their business model. In further extensions to the design logic, George and Bock (2012) use case studies and the IBM survey data on business models in large companies, to describe how CEOs and entrepreneurs create narratives or stories in a coherent manner to move the business from one opportunity to another. They also show that when the narrative is incoherent or the components of the story are misaligned, that these businesses tend to fail. They recommend ways in which the entrepreneur or CEO can create strong narratives for change.

Complementarities of business models between partnering firms

Studying collaborative research and the accessing of external sources of technology, Hummel et al. (2010) found that in deciding on business partners, it is important to make sure that both parties' business models are complementary. For example, they found that it was important to identify the value drivers of potential partners by analyzing their business models, and that it is beneficial to find partner firms that understand key aspects of our own firm's business model.

The University of Tennessee conducted research into highly collaborative business relationships. Researchers codified their research into a sourcing business model known as Vested (also referred to as Vested Outsourcing). Vested is a hybrid sourcing business model in which buyers and suppliers in an outsourcing or business relationship focus on shared values and goals to create an arrangement that is highly collaborative and mutually beneficial to each.

Categorization of Business Models

From about 2012, some research and experimentation has theorized about a so-called "liquid business model".

V4 BM Framework

Al-Debei and Avison (2010) **V4 BM Framework** - four main dimensions encapsulating sixteen elements: Value Proposition, Value Architecture, Value Network, and Value Finance

- **Value Proposition:** This dimension implies that a BM should include a description of the products/services a digital organization offers, or will offer, along with their related information. Furthermore, the BM needs also to describe the value elements incorporated within the offering, as well as the nature of targeted market segment(s) along with their preferences.
- **Value Architecture:** portrays the concept as a holistic structural design of an organization, including its technological architecture, organizational infrastructure, and their configurations.
- **Value Network:** depicts the cross-company or inter-organization perspective towards the concept and has gained much attention in the BM literature.
- **Value Finance:** depicts information related to costing, pricing methods, and revenue structure

Shift from pipes to platforms

Sangeet Paul Choudary (2013) distinguishes between two broad families of business models in an article in *Wired*magazine. Choudary contrasts pipes (linear business models) with platforms (networked business models). In the case of pipes, firms create good and services, push them out and sell them to customers. Value is produced upstream and consumed downstream. There is a linear flow, much like water flowing through a pipe. Unlike pipes, platforms do not just create and push stuff out. They allow users to create and consume value.

In an op-ed on MarketWatch, Choudary, Van Alstyne and Parker further explain how business models are moving from pipes to platforms, leading to disruption of entire industries.

Platform Business Models

In an earlier article in the *Harvard Business Review*, Sangeet Paul Choudary elaborates on the three elements of a successful platform business model. The *Toolbox* creates connection by making it easy for others to plug into the platform. This infrastructure enables interactions between participants. The *Magnet* creates pull that attracts participants to the platform. For transaction platforms, both producers and consumers must be present to achieve critical mass. The*Matchmaker* fosters the flow of value by making connections between producers and consumers. Data is at the heart of successful matchmaking, and distinguishes platforms from other business models.

Chen (2009) stated that the business model in the twenty-first century has to take into account the capabilities of Web 2. 0, such as collective intelligence, network effects, user-generated content, and the possibility of self-improving systems. He suggested that the service industry such as the airline, traffic, transportation, hotel, restaurant, information and communications technology and online gaming industries will be able to benefit in adopting business models that take into account the characteristics of Web 2. 0. He also emphasized that Business Model 2. 0 has to take into account not just the technology effect of Web 2. 0 but also the networking effect. He gave the example of the success story of Amazon in making huge revenues each year by developing a full-blown open platform that supports a large and thriving community of companies that re-use Amazon's on-demand commerce services.

Applications

Malone et al. found that some business models, as defined by them, indeed performed better than others in a dataset consisting of the largest U. S. firms, in the period 1998 through 2002, while they did not prove whether the existence of a business model mattered.

In the context of the Software-Cluster, which is funded by the German Federal Ministry of Education and Research, abusiness model wizard for software companies has been developed. It supports the design and analysis of software business models. The tool's underlying concept and data were published in various scientific publications.

The concept of a business model has been incorporated into certain accounting standards. For example, the International Accounting Standards Board (IASB) utilizes an "entity's business model for managing the financial assets" as a criterion for determining whether such assets should be measured at amortized cost or at fair value in its financial instruments accounting standard, IFRS 9. In their 2013 proposal for accounting for financial instruments, the Financial Accounting Standards Board also proposed a similar use of business model for classifying financial instruments. The concept of business model has also been introduced into the accounting of deferred taxes under International Financial Reporting Standards with 2010 amendments to IAS 12 addressing deferred taxes related to investment property.

Both IASB and FASB have proposed using the concept of business model in the context of reporting a lessor's leaseincome and lease expense within their joint project on accounting for leases. The concept has also been proposed as an approach for determining the measurement and classification when accounting for insurance contracts. As a result of the increasing prominence the concept of business model has received in the context of financial reporting, the European Financial Reporting Advisory Group (EFRAG), which advises the European Union on endorsement of financial reporting standards, commenced a project on the "Role of the Business Model in Financial Reporting" in 2011.

Business Model Design

Business model design refers to the activity of designing a company's business model. It is part of the business development and business strategy process and involves design methods.

Definitions of Business Model

Al-Debei and Avison (2010) define a business model as an abstract representation of an organization. This may be conceptual, textual, and/or graphical, of all core interrelated architectural, co-operational, and financial arrangements designed and developed by an organization presently and in the future, as well all core products and/or services the organization offers, or will offer, based on these arrangements that are needed to achieve its strategic goals and objectives. This definition indicates that value proposition, value architecture, value finance, and value network articulate the primary constructs or dimensions of business models.

ECONOMIC CONSIDERATION

Al-Debei and Avison (2010) consider value finance as one of the main dimensions of BM which depicts information related to costing, pricing methods, and revenue structure. Stewart and Zhao (2000) defined the business model as "a statement of how a firm will make money and sustain its profit stream over time."

Component Consideration

Osterwalder et al. (2005) consider the Business Model as the blueprint of how a company does business. Slywotzky (1996) regards the business model as "the totality of how a company selects its customers, defines and differentiates it offerings, defines the tasks it will perform itself and those it will outsource, configures its resources, goes to market, creates utility for customers and captures profits."

Strategic Outcome

Mayo and Brown (1999) considered the business model as "the design of key interdependent systems that create and sustain a competitive business."

Definitions of Business Model Design or Development

Zott and Amit (2009) consider business model design from the perspectives of design themes and design content. Design themes refer to the system's dominant value creation drivers and design content examines in greater detail the activities to be performed, the linking and sequencing of the activities and who will perform the activities.

Design themes Emphasis of Business Model

Developing a Framework for Business Model Development with an emphasis on Design Themes, Lim (2010) proposed the Environment-Strategy-Structure-Operations (ESSO) Business Model Development which takes into consideration the alignment of the organization's strategy with the organization's structure, operations, and the environmental factors in achieving competitive advantage in varying combination of cost, quality, time, flexibility, innovation and affective.

Design content emphasis of business model design

Business model design includes the modeling and description of a company's:

- value propositions
- target customer segments
- distribution channels
- customer relationships
- value configurations
- core capabilities
- partner network
- cost structure
- revenue model

Business model design is distinct from business modeling. The former refers to defining the business logic of a company at the strategic level, whereas the latter refers to business process design at the operational level.

A business model design template can facilitate the process of designing and describing a company's business model.

Daas et al. (2012) developed a decision support system (DSS) for business model design. In their study a decision support system (DSS) is developed to help SaaS in this process, based on a design approach consisting of a design process that is guided by various design methods.

Examples of Business Models

In the early history of business models it was very typical to define business model types such as bricks-and-mortar or e-broker. However, these types usually describe only one aspect of the business (most often the revenue model). Therefore, more recent literature on business models concentrate on describing a business model as a whole, instead of only the most visible aspects.

The following examples provide an overview for various business model types that have been in discussion since the invention of term *business model*:

- Bricks and clicks business model

Business model by which a company integrates both offline (*bricks*) and online (*clicks*) presences. One example of the bricks-and-clicks model is when a chain of stores allows the user to order products online, but lets them pick up their order at a local store.

- Collective business models

Business system, organization or association typically composed of relatively large numbers of businesses, tradespersons or professionals in the same or related fields of endeavor, which pools resources, shares information or provides other benefits for their members. For example, a science park or high-tech campus provides shared resources (e. g. cleanrooms and other lab facilities) to the firms located on its premises, and in addition seeks to create an innovation community among these firms and their employees.

- Cutting out the middleman model

The removal of intermediaries in a supply chain: "cutting out the middleman". Instead of going through traditional distribution channels, which had some type of intermediate (such as a distributor, wholesaler, broker, or agent), companies may now deal with every customer directly, for example via the Internet.

- Direct sales model

Direct selling is marketing and selling products to consumers directly, away from a fixed retail location. Sales are typically made through party plan, one-to-one demonstrations, and other personal contact arrangements. A text book definition is: "The direct personal presentation, demonstration, and sale of products and services to consumers, usually in their homes or at their jobs."

- Distribution business models, various
- Value-added reseller model

Value Added Reseller is a model where a business makes something which is resold by other businesses but with modifications which add value to the original product or service. These modifications or additions are mostly industry specific in nature and are essential for the distribution. Businesses going for a VAR model have to develop a VAR network. It is one of the latest collaborative business models which can help in faster development cycles and is adopted by many Technology companies especially software.

- Fee in, free out

Business model which works by charging the first client a fee for a service, while offering that service free of charge to subsequent clients.

- Franchise

Franchising is the practice of using another firm's successful business model. For the franchisor, the franchise is an alternative to building 'chain stores' to *distribute* goods and avoid investment and liability over a chain. The franchisor's success is the success of the franchisees. The franchisee is said to have a greater incentive than a direct employee because he or she has a direct stake in the business.

- Sourcing business model

A Sourcing Business Model is a type of business model that is applied specifically to business relationships where more than one party needs to work with another party to be successful. It is the combination of two concepts: the contractual relationship framework a company uses with its supplier (transactional, relational, investment based), and the economic model used (transactional, output or outcome-based).

- Freemium business model

Business model that works by offering basic Web services, or a basic downloadable digital product, for free, while charging a premium for advanced or special features.

Other examples of business models are:

- Auction business model
- All-in-one business model
- Chemical Leasing
- Low-cost carrier business model
- Loyalty business models
- Monopolistic business model
- Multi-level marketing business model
- Network effects business model
- Online auction business model
- Online content business model
- Online media cooperative
- Premium business model
- Professional open-source model
- Pyramid scheme business model
- Razor and blades business model
- Servitization of products business model
- Subscription business model

BUSINESS MODEL FRAMEWORKS

Technology centric communities have defined "frameworks" for business modeling. These frameworks attempt to define a rigorous approach to defining business value streams. It is not clear, however, to what extent such frameworks are actually important for business planning. Business model frameworks represent the core aspect of any company; they involve "the totality of how a company selects its customers defines and differentiates its offerings, defines the tasks it will perform itself and those it will outsource, configures its resource, goes to market, creates utility for customers, and captures profits". A business framework involves internal factors (market analysis; products/services promotion; development of trust; social influence and knowledge sharing) and external factors (competitors and technological aspects). A state of the art review on business model frameworks can be found in Krumeich et al. (2012). In the following some frameworks are introduced.

- [[V[4] Business Model Framework]]
  Developed by Al-Debei and Avison (2010)
- Business reference model
  Business reference model is a reference model, concentrating on the architectural aspects of the core business of an enterprise, service organization or government agency.
- Component business model
  Technique developed by IBM to model and analyze an enterprise. It is a logical representation or map of business components or "building blocks" and can be depicted on a single page. It can be used to analyze the alignment of enterprise strategy with the organization's capabilities and investments, identify redundant or overlapping business capabilities, etc.
- Industrialization of services business model
  Business model used in strategic management and services marketing that treats service provision as an industrial process, subject to industrial optimization procedures
- Business Model Canvas
  Developed by A. Osterwalder, Yves Pigneur, Alan Smith, and 470 practitioners from 45 countries, the business model canvas is one of the most used frameworks for describing the elements of business models.

Related concepts

The process of business model design is part of business strategy. Business model design and innovation refer to the way a firm (or a network of firms) defines its business logic at the strategic level.

In contrast, firms implement their business model at the operational level, through their business operations. This refers to their process-level activities, capabilities, functions and infrastructure (for example, their business processes and business process modeling), their organisational structures (e. g. organigrams, workflows, human resources) and systems (e. g. information technology architecture, production lines).

Consequently, an operationally viable and feasible business model requires lateral alignment with the underlining business operations.

The brand is a consequence of the business model and has a symbiotic relationship with it, because the business model determines the brand promise, and the brand equity becomes a feature of the model. Managing this is a task of integrated marketing.

The standard terminology and examples of business models do not apply to most nonprofit organizations, since their sources of income are generally not the same as the beneficiaries. The term **funding model** is generally used instead.

How do design an e-commerce website?

The design of virtual stores is often the most important factor in the success or failure of online businesses. That doesn't simply mean that e-commerce web sites have to look *attractive* (though they do): they have to be *usable* (quick and easy to navigate around without irritating or confusing people), *reliable* (customers expect sites to be online 24 hours a day, seven days a week, and for pages to load without delay), and *secure* (because no one is prepared to type their credit card details into a website that isn't safe).

Setting up an online store used to be quite an undertaking. Not only did you have to build a dedicated website from scratch, you also had to develop your own **merchant system** that could securely process credit card details and ship transactions to and from bank computers. These days, anyone can set up an online store in minutes. Websites like PayPal make it possible to build a store very quickly and, since they have built-in credit card processing features, handling transactions couldn't be simpler. Many people set up virtual storefronts on the auction site eBay and then use PayPal (now a part of eBay too) to process their transactions. Some websites (notably Amazon) allow you to incorporate mini versions of their store inside your own website—so you make a small commission selling their products within your own site.

It used to be said that the right **domain name** was an essential requirement for a successful online business but some of the most memorably named web sites (including pets. com, etoys. com and garden. com) were early casualties of the dot. com boom and bust. As successful Web businesses such as eBay and Amazon have proved, there doesn't necessarily have to be an obvious connection between the name of a website and things it actually does or sells: all that matters is that, over time, people will come to know, love, and trust the brand and visit the site instinctively when they want to buy something.

Using e-commerce to sell information

There's lots of money to be made online, but not all of this involves selling goods in the traditional way. Many online businesses try to make money by offering a mixture of free and premium services. Yahoo! (which originally stood for Yet Another Hierarchical Officious Oracle), is probably the best-known example of a website like this. Created as a comprehensive directory of other websites, it mutated into a search engine and then a portal, offering a gateway to all kinds of other **premium** services. For example, you can get free e-mail through Yahoo!, but you can also pay extra for a more sophisticated e-mail system; you can store your photographs for free on Yahoo's Flickr site, but you can pay an extra sum to have them printed out or processed in various ways.

Newspapers, magazines, and book publishers also try to make money through a mixture of free and premium services. While most of them offer their basic **content** (the horrible, unappealing name that online businesses give to the words and pictures they publish) for free, using advertising to make money, some also offer a proportion of their articles for a one-off fixed fee or subscription). Buying an article involves a transaction similar to the ones you'd make on Amazon or eBay, so this kind of online publishing is also clearly a variety of e-commerce.

Advantages and disadvantages of e-commerce

Although early reactions to online shopping websites were often mixed ("It takes too long to find what you want", "I'm not sure they're secure", "The things I want are never in stock", "You can't see what you're buying"), things have improved greatly over the last decade and online businesses have found ways round most of the drawbacks. (For example, some online clothing stores sensibly offer free returns if you don't like the clothes you've bought or if they turn out not to fit.) Many people now swear by online shopping and wouldn't dream of setting foot in a real-world store where prices are often higher, waiting lines are longer, and the doors open only during normal business hours.

For businesses too, e-commerce has opened up all kinds of new opportunities. Not many can compete with huge businesses like Amazon or eBay, but anyone can open an online store and start trading within a matter of minutes. Small local stores, long threatened by the growth of giant retailers like Wal-Mart and Tesco, have found a new lease of life by trading online and selling their products mail order.

Electronic Cash and Electronic Payment Schemes ecash

Using cryptography, **ecash** was conceived by David Chaum as an anonymous electronic money or electronic cash system in 1983. It was realized through his corporation Digicash and used as micropayment system at one US bank from 1995 to 1998.

Design

Chaum published the idea of anonymous electronic money in a 1983 paper; eCash software on the user's local computer stored money in a digital format, cryptographically signed by a bank. The user could spend the digital money at any shop accepting eCash, without having to open an account with the vendor first, or transmitting credit card numbers. Security was ensured by public key digital signature schemes. The RSA blind signatures achieved unlinkability between withdrawal and spend transactions. Depending on the payment transactions, one distinguishes between on-line and off-line electronic cash: If the payee has to contact a third party (e. g., the bank or the credit-card company acting as an acquirer) before accepting a payment, the system is called an on-line system. In 1990, Chaum together with Moni Naor proposed the first off-line e-cash system, which was also based on blind signatures.

History

Chaum started the company DigiCash in 1989 with "ecash" as its trademark. He raised $10 million from David Marquardtand by 1997 Nicholas Negroponte was its chairman. Yet, in the United States, only one bank -the Mark Twain bank in Saint Louis, MO- implemented ecash, testing it as micropayment system; Similar to credit cards, the system was free to purchasers, while merchants paid a transaction fee. After a three-year trial that signed up merely 5, 000 customers, the system was dissolved in 1998, one year after the bank had been purchased by Mercantile Bank, a large issuer of credit cards. David Chaum opined then "As the Web grew, the average level of sophistication of users dropped. It was hard to explain the importance of privacy to them".

In Europe, with fewer credit cards and more cash transactions, micropayment technologies made more sense. In June 1998, ecash became available through Credit Suisse in Switzerland, was available from Deutsche Bank in Germany, Bank Austria, Sweden's Posten AB, and Den norske Bank of Norway, while in Japan Nomura Research Institute marketed eCash to financial institutions. In Australia, ecash was implemented by St. George Bank and Advance Bank, but transactions were not free to purchasers. In Finland Merita Bank/EUnet made ecash available.

DigiCash went bankrupt in 1998, despite flourishing electronic commerce, but with credit cards as the "currency of choice".

DigiCash was sold to eCash Technologies, including its eCash patents.

In 2000 eCash Technologies sued eCash. com, alleging trademark infringement and unfair competition. eCash. com counterclaimed that eCash Technologies' trademark registration was fraudulently obtained, because it failed to disclose eCash. com's registration of the "ecash. com" domain name to the U. S. Patent and Trademark Office. The court rejected eCash. com's counterclaim saying a trademark applicant must disclose a third party's rights only if they are "clearly established." The court argued because the "mere registration of a domain name does not confer trademark rights, let alone "clearly established" rights, ECash Technologies had no duty to disclose defendant's registration of the "ecash. com" domain name to the PTO.

In 2002 eCash Technologies was acquired by InfoSpace, currently known as Blucora.

WHAT IS E PAYMENT

E payment is a subset of an e-commerce transaction to include electronic payment for buying and selling goods or services offered through the Internet. Generally we think of electronic payments as referring to online transactions on the internet, there are actually many forms of electronic payments. As technology developing, the range of devices and processes to transact electronically continues to increase while the percentage of cash and check transactions continues to decrease. In the US, for example, checks have declined from 85% of non-cash payments in 1979 to 59% in 2002, and electronic payments have grown to 41%.

The Internet has the potential to become the most active trade intermediary within a decade. Also, Internet shopping may revolutionize retailing by allowing consumers to sit in their homes and buy an enormous variety of products and services from all over the worlds. Many businesses and consumers are still wary of conducting extensive business electronically. However, almost everyone will use the form of E Commerce in near future.

Master card/visa secure electronic transaction

Secure Electronic Transaction (**SET**) was a communi-cations protocol standard for securing credit card transactions over insecure networks, specifically, the Internet. SET was not itself a payment system, but rather a set of security protocols and formats that enabled users to employ the existing credit card payment infrastructure on an open network in a secure fashion. However, it failed to gain attraction in the market. VISA now promotes the 3-D Secure scheme.

History and development

SET was developed by the **SET Consortium**, established in 1996 by VISA and MasterCard in cooperation with GTE, IBM, Microsoft, Netscape, SAIC, Terisa Systems, RSA, and VeriSign. The consortium's goal was to combine the card associations' similar but incompatible protocols (STT from Visa/ Microsoft and SEPP from MasterCard/IBM) into a single standard.

The first review draft of the protocol was published February 1996 and the v1. 0 standard document was published in May 1997. Although there were several attempts to update or revise the protocol, no official version was produced beyond 1. 0. An official reference implementation developed by Terisa Systems was announced in 1997.

In December 1997 Visa and MasterCard created an independent company, *SET Secure Electronic Transaction LLC* (a. k. a. **SETco**), announcing American Express and JCB as cooperating members. SETco managed the development and deployment of the protocol and was responsible for branding and certification. Unofficial and informal interoperability testing among vendors occurred during 1997. Formal pilot tests began in 1998, but they were reportedly problematic.

SET allowed parties to identify themselves to each other and exchange information securely. Binding of identities was based on X. 509 certificates with several extensions. SET used a cryptographic blinding algorithm that, in effect, would have let merchants substitute a certificate for a user's credit-card number. If SET were used, the merchant itself would never have had to know the credit-card numbers being sent from the buyer, which would have provided verified good payment but protected customers and credit companies from fraud.

SET was intended to become the de facto standard payment method on the Internet between the merchants, the buyers, and the credit-card companies. Despite heavy publicity to win market share, it failed to gain widespread use. Reasons for this include:

- Network effect - need to install client software (an e-wallet).
- Cost and complexity for merchants to offer support, contrasted with the comparatively low cost and simplicity of the existing SSL based alternative.
- Client-side certificate distribution logistics.

Key features

To meet the business requirements, SET incorporates the following features:

- Confidentiality of information
- Integrity of data
- Cardholder account authentication
- Merchant authentication

Participants

A SET system includes the following participants:

- Cardholder
- Merchant

- Issuer
- Acquirer
- Payment gateway
- Certification authority

Transaction

The sequence of events required for a transaction is as follows:

- The customer obtains a credit card account with a bank that supports electronic payment and SET
- The customer receives a X. 509v3 digital certificate signed by the bank.
- Merchants have their own certificates
- The customer places an order with the merchant.
- The merchant sends the customer his public key and a copy of his certificate so that the customer can verify that it's a valid store.
- The customer sends the merchant:
- His certificate.
- His order details, unencrypted.
- His bank account details encrypted with the bank's public key.
- The merchant requests payment authorization by sending the bank:
- The payment details encrypted with the bank's public key.
- The customer's bank account details encrypted with the bank's public key.

Note that the merchant doesn't know the client's payment and bank account details.

- The bank sends the merchant a confirmation encrypted with the merchant's public key.
- The merchant sends the client the bank's response encrypted with the client's public key.
- The merchant ships the goods or provides the service to the customer.
- The merchant sends the bank a transaction request encrypted with the bank's public key.
- The bank transfers the payment to the merchant.

Dual signature

An important innovation introduced in SET is the *dual signature*. The purpose of the dual signature is to link two messages that are intended for two different recipients. In this case, the customer wants to send the order information (OI) to the merchant and the payment information (PI) to the bank. The merchant does not need to know the customer's credit-card number, and the bank does not need to know the details of the customer's order. The customer is afforded extra protection in terms of privacy by keeping these two items separate. However, the two items must be linked in a way that can be used to resolve disputes if necessary. The link is needed so that the customer can prove that this payment is intended for this order and not for some other goods or service.

The message digest (MD) of the OI and the PI are independently calculated by the customer. The dual signature is the encrypted MD (with the customer's secret key) of the concatenated MD's of PI and OI. The dual signature is sent to both the merchant and the bank. The protocol arranges for the merchant to see the MD of the PI without seeing the PI itself, and the bank sees the MD of the OI but not the OI itself. The dual signature can be verified using the MD of the OI or PI. It doesn't require the OI or PI itself. Its MD does not reveal the content of the OI or PI, and thus privacy is preserved.

3

E- Marketing in Tourism

E-marketing refers to the use of the Internet and digital media capabilities to help sell your products or services. These digital technologies are a valuable addition to traditional marketing approaches regardless of the size and type of your business. E-marketing is also referred to as Internet marketing (i-marketing), online marketing or web-marketing.

As with conventional marketing, e-marketing is creating a strategy that helps businesses deliver the right messages and product/services to the right audience. It consists of all activities and processes with the purpose of finding, attracting, winning and retaining customers. What has changed is its wider scope and options compared to conventional marketing methods.

E-marketing is deemed to be broad in scope, because it not only refers to marketing and promotions over the Internet, but also includes marketing done via e-mail and wireless media. E-marketing also embraces the management of digital customer data and electronic customer relationship management (ECRM) and several other business management functions.

E-marketing joins creative and technical aspects of the Internet, including: design, development, advertising and sales. It includes the use of a website in combination with online promotional techniques such as search engine marketing (SEM), social medial marketing, interactive online ads, online directories, e-mail marketing, affiliate marketing, viral marketing and so on. The digital technologies used as delivery and communication mediums within the scope of e-marketing include:

- Internet media such as websites and e-mail
- Digital media such as wireless, mobile, cable and satellite.

EMAIL MARKETING

Email marketing is directly marketing a commercial message to a group of people using email. In its broadest sense, every email sent to a potential or current customer could be considered email marketing. It usually involves using email to send ads, request business, or solicit sales or donations, and is meant to build loyalty, trust, or brand awareness. Email marketing can be done to either sold lists or a current customer database. Broadly, the term is usually used to refer to sending email messages with the purpose of enhancing the relationship of a merchant with its current or previous customers, to encouragecustomer loyalty and repeat business, acquiring new customers or convincing current customers to purchase something immediately, and addingadvertisements to email messages sent by other companies to their customers.

Madison Logic posted global data in April 2014 that claimed 122 billion emails are sent every hour.

Types of Email Marketing

Email marketing can be carried out through different types of emails:

Transactional Emails

Transactional emails are usually triggered based on a customer's action with a company. To be qualified as transactional or relationship messages, these communications' primary purpose must be "to facilitate, complete, or confirm a commercial transactions that the recipient has previously agreed to enter into with the sender", along with a few other narrow definitions of transactional messaging. Triggered transactional messages include dropped basket messages, password reset emails, purchase or order confirmation emails, order status emails, reorder emails and email receipts.

The primary purpose of a transactional email is to convey information regarding the action that triggered it. But, due to its high open rates (51. 3% compared to 36. 6% for email newsletters), transactional emails are an opportunity to engage customers: to introduce or extend the email relationship with customers or subscribers, to anticipate and answer questions or to cross-sell or up-sell products or services.

Many email newsletter software vendors offer transactional email support, which gives companies the ability to include promotional messages within the body of transactional emails. There are also software vendors that offer specialized transactional email marketing services, which include providing targeted and personalized transactional email messages and running specific marketing campaigns (such as customer referral programs).

Direct Emails

Direct email or interruption based marketing involves sending an email solely to communicate a promotional message (for example, an announcement of a special offer or a catalog of products). Companies usually collect a list of customer or prospect email addresses to send direct promotional messages to, or they can also rent a list of email addresses from service companies, but safe mail marketing is also used.

Comparison to Traditional Mail

There are both advantages and disadvantages to using email marketing in comparison to traditional advertising mail.

Advantages

Email marketing is popular with companies for several reasons:

- An exact return on investment can be tracked ("track to basket") and has proven to be high when done properly. Email marketing is often reported as second only to search marketing as the most effective online marketing tactic.
- Email marketing is significantly cheaper and faster than traditional mail, mainly because of high cost and time required in a traditional mail campaign for producing the artwork, printing, addressing and mailing.
- Advertisers can reach substantial numbers of email subscribers who have opted in (i. e., consented) to receive email communications on subjects of interest to them.
- Almost half of American Internet users check or send email on a typical day, with email blasts that are delivered between 1 am and 5 am local time outperforming those sent at other times in open and click rates.
- Email is popular with digital marketers, rising an estimated 15% in 2009 to £292 m in the UK.
- If compared to standard email, direct email marketing produces higher response rate and higher average order value for e-commerce businesses.

Disadvantages

A report issued by the email services company Return Path, as of mid-2008 email deliverability is still an issue for legitimate marketers. According to the report, legitimate email servers averaged a delivery rate of 56%; twenty percent of the messages were rejected, and eight percent were filtered.

Companies considering the use of an email marketing program must make sure that their program does not violate spam laws such as the United States' Controlling the Assault of Non-Solicited Pornography and Marketing Act (CAN-SPAM), the European Privacy and Electronic Communications Regulations 2003, or their Internet service provider's acceptable use policy.

Opt-in email advertising

Opt-in email advertising, or permission marketing, is a method of advertising via email whereby the recipient of the advertisement has consented to receive it. This method is one of several developed by marketers to eliminate the disadvan-tages of email marketing.

Opt-in email marketing may evolve into a technology that uses a handshake protocol between the sender and receiver. This system is intended to eventually result in a high degree of satisfaction between consumers and marketers. If opt-in email advertising is used, the material that is emailed to consumers will be "anticipated." It is assumed that the consumer wants to receive it, which makes it unlike unsolicited advertisements sent to the consumer. Ideally, opt-in email advertisements will be more personal and relevant to the consumer than untargeted advertisements.

A common example of permission marketing is a newsletter sent to an advertising firm's customers. Such newsletters inform customers of upcoming events or promotions, or new products. In this type of advertising, a company that wants to send a newsletter to their customers may ask them at the point of purchase if they would like to receive the newsletter.

With a foundation of opted-in contact information stored in their database, marketers can send out promotional materials automatically using autoresponders—known as Drip Marketing. They can also segment their promotions to specific market segments.

Legal requirements

Canada

The "Canada Anti-Spam Law" (CASL) went into effect on July 1, 2014. CASL requires an explicit or implicit opt-in from users, and the maximum fines for noncompliance are CA$1 million for individuals and $10 million for businesses.

European Union

In 2002 the European Union (EU) introduced the Directive on Privacy and Electronic Communications. Article 13 of the Directive prohibits the use of personal email addresses for marketing purposes. The Directive establishes the opt-in regime, where unsolicited emails may be sent only with prior agreement of the recipient, this does not apply to business email addresses. The directive has since been incorporated into the laws of member states. In the UK it is covered under the Privacy and Electronic Communications (EC Directive) Regulations 2003 and applies to all organizations that send out marketing by some form of electronic communication.

United States

The CAN-SPAM Act of 2003 was passed by Congress as a direct response of the growing number of complaints over spam e-mails. Congress determined that the US government was showing an increased interest in the regulation of commercial electronic mail nationally, that those who send commercial e-mails should not mislead recipients over the source or content of them, and that all recipients of such emails have a right to decline them. The act authorizes a US $16, 000 penalty per violation for spamming each individual recipient. However, it does not ban spam emailing outright, but imposes laws on using deceptive marketing methods through headings which are "materially false or misleading". In addition there are conditions which email marketers must meet in terms of their format, their content and labeling. As a result, many commercial email marketers within the United States utilize a service or special software to ensure compliance with the Act. A variety of older systems exist that do not ensure compliance with the Act. To comply with the Act's regulation of commercial email, services also typically require users to authenticate their return address and include a valid physical address, provide a one-click unsubscribe feature, and prohibit importing lists of purchased addresses that may not have given valid permission.

In addition to satisfying legal requirements, email service providers (ESPs) began to help customers establish and manage their own email marketing campaigns. The service providers supply email templates and general best practices, as well as methods for handling subscriptions and cancellations automatically. Some ESPs will provide insight/assistance with deliverability issues for major email providers. They also provide statistics pertaining to the number of messages received and opened, and whether the recipients clicked on any links within the messages.

The CAN-SPAM Act was updated with some new regulations including a no fee provision for opting out, further definition of "sender", post office or private mail boxes count as a "valid physical postal address" and definition of "person". These new provisions went into effect on July 7, 2008.

ONLINE MARKETING FOR TOURISM

Technology and the Internet have created a revolution in tourism marketing. The Internet not only inspires and provides consumers with information on potential travel destinations, but enables them to take immediate action by booking online. And, this is only the beginning of their online engagement, as the Internet continues to play a role during the vacation as well as long after the visitor returns home.

This Online Marketing for Tourism guide will take you through:

- Understanding your customer's online habits
- How to build an online marketing plan
- How to analyze your website
- The basics of Search Engine Optimization (SEO) and Search Engine Marketing (SEM)
- Using social media to communicate with your customers
- Email marketing
- Using third party websites to expand your visibility

The Online Marketing guide is written for small and medium tourism operators in British Columbia. It does not matter if you run a restaurant, a B&B, or a small kayaking tour operation. Based on your type of business, and the money and time you can invest in online marketing, this guide will help you maximize the return on your efforts.

E-marketing pointers for the tourism trade

If you don't have a website that offers quality information, real-time interaction and a booking process, you're going to lose out on converting web activity to sales.

First discover who you are selling to

Research show that the tourism buyer's age increases every year, and products are in effect selling to an increasingly ageing demographic. The current and future markets are aged 11 to 30. The best way to reach THEM is online, the space in which they spend the most time.

What this means is that you need to target your approach to an online (and mobile) audience. Instead of spending outrageous sums of cash advertising in high-end glossy magazines and printing expensive flyers, use your money wisely to reach your target market on the web.

Develop a website that offers bookings online, and develop a mobile version so your website is searchable via smartphone.

Make sure you develop and maintain your social media accounts, too. Social media is way more powerful and popular than TV!

The more choice you offer, the better

Gone are the days of standard travel packages. Today's travellers want to do it their own way. This means that products and tour operators need to build in options in every node of the travel value chain, from the booking to the feedback; and from the breakfast menu to the accommodation package.

If possible, enable your website with individual customisable packages so travellers can build and maintain their own itinerary (and give honest feedback immediately), constructed from their personal interests.

Internet Marketing for Tourism

Internet marketing in the tourism industry can help you connect with your clients, show them the visual appeal of your destination, and possibly get more exposure than you would with traditional print advertising. Use both natural and paid search to promote your destination, and you are sure to see results.

Photos

Photos are an effective marketing method, especially in tourism, providing a strong visual experience for the consumer and helping you to build an online presence. Use keywords in the photo tags and descriptions to help the pictures come up in the search engines' image results. Hire a professional photographer to take beautiful pictures of your location. Explain to him the "feel" that you want to depict with your location, such as cozy, tropical, exotic, party or family-oriented. Upload the photos to websites such as Flickr, and use its Creative Commons area, allowing others to use the images in blogs and articles. This gives your images, and therefore your location, more exposure.

Videos

Use video to give viewers valuable information that benefits them as opposed to your business. Do not use videos to give a monologue on how great your resort is. For example, if you are marketing a beach resort, create a tutorial on how to make your own aloe vera gel, or how to train to be a scuba diver. Link these videos to your website, blog and photo collection for ultimate exposure.

Online Business Listings

Google Maps and Yahoo Business Listings are often overlooked methods of tourism Internet marketing. Registering your business with Google Maps and Yahoo Business Listings will help it come up in the top of the search results when consumers search for keywords that relate to your business. It's free and only takes a few minutes.

Blogs and Articles

Produce large amounts of informative, keyword-rich content about your destination that will attract attention and establish you as an expert in your field, but do not write blogs and articles that promote your business directly. Instead, write about the "Ten Places You Must Go In the Bahamas" or "The Biggest Roller Coasters In the World," for example. Relate the articles back to your location without giving an advertising spiel that will offend people.

Social Media

Create Facebook, LinkedIn and Twitter profiles in the name of your tourist destination. Post links to your blogs, articles, photos and video. Update followers of your profile about special events and promotions at your destination, and link to interesting articles about the industry, the area and activities that your fans may enjoy. By providing valuable information to your followers, you will make them want to continue reading your updates. And the larger the audience, the more exposure your resort receives.

Email Marketing

Gather contacts from your Facebook fans, Twitter followers and past customers. Send weekly or monthly email newsletters with updated information about your destination, new activities and special travel offers.

Types of e-commerce

Various types of e-commerce platforms fall into several industry classifications based upon their licensing model, sales scenario and data exchange.

Types of licensing models

On-premise e-commerce

On-premise e-commerce software usually requires initial one time purchase investment in terms of licensing fees. Also, it implies extra costs related to hardware and installation services as well as data migration and on-going maintenance fees that are usually charged on a yearly basis for software updates and support. Some examples of typical on premise E-commerce platforms are Hybris (company), Intershop Communications, Sana Commerce., Oorjit. and IBM Web Sphere.

Advantages

1. Easily customizable;
2. Data security;
3. High performance;

Disadvantages:

1. Large initial investment;
2. Self-maintenance;
3. Technical knowledge

Software as a service (SaaS) E-commerce

Software as a Service (SaaS)- is a cloud based delivery model in which applications are hosted and managed in a service provider's datacenter, paid for on a subscription basis and accessed via a browser over an internet connection. Two examples of typical SaaS E-commerce solutions are Shopify and Demandware.

Advantages

1. Affordable low-cost solution;
2. Hosted/upgraded by E-commerce provider;
3. Easily scalable

Disadvantages:

1. Limited integration with back-end systems;

2. Lack of data security;
3. Limited control over the system;

Open source E-commerce

Open source e-Commerce is a free of charge platform that doesn't imply licenses fee. Furthermore, open source users are also responsible for installing, maintaining, securing and configuring the software on their own servers. In order to set up an open source platform, basic technical expertise is required in the areas of web design and development. Software products that are distributed as open source are generally free, and users can access and modify the source code. Several examples of typical open source E-commerce platforms are PayCart, PrestaShop, osCommerce, Magento, Thelia and Cart42

Advantages

1. Free of charge system;
2. Wide variety of available addons/plugins/extensions;
3. Better flexibility with a customizable source code;

Disadvantages

1. More technical knowledge required;
2. Performance depends on hosting costs
3. No standard integration with back-end system;

Sales Scenario

There are multiple types of sales scenario that eCommerce system can combine depending on a company's sales approach towards their customers.

Business-to-Consumer (B2C)

In a Business-to-Consumer E-commerce environment, companies sell their online goods to consumers who are the end users of their products or services. Usually, B2C E-commerce web shops have an open access for any visitor, meaning that there is no need for a person to login in order to make any product related enquiry.

Business-to-Business (B2B)

In a Business-to-Business E-commerce environment, companies sell their online goods to other companies without being engaged in sales to consumers. In most B2B E-commerce environments entering the web shop will require a log in. B2B web shop usually contains customer-specific pricing, customer-specific assortments and customer-specific discounts.

Consumer-to-Business (C2B)

In a Consumer-to-Business E-commerce environment, consumers usually post their products or services online on which companies can post their bids. A consumer reviews the bids and selects the company that meets his price expectations.

Consumer-to-Consumer (C2C)

In a Consumer-to-Consumer E-commerce environment consumers sell their online goods to other consumers. A well-known example is eBay.

Types of data exchange

Many E-commerce software retrieve the information from a certain back-end system, such as an Enterprise resource planning (ERP) or Customer relationship management (CRM) system. This information is stored in the **database** of that system. The Business logic contains all of the business rules that define the way data is stored, created, displayed, calculated and is being recreated inside an ERP or CRM system. For example: different product discounts are applied for different customer accounts. In order to retrieve the information, two types of data exchange are taken into account.

Integrated E-commerce

In integrated E-commerce, a part of the software solution is installed inside the back-end system. This means that the connection between the business logic and database of a back-end system is configured **automatically**. Information that is available in the back-end system is being **re-used** and displayed in the front/back end of the E-commerce system. An integrated E-commerce software product thus doesn't require to invest in recreating a separate database or business logic. Instead, it re-uses those of the back-end system. Integrated E-commerce software is mostly used in a B2B and B2C scenario. A typical example of an integrated E-commerce software is Sana Commerce.

Interfaced E-commerce

In interfaced E-commerce, the software solution is installed on top of the back-end system. This means that the connection between the business logic and database of a back-end system is setup **manually**. Information that is available in the back-end system is being **duplicated** into the E-commerce software. An interfaced E-commerce software product thus has their own **database** and **business logic** that are being synchronized constantly through a connection to a certain back-end system. Interfaced E-commerce is mostly used in a B2C scenario. An example of an interfacing E-commerce software isMagento.

B2C e-Tourism

Definition

Business that sells products or provides services to end-user consumers.

Information

While business-to-consumer activity exists both online and offline, the acronym B2C has primarily been used to describe the online variety.

B2C businesses played a large role in the rapid development of the commercial Internet in the 1990s. Large sums of venture capital flowed to consumers in the form of free online services and discounted shopping, spurring adoption of the new medium. When the capital markets turned sour, however, the B2C companies were among the first to fall, and they fell fast. Many companies tried to follow the herd of investors by undergoing a B2C to B2B makeover.

For awhile after the. com bubble, B2C was used infrequently except when it was followed by "...is dead." However, with more people online, new technologies and new online revenue models, many types of B2C companies are now flourishing online.

E-Commerce - B2C Model

In B2C model, business Website is a place where all transactions take place between a business organization and consumer directly.

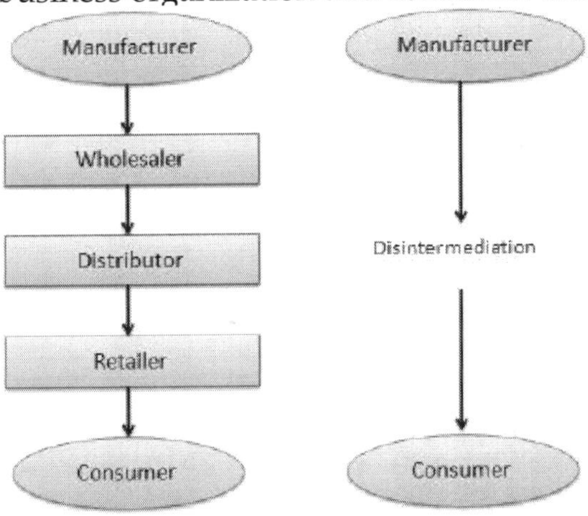

Traditional Distribution System   Direct Marketing System

In B2C Model, a consumer goes to the website, selects a catalog, orders the catalog and an email is sent to business organization. After receiving the order, goods would be dispatched to the customer. Following are the key features of a B2C Model

- Heavy advertising required to attract large no. of customers.
- High investment in terms of hardware/software.

- Support or good customer care service
  Consumer Shopping Procedure
  Following are the steps used in B2C e-commerce "
  A consumer
- determines the requirement.
- searches available items on the website meeting the requirment.
- compares similar items for price, delivery date or any other terms.
- gives the order.
- pays the bill.
- receives the delivered item and review/inspect them.
- consults the vendor to get after service support or returns the product if not satisfied with the delivered product.

Disintermediation and Reintermediation

In traditional commerce, there are intermediating agents like wholesalers, distributors, retailers between manufacturer and consumer. In B2C website, manufacturer can sell products directly to consumers. This process of removal of business layers responsible for intermediary functions is called Disintermediation.

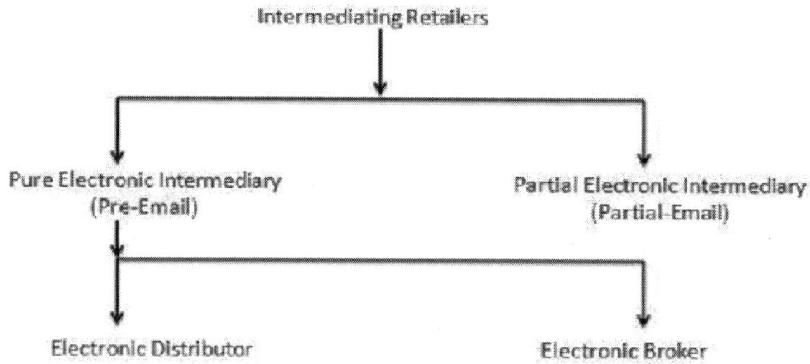

Now-a-days, a new electronic intermediary breed is emerging like e-mall and product selection agents are emerging. This process of shifting of business layers responsible for intermediary functions from traditional to electronic mediums is called Reintermediation.

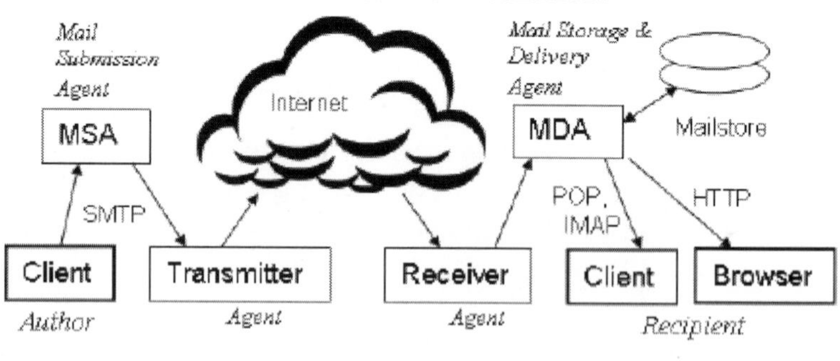

4

Strategic E-Tourism Marketing Planning

The Strategic Marketing Plan strives to extend the reach of the state's strategic marketing effort through collaboration and cooperative partnerships with the culture and tourism industries at large, reaching the arts, history, film and tourism entities. Tourism can be defined as a combination of activities, services and industries that delivers a travel experience to customers. Effectively marketing these experiences to potential visitors can be challenging, especially if you are not aware of the strengths and weaknesses of your business or what your competition is doing.

Market planning in the fifties and the sixties was not really feasible because the base of Indian tourism was narrow. The resources for promotion were even more limited and, tourism being a new industry, personnel were not well-trained.

For preparing any successful marketing plan, we deal with four variables, popularly known in the marketing jargon as the four Ps.

Product: It means attractions or tourist resources that a country can offer - beautiful monuments, scenic beauty, beach and mountain resorts, transportation services, good hotel accommodation, polite and friendly people, etc.

Price: It implies the optimal rates at which the tourism product (holiday) can be sold.

Place: Most suitable distribution channels. In other words, the markets where the product should be sold and the network through which it is sold.

Promotion: It implies the communication process, public relations, advertising, promotion, etc.

To begin with, the Indian tourist 'product' had several drawbacks. The major shortcoming was the image. India did not enjoy the image of a holiday destination.

Indians were often shocked to see the results of surveys conducted by organisations like PATA showing India in a terribly bad light. Despite the shock the fact remained that India had an image problem about its tourist product everywhere, especially in the USA. The picture in Western Europe was not very different. In 1961, the London Observer questioned its readers where they were planning to spend their holidays in 1962. India was not even mentioned among the first twelve popular destinations. A member of the Indian Parliament on return from England in 1966 quoted a placard shown in London which read:

Positive news came from Germany. In a survey carried out in the Federal Republic of Germany, the respondents were asked in the early sixties: 'If you could do as you liked, where would you go and what would you like to see and do most of all'? They were given the choice of twenty two places and activities; for example:

- The Egyptian Pyramids
- The ruins of ancient Greece
- The skyscrapers of New York
- The Kremlin in Moscow
- The Hollywood film studios
- A journey across the ocean in a sailing ship
- To watch a nuclear explosion
- The Isle of Capri
- Paris
- St. Peter's in Rome
- Tour to India

Surprisingly, India was the most popular country outside the European continent.

The image problem was further complicated by the inadequacy of transport and hotel accommodation, both in quality and quantity. In 1967, the Director of the Government of India tourist office in San Francisco called on a major travel agency and the following conversation took place with the President of the company, with the President doing the most of the talking.

"Sir you have beautiful, colourful literature on India. I must compliment you on its production."

"Thank you very much. How is the business?"

"You have a great country with varied tourist attractions."

"Thank you again for saying that."

"You have a very nicely located office in a central place in San Francisco. Your staff is polite and efficient."

"Well you are making my day...."

"But, Sir, why don't you close down your office?"

"Now, tell me, why do you say that after paying me all these compliments this morning?"

"Better buy some planes for Indian Airlines for tourists. I cannot get confirmation on Indian Airlines for my clients for months. How can I sell India?" he asked. "Presently, what you need is capacity on Indian Airlines and not promotion. Close your shop and go back home," he advised.

This was duly reported to the Government of India, but the government had its own priorities. It was a time when Indian Airlines had not bought its

Boeings and Airbuses, and the capacity on most routes was limited.

No amount of marketing and promotion could help India with these constraints.

The Indian Airlines' capacity was increased in December 1970 when Boeing 737s were bought; later their fleet was augmented by the addition of more such planes and in 1988 and after by the purchase of 19 Airbuses. Despite these purchases, Indian Airlines' capacity did not catch up with the increasing demand. The situation is a little better today though popular tourist routes are still overcrowded during the season. By 1997, the Indian Airlines had more planes than pilots, and Indian Airlines fleet was underutilised- the other extreme.

The introduction of a Hotel Loan Development Fund in 1968 eased the accommodation situation somewhat. While marketing India's tourist product, price too was an important factor to be taken into consideration. Although India's tourist facilities were relatively inexpensive, the high airfares were a negative factor in the major tourist markets of the world. The majority of tourists to India come by air from long distances - an expensive way of travelling compared to road or rail travel as in Europe.

It would be seen that India's share in world tourism cannot be very large till there is a significant inter-regional movement. If the experience of other countries provides a clue, large-scale tourism cannot originate from long-distance markets. European countries and Canada, Mexico and the Carribbean receive a majority of their tourists from the neighbouring areas. East Asia - Thailand, Singapore, Hong Kong, the Philippines and Malaysia - receives a sizeable number of visitors from neighbouring countries. Till such time as India develops large-scale inter-regional traffic, it cannot have "mass tourism" or even tourism on a large-scale. Tense political relations and economic weaknesses of India's neighbours preclude any such possibility in the coming years.

Keeping in mind these factors, Indian advertising strategy in the sixties was essentially to tell American travellers they could break their journey in India on round-the-world tours, and to the Europeans that India was a home of a great civilisation, culture and architectural wonders. A market study conducted in the United States through the Stanford Research Institute in the early sixties revealed that Americans having an annual income of US $ 10,000 to 15,000 per year alone could afford to travel to India and in addition, only those who had a lot of intellectual curiosity. Indian advertising was, therefore, targeted to the people in this income bracket and among them also to those who had already travelled to Europe.

PRINCIPLES OF TOURISM MARKETING

You may have heard people talking about the four 'P's of marketing -

product, place, price and promotion. An integral part of any marketing plan, these four 'P's' have specific implications for tourism businesses.

Marketing is a human activity. All the activities of tourism marketing bear a glaring testimony to this fact. In tourism marketing, we deal with mobile, enthusiastic and pleasure-seeking humans. They are on travel sprees. They want to enjoy the nice places of the world! They are efficient (at least during the courses of their journeys), conscious of the environs they visit, always careful about the money they spend, keen to explore and receptive to every phenomenon/product/service that makes comfortable or ecstatic.

We have defined Marketing in this chapter. Let us now define the term Tourism Marketing. According to Krippendorf, "Marketing in tourism is to be understood as the, systematic and coordinated execution of business policy by a tourist undertaking, whether private_ or State, owned at local, regional, national and international levels, to achieve the optimal satisfaction of the needs of identifiable consumer groups and in doing so, achieves an appropriate return."

Product

You need to have a clear understanding of your potential business, its different elements, who your 'typical' customer will be, as well as the level of service or standards you intend to provide. It helps to identify your unique selling point to help you stand out from your competitors.

It's important to note that product life cycles are getting shorter so the offerings of any given tourism business in two or three years time is increasingly likely to be different than those offered today. What this means for tourism businesses is that to continue to be viable, they need to allocate resources to product improvement and new product development. Market research is therefore of ongoing significance to all tourism businesses, both new and established, so that the needs and desires of the market can be monitored and problems or opportunities identified in advance.

Place

'Place' also refers to 'channels' and 'distribution'. The tourism industry has particular distribution channels both nationally and internationally - including retail travel agents, wholesalers and Inbound Tour Operators (ITOs) - which has implications for how your tourism product needs to be priced and packaged. And with the growth of online, an ever-increasing number of consumers are cutting out these intermediaries and booking directly with providers. You need to be there where they look for you.

Price

All businesses have to ensure that their prices are right if they are to stay in business. But the costing and pricing of tourism product has some characteristics which can be a little confusing to new industry players.

The net rate is what you must receive when selling your product. This figure will be the operating costs attributable to the product (not including commissions) plus a profit margin. The retail price (or rack rate) is the net rate plus distribution/commission costs plus GST (good and services tax).

Commissions are the cost of distributing your product, and the rates vary depending on the intermediary. Retail travel agents expect a commission between 10 and 20 per cent, commissions for wholesalers are typically between 20 and 30 per cent, and ITO commissions are generally between 25 and 35 per cent. For further information see Distribution Channels: How do they work?

Promotion

Promotion is the communication link between sellers and buyers for the purpose of influencing, informing, or persuading a potential buyer's purchasing decision. Without promotion, nobody will find out about your business and your product.

There are two broad categories of promotional activities - above the line and below the line.

Above the line: Promotion in the media (e.g. TV, radio, newspapers, magazines, websites, mobile phones) in which the advertiser pays to place an advertisement of a predetermined size/length/format.

Below the line: All other promotion, including your corporate website and social media presence, web listings sponsorship, endorsements, sales promotions, merchandising, direct mail/e-newsletters, personal selling, public relations and media liaison, trade shows, presence at the CRVC and more.

Salient Features

The following features are important :

- Tourism marketing activities are executed at regional, national and international levels.
- It leads to creation of a service or set of services. Some products are also included in its gamut but the "service aspect" of this gargantuan field is more important.
- It is a managerial process and is designed to earn profits for the tourism marketing firm or the producer who manufactures products/services related to tourism.

- The basic tenet of tourism marketing is the satisfaction of needs of tourists (or would-be tourists).
- New products/services can be created and marketed from a scratch and also, old products/services can be marketed/sold to customers.
- The nature of tourism product/service is perishable. Hence, tourism marketers are always on their toes to market these products/services to the prospective buyers so that marketers are able to sell as much of these within the given time frames.
- Just like they try to do in other marketing programmes, tourism marketers try to create new users, convert light users into medium users and convert medium users into heavy users.
- Links of tourism marketers are at regional, national and global levels. They cannot survive in the markets without associating with their counterparts in other regions of the world. They have to depend, unlike conventional marketers, on such persons or firms for ensuring that their clients (tourists) get the coveted sets of products/services. Thus, distribution of the product or service is done by many players, each one of them claiming a small share in the profit cake. In conventional marketing, the distribution channels take a share of profits after the sale has been effected. In tourism marketing, various components of tourism get their respective shares in advance. Example: The airline, hotel, local transporter etc. get their amounts in advance. Shopping is done by the tourist either through a credit card or by paying cash at the counter. Other hotel expenses like bar, restaurant are paid for by the tourist when he checks out of the hotel. In some cases, tickets to various forts, palaces, parks etc. are to be purchased by the tourist at such spots. Hence, some components of the itinerary are prepaid while some other have to be paid for at the time of purchasing those components.

  Thus, the system of extending credit does not exist in tourism marketing, especially in international tourism marketing. There are 3 exceptions to this rule. Firstly, in the operations of time share resorts, tourists-to-be because members and use the tourist spot for a limited number of days. They pay some amount in advance and pay the balance in convenient installments. Secondly, some tourists may take loans from banks and private lenders and pay back to them after they have completed the tours.

  In the second case, the payments are made to tour operators in advance. Thirdly, some tour operators have also started extending credit facilities to tourists; they charge interest and deliver services related to transport, accommodation and leisure before actually receiving the payments. However in general, the tourism industry is the "first pay avail later" type of industry.

- Tourists have to be guided throughout the course of an itinerary. That is because they' are new to the tourist spot. Language, cultural differences and individual motivation are some of the factors that affect their actions and desires lour guides, hotel staff, transporters and operative staff at fun parks, theme parks and other places of leisure help these tourists so that they could enjoy their stints at such places. So, tourism marketing does not end with sale of tickets or booking of hotel rooms. It must be executed in a professional manner till the last phase of the tour itinerary.
- As already stated, differences in life-styles, languages, cultures, cuisine, daily habits religions and perceptions (of tourists) force marketers to adopt varying strategies during the course of an itinerary. Each one of tourists ought to be looked after in a different manner. In the parlance of Group Inclusive Tours (GITs), individual attention cannot be given. But in individual and family tours, the needs of an individual or a family can be addressed with professional finesse. However, GITs are cheap and individual/family tours (or those that are organised according to special programmers) are very costly.
- Production and consumption of tourism services are closely interrelated. Most of the tourism services cannot be consumed incrementally. So, consumption, once started, cannot be stopped are modified. So, risk or uncertainty is higher for the customer. So, he seeks precise information sets or data before he undertakes a tour. He cannot see, feel, touch or inspect the services/products related to tourism before he decides to use them. But he can make comparisons of services offered by different competitors, namely, resorts, airlines, hotels, bars, discotheques etc. But here lies the crux of the problem. He does not know much (or anything) about the tourist place he intends to visit. He can only use a few criteria, namely, grade of the hotel, location of the hotel, class of airline (executive, royal executive, economy etc.), duration of the tour, reputation of the travel agency and image of the tourist spot! country, to take a decision. When he actually goes through the tour, then only he realises what were the wrong decisions in his selection.
- Different manufacturers join hands to form a tourism product. An airline considers seats flown or passenger miles covered as its product. A hotel produces guest nights. A theatre considers the number of visitors as its product. All these components form a whole that we call Tourism Product. As already stated, services form a major part of this product. Marketing efforts are needed not only to sell all these components as a whole, but also to execute these components when the tourist places an order to buy the package. Once an order has been placed (and money received), neither the buyer nor the seller can withdraw from the contract. Products and services cannot be rejected in tourism. However, these can

be modified (at a cost to the customer) but within the limits imposed by the itinerary, various producers of products and services, law of the land and financial resources of the customer (tourist).

- Tourism demand is unstable. It depends upon seasons political upheavals, wars, modes of transport, accessibility to the tourist spot, financial resources of the customer (tourist), currency fluctuations, international relations force mejeure' etc.
- Travel motivations are diverse in nature. Different people take up tours for different reasons.

Instance: For the youth, fun could be the criterion to visit London. But for an old couple, ancient monuments, the Big Ben and Stonehenge could be the places to be visited (and not fun parks and night life). Humans are different in terms of motivations, perceptions and actions. So, they ought to be treated as individuals. Tour programmers are costly. Individual tour programmes are much more costlier than GITs. The marketer must, therefore, identify some common motivations of the tourist group. He should segregate customers on the basis of these travel motivations. It would be easier for him to understand their precise needs and serve them.

DESTINATION BRANDING: BUILDING BRAND EQUITY

It is widely acknowledged in marketing literature that brands can command enormous value and, consequently, they need to be managed as a strategic asset. Some have viewed brands as simply an expectation of a promise or experience and whilst this may very well be true, the implications for marketers are profound - their business' survival and ultimate success or failure depends on brand health. Consider an iconic brand such as Coca-Cola and the enormous market power it commands through its enduring consumer 'pull'.

What is less commonly understood is how this power should be measured and, by extension, how it should be professionally managed.

According to marketing guru Philip Kotler, brand building and management are essential skills in the marketing of any product, service, organisation, person, place, or cause. A brand is not just the name put on an offering; it is the driving force that shapes the marketing mix, providing a platform for an organisation's strategies and tactics.

Indeed, building a strong brand position and managing it requires:

- Planning and implementing of brand building programmes;
- Determining of brand positioning and value proposition;
- Strengthening of consumer-brand relationships and measuring brand performance.

However, whilst the concept of branding has been used extensively in the context of products and services with more than a century of thinking behind it, it is a relatively new concept when applied to destination or places (countries, regions, cities etc.).

What is a brand?

Branding as a word originates from Medieval England where it referred to the practice of marking goods, livestock and other products with a hot iron as a means of establishing proof of ownership. As a common business practice, branding took off when manufacturing got into full swing in the 19th century and has subsequently evolved into the symbolic embodiment of all the information connected to a product service or organisation.

Kotler et al (Principles of Marketing, 2005) defines it as 'a name, term, sign, symbol or design, or a combination of these, intended to identify the goods or services of one seller or group of sellers and to differentiate them from the competitors'.

In this context, the work of Noam Chomsky, and one of his subsequent disciples, Stephen Pinker, on evolutionary psychology can be seen as particularly pertinent. Chomsky asserts that language is not a cultural artefact but a distinct piece of the biological make-up of the brain. Words are divided into "naming" and "doing" words. People organise their sense of reality by tagging bits of experience with "names", and by describing what the "names" might do. Therefore, branding was intended, whether consciously or not, to exploit this natural tendency. Manufacturers who were confident that proof of origin would help to create sales knew that branding would help - both as a guarantee and as an aid to memory. Those who were less confident knew that one way to generate sales was to counterfeit well-known brands (Jannie Hofmeyr).

Brand Equity

Where we get into somewhat more murky territory is when we try to define (let alone operationalise) the notion of brand equity. In Aaker's seminal book 'Managing Brand Equity', he talks about the value of a brand as a strategic asset and a company's primary source of competitive advantage. He defines brand equity as "a set of brand assets and liabilities linked to a brand, its name, and symbol that add to or subtract from the value provided by a product or service to a firm and/or to that firm's customers". These assets and liabilities, according to Aaker (1991), have five dimensions - brand loyalty, brand awareness, perceived quality, brand associations, and other proprietary brand assets.

If a brand fails to develop or maintain differentiation, consumers have no basis for choosing it over others. The product's price will then be the determining factor in the purchase decision. In the absence ofAbsent differentiation, says Aaker, the core of any brand - a loyal customer base - cannot be created or sustained. Brands must differentiate through features, service, programme, or ingredients in a way that is meaningful to customers.

What Aaker and others in the marketing community are mostly referring to is a research orientated conceptualisation of brand equity - for measuring a brand's strength and ability to compete in its marketplace. Other approaches have concentrated more on the financial aspect of the valuation - i.e. brand valuations in the context of brand sale or acquisition. From this perspective, brand equity is that incremental value that accrues to a product when it is branded - the premium, or value-add from the brand financially in comparison to equivalent products. This can be carried out either in terms of gross margin, or in wider measures such as EVA (Economic Value Added).

Brand commitment expert, Jannie Hofmeyr, talks about brands as a 'cognitive set of hooks' that the mind uses to organise our experiences with products or services. These experiences can result from the use of the brand or exposure to brand related messages and stimuli (whether part of structured marketing efforts or more informal means - word of mouth, etc).

Deciphering what is on the mind is not at all straightforward as it involves delving into the web of images, memories, emotional triggers that brands evoke. In the commerical mileu (for brands to be preferred and bought by consumers) this is then mediated by the level of interest one has for the category (involvement) and the brand's market clout (distribution, promotions, etc).

Kent Wertime (Building Brands & Believers: How to Connect with Consumers Using Archetypes) argues that while products are becoming more alike, brands can avoid 'commoditisation' by drawing on the rich language of archetypes to tap into more unconscious and emotional levels that influence consumer perception and preference.

The Benefits of Brand Equity

A number of tangible and intangible benefits can be identified as a result of brand equity. Strong brands drive price premiums, encourage greater customer loyalty, and foster higher employee commitment to the companies that own them, as well as attracting higher skilled employees. A strong brand can out-perform the market when economic times are good, and can protect a company when prevailing economic conditions are less beneficial or when there have been marketing mistakes. A company with strong brands also has increased visibility on stock markets.

Increasingly, owners of successful brands have to look beyond their narrow focus on customers and their own bottom-line, and consider the impact of their brands on society at large. There is a large element of self-interest in this, as brands with clear and strong values can leap product categories and compete in markets outside their core competence e.g. Virgin moving from music to airlines.

The indications are that if a brand is likely to be successful and valuable in future, it will need to think and behave like a leader: at the basic level of product and service delivery and quality; and at the emotional level of creativity, values and social contribution. Branding is a powerful tool; but if it is not based on solid foundations, it will not succeed in the long-term.

Why the Need for Destination Marketing?

The underlying concept of Destination Marketing, which was pioneered as an area of study by authors such as Philip Kotler, Donald Haider and Irving Rein, is that all places - cities, regions, countries - are subject to challenges as a result of global, political and economic changes, as well as normal processes of evolution and decay. Faced with scarce resources, and a growing number of competitors, destinations have to rely increasingly on their own local resources if they are to survive and prosper. Despite the powerful internal and external forces that challenge them, however, destinations have the collective resources and people to improve their relative competitive positions.

Many places have fallen on hard times as a result of economic and social changes. External factors such as exhaustion of natural resources, competition from cheaper markets, technological change, global restructuring, environmental and social pressures, can all lead to industrial decline. Internal factors also come into play often as a result of these external elements, such as major companies leaving, and economic recession. This has a detrimental impact on employment which results in a stagnating or declining community tax base, leading to conditions of infrastructure breakdown and reductions in services. The place loses its ability to attract new businesses, residents and tourists, and the downward spiral continues. Communities where this have occurred include, for example, the Rust Belt in the US, the South Wales mining community, the coal producing areas of France and Belgium.

Destinations in trouble often resort to palliatives such as national or local government grants, bidding for smokestack industries, building convention centres and exotic attractions. The evidence suggests, however, that "place wars" such as battles for Japanese factories, government projects, Olympic Games, baseball team franchises, convention business and other economic prizes are often misguided and end in wasted money and effort, if the necessary investment is not made in improving the industrial and infrastructure base and marketing the area effectively.

Kotler et al argue that the hidden key to combatting these challenges is for destinations to learn how to compete, and to learn how to think more like businesses, developing products, markets and customers. A strategic market planning perspective provides destinations with the marketing tools and opportunities to respond to challenges, coupled with fundamental policies such as rebuilding the infrastructure, creating a skilled labour force, stimulating local business entrepreneurship and expansion, developing companies and industries, creating local attractions, and building a service-friendly culture.

Strategic marketing of places requires a deep understanding of how "place buyers" - tourists, new residents, factories, corporate headquarters, investors - make their location decisions. Once they have this understanding, "place sellers" can compete aggressively for "place buyers".

Destination Marketing

As with any other product or service, the effective promotion of a destination requires a strategic marketing analysis. This should start with identifying what needs and whose needs the destination can meet and satisfy. What preference groups (investors,for example) or market niches (e.g. skiers) should be targeted to optimise economic outcomes? A Segmentation, Targeting and Positioning (STP) model can be created which will help determine priorities and target audience.

Segmentation requires potential customers to be identified - such as foreign direct investors, expatriates, or the diaspora. Clients can then be targeted selecting those who can be served most effectively, will receive the most value or can be charged the most for services offered. Positioning then demands effectively communicating the main benefits offered to the main target group.

A destination needs to be positioned in relation to its competitors, emphasising its natural and human endowments and its relative advantages. The process of positioning should aim to identify the destination with an image, perception, concept or characteristic which captures its essence and broadens its appeal to its targeted clients. However, as with any other form of branding, it is important to ensure that positioning messages are attuned with realities on the ground. Anything that is subsequently perceived to be a lie or an exaggeration will rebound and have a negative impact on a destination's subsequent image.

Marketing is about optimal allocation of resources in view of objectives and opportunities. There are four principles underpinning a successful marketing campaign which can be applied as well to destinations as other products and services.

- Product - The "products" for a destination are issues such as infrastructure, natural endowments, geographic vantage point, climate;
- Price - Can the destination demonstrate a relative or absolute advantage in terms of cost or return on investment compared to competing places?
- Place - Demonstrate how the destination faciliates investment through programmes such as the unhindered exchange of goods, services and capital (tax holidays, free trading zones, double taxation agreements, helpful laws and regulations etc.); and
- Promotion - The advertising and dissemination of news and information about the destination, public relations and lobbying activities, media campaigns etc.

Destination marketing comprises a number of strategies that communities and regions can use to embrace their competitive positions: attracting tourist and business visitors; attracting businesses from elsewhere; retaining and expanding existing businesses; promoting small business expansion and encouraging new business start-ups; expanding exports and outside investments; and expanding the population or changing the mix of residents.

Topophilia

The Chinese-American geographer, Yi-Fu Tuan, retired Professor Emeritus at the University of Wisconsin, invented the concept of Topophilia, which is very relevant to the concept of branding when applied to destinations and places. Topofilia is defined as the affective bond with one's environment - a person's mental, emotional and cognitive ties to a place. It concerns itself with environmental perceptions and values at different levels: the species, the group and the individual.

Yi-Fu Tuan holds culture and environment, and topophilia and environment as distinct in order to show how they mutually contribute to the formation of values. Topophilia examines the search for environment in the city, suburb, countryside and wilderness from a dilatectical perspective, distinguishing different types of environmental experience, and describing their character.

The concept of Topophilia can be linked to destination marketing because such marketing succeeds when stakeholders such as citizens, workers and business firms derive satisfaction from their community, and when visitors, tourists, new businesses and investors find their expectations met. This cements their affective bond with their environment.

Destinations as Brands

There is increasing interest and demand for destinations - countries, regions, cities - to develop and market themselves as brands. These destinations, often through the form of a Tourist Board or a similar, quasi-governmental organisation, seek to differentiate themselves from the competition - other destinations - through their unique selling points, appealing to both national and international audiences. Destinations have to adopt techniques based on challenger branding principles, enabling them to stand out from the crowd, with marketing aimed at various audiences - individuals, tourists, business. While different triggers are used for different audiences, the value of the brand should be consistent with the same messages.

Increasingly, destinations are being forced to adopt a market perspective towards their product and consumers, and need to effectively communicate and promote their competitive advantages. This requires the development of a full marketing plan and roll-out programme to sell the destination to whatever audience it may be seeking to attract e.g. investors, tourists, potential citizens.

Conclusion

From its initial roots as a sign of ownership, branding has evolved and developed to the point where it can be used as a significant measure of distinction, with the ability to command price premiums, engage consumer loyalty - both at the rational and emotional level - and create a strong attatchment in the mind's of consumers.

In recent years the concept has begun to be extended to destinations or places - countries, regions, cities. This reflects the fact that destinations are increasingly at risk to the challenges posed by global, political and technological changes, and are finding themselves competing against a plethora of alternatives, some of which are priced very aggressively. To face these challenges, destinations need to establish a strategic vision and establish a market-orientated strategic planning process, adopting a market perspective toward their product and consumers. Destination branding helps define a place and create a unique identity with clear and strong values, appealing to both our rational and emotional motivations. However, as with any other brand, destinations need to be backed up by product, service delivery and quality, plus an appeal to that sometimes elusive emotional side of the human psyche. If the infrastruture, economic base, level of service and attitudes are not there on the ground, the brand promise will quickly be undermined and wither.

As globalisation gathers pace in the 21st century, no destination is assured of immunity from external and internal pressures. Destination branding, supported by appropriate support programmes and investment can help a place respond to these challenges, distinguish itself from the competition, and guarantee a better chance for survival and long-term prosperity.

INFORMATION AND COMMUNICATION TECHNOLOGY IN E-TOURISM MARKETING

Tourism is essentially an expression of natural human instinct for experience, education and entertainment. The motivations for tourism also include social, religious and business interests. The economic consequences of this phenomenon are wide ranging. International tourism was worth about 321 billion U.S. Dollars during 1994 involving 528 million tourist visits (WTO, 1994).

With the explosion of technological advancements in the mid and late 20th century, tourists discovered increasing access to a growing array of destinations. From promoting destinations and attracting traveler attention to enabling instant reservations and payment collection, communication technology continues to exhibit a significant impact on the tourism industry and travel in general.

Information Technologies (ITs) have revolutionized the tourism industry and altered the competitiveness of organizations and destinations. The rapid development of both tourism supply and demand makes ITs an imperative partner of the industry, especially for the marketing, distribution, promotion and coordination of the industry. In the late 1990s the proliferation of the Internet and the World Wide Web in particular revolutionized communications as it enabled organizations to demonstrate their offerings globally using multimedia interfaces. As a result, most of tourism enterprises and destinations had to readdress their strategic management and marketing and to redesign their practices in order to take advantage of the new tools. In addition, several new organizations emerged to satisfy the emerging demand. This paper examines the paradigm-shift experienced in the industry and illustrates the business reasons for ITs adoption as well as the emerging trends and opportunities. It is contended that organizations which fail to take advantage of the emerging tools will lose market share and perhaps suffer competitive disadvantages.

Communication technology plays a considerable role in travel and tourism, as much of modern tourism revolves around the ability of tourist destinations to communicate their benefits to potential visitors and the ability of those visitors to reach out to points of interest at the destination. According to a review of literature conducted by the Learning and Teaching Support Network (LTSN), the communication technology that powers systems like the Semi-Automated Business Research Environment (SABRE) airline reservation system has driven a considerable increase in tourism since at least 1953. In addition, more modern communication technologies that employ Internet connectivity continue to exhibit profound affects on the tourism industry.

SIGNIFICANCE OF TOURISM

International tourism receipts form part of the balance of payment accounts of individual countries and are of major significance to both developed and developing countries. The main consideration for the development of tourism in several countries is, therefore, its balancing impact on the foreign trade account.

Tourism generates income and employment in the tourist receiving regions, be it a country, region, town or village. It makes the best use of resources which may not be used otherwise. Tourism can, thus, become an effective instrument of growth if it is developed through proper planning as a positive force to stimulate economic activity, improve ecology, foster national integration and mutual understanding of people of every nation.

The spectrum of employment generated by tourism varies from highly trained communication and computer specialists to room boys, sales girls, receptionists, waiters and unskilled workers. The airlines, travel agencies and tour operators also need several men and women with a variety of skills which are not too difficult to master. Tourism also provides high potential for self employment in a variety of ancillaries such as horticulture and handicrafts.

Tourism is also a source of amenities for the resident population of the tourist destinations. Because of visitor's arrival, the residents may enjoy a higher standard of public transport, shopping and entertainment facilities than they would be able to support otherwise (Burkart, A.J. and Medlik, S., 1976). The provision of employment, income and amenities for the resident population are, thus, the three main beneficial effects of tourism which apply to a greater or lesser extent to any tourist destination. These benefits are of particular significance to developing countries as no sophisticated technology is required to establish such facilities.

In some locations, tourism may provide an infrastructure, which in turn forms the base and stimulus for the diversification of the economy and for the development of other industries. Over and above, an established infrastructure often acts as an attraction to new and less directly related economic activities. Tourism expenditure, thus, stimulates an economy beyond the sectors concerned with tourism.

Apart from its direct contribution to the economy, tourism has significant linkages with several other sectors of the economy like agriculture, horticulture, poultry, handicrafts, construction, etc. Several items of tourist expenditure induce a chain of transactions in various other sectors. Each such transaction calls for the supply of some kind of goods and services. Further those directly or indirectly employed following the development of tourism may also demand more goods and services as a result of such employment that what they would have demanded otherwise. The additional consumption demand, thus emanating from tourist expenditure, will not only induce more employment, but also generates a further multiplier effect through a successive chain of transactions. As a result of this twin set of multiplier effects-indirect and induced-additional income and employment opportunities are generated through each successive transaction.

The impact of tourism on regional development and distribution of income is also significant. Tourists normally seek out areas in the interior of the countries for reasons of purity of environment, privacy, scenic beauty and its outdoor appeal. These national resources would otherwise be rganized d as there are few competing claims for their use. Tourism, thus, offers itself as a way of economically rganized resources which would otherwise remain either idle or rganized d , but attract the attention of visiting tourists. The exploitation of rural areas and the less developed countrysides through schemes such as outdoor treks, beach and mountain resorts, etc. far from the maddening crowds of urban areas will lead to the development of such areas. Such an involvement of the rural and interior areas can have a constructive effect on re-distributing the earnings from tourism.

Tourism also contributes significantly to the development of art and handicrafts. The millions of international tourists who are constantly on the move in search of recreation and pleasure support the promotion of such arts and crafts, while contributing substantially to the economy of the region.

TOURISM IN INDIA

India is a democracy at its best with more than 900 million people steering the path of progress. This vast land with its enormous diversity of history, people, culture and human life, makes for a product mix that can take in almost the entire world. The rich beauty of its ancient monuments, the beat and rhythm of its folk and classical dances, its colourful crowded rganiz, the grandeur of its snow-capped mountain tops, the quiet back waters and beautiful beaches and above all its friendly and charming people make India a land of tourist paradise. It is also a secular country with a heritage of an all encompassing ancient culture and cosmopolitan tinge. Despite these favourable factors, the international tourist traffic to the country still continues to be comparatively less though there has been considerable growth over the years and it has emerged as one of the largest foreign exchange eraners of the country.

Tourism is presently the third largest export industry in India - the first two being gem and jewellery and ready made garments. The foreign exchange earning from tourism is estimated to be about Rs. 7400 crores as against Rs. 7.7 crores in 1951.

The most beneficial impact of tourism is its capacity to generate large scale employment opportunities, particularly in remote and backward areas. The direct employment in the sector during 1994-95 was about 7.8 million persons accounting for about 2.4% of the total labour force. The labour-capital ratio per million rupee of investment at 1985-86 prices in the hotel and restaurant sector is 89 jobs as against 44.7 jobs in the case of agriculture and 12.6 jobs in the case of manufacturing industries. In the case of tourism, after combining the relevant individual segments. The ratio becomes 47.5 jobs and is still higher than most other segments. It is thus clear that tourism can play a major role in resolving the problem of large scale unemployment in the country provided it is developed on the desired lines with major inputs and initiatives from the Central Government.

A third impact of tourism, which is of particular significance to India is its contribution to national integration. Over 100 million domestic tourists visiting different parts of the country every year return with a better understanding of the cultural diversity of people living in different regions and carry with them a feeling of friendship and peace.

Technology & Tourism

Tourism in its present form is a post war phenomenon developed essentially as a consequence of technological developments in the fields of rganized , railways, ships, aircrafts, computers and communication systems. Although sails were the earliest means of transport, the invention of steam powered automobile by Nicholas Joseph Cugnot in 1769, the assembly of the first commercial steamer by Robert Fulton in 1807 and the production of first successful locomotive by George Stephenson in 1814 introduced several means of mass transport. It was, however, the advent of air transportation during twentieth century which revolutionalised the phenomenon of international tourism. It reduced the distances between the nations to a matter of few hours.

The developments in computer and communication technologies have made it possible to have rental cars with rganized d driving directions and self-service video-terminals at rental counters in high traffic airports. Fully automated rental transaction systems n - National's "Smart Key" machine and Budget's "Remote Transaction Book" came into existence. Yet another major contribution of technological developments in computers and communication systems to tourism is the rganized d reservation systems (CRS). These systems can now inform subscribers about schedules, fares and seat availability, issue tickets and boarding passes, record bookings, maintain waiting lists, display preferred airlines or classes, search for the lowest fare available or the first available non-stop flight and calculate fares for domestic and international itineraries. The system can also make reservations for other services like hotels, car rentals, cruises, railways, tours, boat charters, theartres and sporting events.

Information Needs in Tourism

Travel is a basic human instinct. Technological revolutions in the last few decades and the consequent changes in the social systems accelerated its intensity in the current century. Thus, tourism is presently a mass phenomenon involving every human being in the world. They need detailed information about each place they intend to visit. The specific elements of such information needs are :

- Geographical information on location, climate, landscape, etc.
- Attraction features
- Social customs, culture and other special features of the place
- Accessibility though air, water, rail and road and availability of scheduled means of transport
- Accommodation, restaurant and shopping facilities
- Activities and entertainment facilities
- Seasons of visit and other unique features
- Quality of facilities and their standard prices including exchange rates
- Entry and exit formalities and restrictions if any on tourists, etc.

Though the ultimate users of this information are the consumers ie. The tourists, the actual benefits in money terms accrue to the tourism industry consisting of the destination managers and service providers. There is, therefore, a strong competition amongst various destination countries in the world to produce and package such information in the most attractive format to attract the consumers from the tourist generating countries.

The travel intermediaries like travel agents, tour operators, and reservation system store such information in respect of each destination to service their clients and improve their business. They need the information in the easiest retrieval format so that the information needs of the clients are met as quickly as possible.

Tourists generally need both static and dynamic information. Information on those features which do not change rapidly over time is termed as static information. It includes details information about location, climate, attraction features, history, facilities available, etc. Information about airline, train and bus schedules, tariffs of transport and accommodation units and current availability of such facilities is considered as dynamic as they can change very frequently. These items of information have to be gathered, stored and disseminated on a real time basis. All types of reservation systems including air, rail and accommodation sectors contain such information.

APLICATION OF INFORMATION TECHNOLOGIES

Till a few years ago, the basic sources of information in the tourism sector were pamphlets, brochures, directories, guide books, etc. produced and published by different countries. These sources prevail even today, though they are the most inefficient means of information.

The last few decades witnessed the application of computer and communication technologies in the field of tourism. Two distinct streams of information sources viz, (i) online and (ii) offline came into existence. Databases containing information about places, tourist attractions and facilities became available for online access in several countries. The emergence of rganized d reservations system (CRS) like Galileo, Amadeus, Sabre, PARS, JALCOM, QAMTAM and ABASUS, etc. opened up a new source of online information on tourism and are being expanded continuously. The latest sources of online information is INTERNET which contains some pages on most of the tourist destinations in the world.

The CD-ROM technology also took the tourism industry by storm. CD titles which came in the market during the initial period mostly contained geographical information. Soon multimedia CDs on specific tourism products made their appearance. Several such titles are presently available in the market. The next few years are likely to witness a rapid growth in CD titles covering every aspect of tourism due to improved marketing efforts and increased competitions. Further hotel management and catering technology is fast emerging as an area of information technology application in the field of tourism.

The Indian Scenario

In India, the Department of Tourism took the first initiative to introduce information technology in tourism in the year 1989 by establishing TOURNET with the technical assistance of CMC Ltd. The network consisted of 35 information nodes installed in the field offices of the Department of Tourism located in different parts of the country. Each node contained a CD-drive apart from the usual configuration of floppy drives and hard discs. Each node was provided with a CD containing textual database on all the major tourist destinations in the country.

Recently, multimedia databases on tourism have been developed by Rajasthan and Maharashtra Tourism Departments with the assistance of some of the private software development firms. Apart from the government initiatives, a few private firms are also active in the field and a few CDs on Indian tourism are already available through their efforts.

The Central Department of Tourism is presently trying to tie-up with some of the private software development firms to produce a series of multimedia CDs covering all the tourist destinations in India. The intention is to bring out a marketable product for sale within India and abroad.

In the online field, the CRS Amadeus and PARS are already operational in India. Amadeus was established in 1993 and PARS came in 1995. INTERNET facilities are also presently available in India.

INTERNET AND TOURISM INDUSTRY

The easy access to information and its worldwide dissemination have been rganized d with Internet taking big strides with each passing day and gaining immense popularity the world over. The invention of internet has opened a new world of information and ushered in a great knowledge era. Its effect has been felt in many sectors like health, commerce, education industry etc. The tourism sector has also felt its effects. Internet, in fact, has brought in a big change in the methods of sales and marketing of different tourism products, reservation systems in airlines, railway, hotels etc.

The Internet today caters to travel activity of all kinds ranging from virtual sightseeing and offering detailed information on travel sights to allowing users to plan their own itinerary, make travel reservations online, offering help with special needs and even maintain online travel diaries. Internet, by way of putting control in the hands of the users and offering discounts unheard of in real life, is fast tempting users to fulfil their travel-related needs online. Virtual sightseeing is the most simplistic form of using the Internet for travel. With users visiting several websites that offer detailed information about travel destinations, and virtually tour these places by pictures and commentaries offered by sites. This is also the fastest and most inexpensive way to go sightseeing today with the only cost being that of Internet access.

Computer Technology in Tourism

In the field of tourism, the computer has made entry in a big way. A computer is a managerial tool capable of processing large volumes of data rapidly. It can perform basic arithmetic functions (addition, subtraction, division and multiplication) and logical operations (sorting, ranking and assembling) in a fraction of a second. A computer dispenses results in a large variety of formats. These are capable of repeating programmed instructions almost endlessly without an error, and maintaining a vast database of stored information for possible future use. Today a computer can be put to a variety of uses in the day to day activities.

Although the computers were in use in some way or other in various branches of tourism industry since the early Sixties, today these are considered indispensable. These are extensively used in almost all branches of the travel industry. They are part and parcel of a travel agency and are playing a key role in making the task of providing travel services an easy affair. Computers lately are undertaking, among other jobs, the planning of vacations for an individual and his family through home terminals.

Computer in Airlines

Today almost all the airlines use computers for their entire reservation work. The sudden growth, about forty years ago, in global travel, put a big pressure on the handling of air traffic, especially the passenger traffic for the airlines, both international and domestic. Growth patterns in passenger traffic had begun to indicate that handling reservation manually could not be sustained long without affecting efficiency in the customer service. It was then that a need to rganized passenger reservation systems was felt by the major airlines of the world. IBM took the initiative and developed a rganized d reservation system known as Programmed Airlines Reservation System (PARS). This system was developed in the early 1960s. However, PARS was not developed exclusively for or with any one particular airline. The system was designed as an all-purpose software package that would fit the requirements of any domestic airline. It was designed around IBM's new hardware range system 360, which was subsequently to revolutionise the entire computer industry.

The first airline to use PARS was the United States based Continental airlines in the year 1967. This was followed by most major US airlines which used the system making PARS the most popular and successful software product of the time. This was a major achievement for IBM. The system later expanded to meet the needs of several other airlines outside the United States of America resulting in the creation of International Programmed Airlines Reservation System (IPARS). Initially this system was a joint venture between IBM and British Overseas Airways Corporation (BOAC) and aimed at adapting PARS to the needs of airlines that had mainly international operations.

Subsequently, many airlines adopted the system. The international package became almost as much of a standard as PARS. Although many airlines modified the system extensively, IPARS was at the base of most international airlines system. By the late 1960s, the system developed was known as CPARS (C for Compact). This system was followed by a system known as Univac Standard Airline System, USA. With the passing of the years more and more systems developed, incorporating more functions to enable the airlines to have more transactions and instructions. The functions of various systems are basically identical across all airline reservation systems. The differences between them are in areas not apparent to the passengers, such as the flexibility with which they can handle control of space of flights, particularly where multiple classes and multiple sectors are involved.

The popularity of any system to a large extent depends on its coverage and online reservation network. The number of terminals which a system has is also an important consideration. The more the terminals a system has, the larger will be the online reservation network. The number of reservation transactions carried out by a system in a given time is another important aspect. However, it became obvious that the system was too costly, for smaller international airlines developed their own IBM oriented reservation systems in the early 1970s to be considered by an airline before using a system. To sum up, the following main aspects are important to make a system perfect and universally acceptable:

- Number of reservation transactions to be handled,
- Data links with other airlines,
- Number of terminals,
- Information processing capacity, and
- Data volume capacity.

Computer in Air Cargo

Most of the airlines are now using computers for cargo handling operations as well. The handling of cargo shipments on ground is a costly affair and the cost has been increasing over the years.

Almost 50 per cent of the handling of cargo shipment reflect the cost of manual information processing. Freight rate increases have not kept pace with cost increase, so airlines had either to accept reduced margins or take steps to reduce overheads. Computerisation of cargo has helped reduce costs as this speeds up the handling of information related to consignments and also reduces the time the cargo spends on the ground. The pioneer in cargo rganized d on was Alitalia, whose PO 4-cargo system was adopted and modified by many major airlines, such as Swissair, TWA and British Airways. Univac's USAS has a fully developed cargo module. Almost all the major airlines in the world have now adopted one system or another of cargo rganized d on.

Advantage to Travel Agents

Today several airlines have developed and adopted sophisticated computer systems for their use. The airlines also make available their system to their appointed sales agents who are equipped with an appropriate terminal and receive the necessary instructions and procedures. Airlines have thus greatly benefited from the use and adaptation of computers. Some of the major advantages of use of computers by airlines include:

- High profile applications like passenger reservations;

- Applications of departure, control and cargo;
- Accounting, budgeting, forecasting and planning;
- Engineering management;
- Cargo management;
- Revenue accounting;
- Fare quotations and construction;
- Ticket printing;
- Crew scheduling;
- Crew management; and
- Yield rganized d

COMPUTER RESERVATION SYSTEMS (CRS)

Computer Reservation Systems (CRS) in recent years has made a major advance in the airline reservation system. Different Computer Reservation systems companies which are global giants in their own rights form a link between the airline and the travel agent by offering online flight bookings and availability details. This system was first introduced in Germany. A system capable of carrying out as many as one thousand reservation transactions every second involving data links with 28 airlines, a host of car hire agencies and hotels and about 20,000 travel agencies in Europe alone was set up in Erding in the southern part of Germany. The System known as "Amadeus" was developed jointly by four airlines-Air France, Iberia, SAS and Lufthansa. The information processing capacity of the mainframe IBM and Unisys computers installed at Erding, the world's largest computer centre involves a data volume of hundreds of thousands of books.

In addition to Amadeus, Galileo and Sabre are two other global giants in Computer Reservation System. CRS can now be used through Internet as well. This has brought the details of online flight booking and availability of seats within the reach of every passenger having an internet connection. The impact of the net can be gauged by the fact that CRS companies have now redesigned themselves as GDSs (Global Distribution Systems). The business is no longer limited to airline bookings alone but covers a broader horizon with value - added travel information.

Role of SITA

Airline industry had, however, laid the foundation for global communication long before the internet was even considered to be of any great value by its pioneers. It has been using networks like SITA 'Societe International de Telecommunications Aeronautiques' set up as early as the year 1949. The role of SITA in airlines automation has been very crucial. Automation is the key to achieving a higher level of productivity in any industry, especially in the airlines industry, and this will continue with more emphasis being put on achieving short-term benefits.

SITA is responsible for providing Data Processing Services. In fact, it is the major supplier of information - handling services for the airline industry. Its aims are to foster efficient telecommunications, data processing and transmission means for all categories of information required in the operation of air transport enterprises, with the specific aim of promoting safe and regular air transport in all countries.

- Passenger Reservations
- Departure Control
- Meteorological Data
- Credit Authorisation and Document Verification v) Baggage Tracing (BAGTRAC)
- Share Cargo Service
- Shared Flight Operations data base viii) Flight Planning
- Baggage Handling and Management Service x) Common Customs Interface System
- Fuel Management
- Airline Schedules and Flight Availability database
- IATA Passenger Tariff Conference Support

SITA is providing a valuable service to the airlines. Almost all the information required in the operation of air transport in the world is being provided to the airlines industry. The range of services. Offered by SITA is very extensive and new services are being added as and when these are required. The network today is the world's largest private network serving a large number of countries.

Computer in Hotels

Like in airlines, the computer technology has entered the hotel industry in a big way. A hotel's most crucial internal resource is information and with the use of computers the information is available in a way that saves labour and ultimately increases the profits.

Although computers in the hotel industry started being used as far back as the late 1960S; it was only in the 1970s that the technological advances in computer technology made possible the right combination of compactness and versatility for different sizes of hotels. The lower cost encouraged many individual hotels to install the system. Today computers are installed in large numbers and are widely accepted in the hotel industry. One of the most important factors or its large-scale acceptance in the industry has been its reliability. The computer system has been found to be very reliable in the dissemination of the right kind of information at the push of a button.

Today, the hotel industry is a major market for the computer manufacturers and the software vendors. It has been increasingly rganize that the hotel computer systems achieve better internal and external control and, through the use of analysis methods, provide the opportunity to improve the overall profitability of the unit. Like in the airlines, the computers offer substantial advantages for reservation systems in terms of speed and accuracy. The errors are almost negligible.

Application Areas

Hotel systems all over the world have traditionally been divided into the following two main areas:

(1) Front Office Application Areas.

(2) Back Office Application Areas.

Front Office Application Areas incorporate the following:

- Reservations
- Registration
- Guest accounting
- Night auditing
- Communication operations (telephones, telex, fax).

Back Office Application Areas incorporate the following:

- Financial management
- Inventory control systems accounts
- Profit/loss rganize
- General ledger
- Credit card verifications

The computer system streamlines the functioning of all the above areas in a hotel set-up. It helps in the smooth functioning of the hotel, better guest relations, increased efficiency of staff and the overall profitability of the hotel. The key to successful operation of a hotel lies in the operation of an efficient information system. With the introduction of computers in the hotel the information system has become more accurate and efficient. The guest has an access to the required information with a push button convenience. Since the computer is used as a communication medium, there is better coordination between various departments. The computer has relieved the staff of many routine jobs enabling them to devote more time and attention to the needs of the guests.

The computers have made guest accounting systems more sophisticated and reliable. It automatically collects and calculates, receipts and payments and consolidates and verifies credit card payments and cash controls. The sales outlets, like restaurants, automatically record the guest's expenditure at the point of sale, while direct electronic links to the telephone system in the guest rooms can monitor guest calls for instant charging to their accounts. The computers have eliminated cumbersome accounting machines often seen at the cashier's desk giving a front office system a modern and sophisticated look, resulting in greater guest satisfaction and adding to the prestige of a hotel.

Back office systems have a large number of areas having great potential for cost control where computers are used to a great advantage for the hotel. With the use of computers, management can monitor the progress of individual restaurants and other sales outlets against targets and budgets which may be set for various items. Daily reports on inventory usage become available by way of rganized input from each centre collected at regular intervals throughout the day.

Computer Terminals. The modern day business rganize is increasingly getting used to having a computer in his hotel room. In fact, many such business rganized in countries like USA, Belgium, Holland, France, Switzerland, Germany, Japan, Canada and many other countries are inquiring before booking a room as to whether guest rooms where they are planning to stay have an in-room computer terminal. The computer has thus entered the guest rooms of many hotels in the west and become the latest novelty of a luxury hotel. A number of individual hotels as well as hotel chains have introduced in-room terminals that are hooked by television and telephone into a data system that includes official airline guides, news agencies, stock market agencies, weather bureau, shopping services, travel, club, entertainment guide, electronic games and even job listing features. Access to the computer terminal is gained by the guest by way of punching a credit card number which is charged for their time at the terminals on sliding rates roughly equivalent to those for long distance telephone calls.

HOTELS AND GLOBAL DISTRIBUTION SYSTEMS (GDS)

The hotel industry is today making extensive use of GDS internationally. The GDS basically is a whole gamut of providers who actually started off for the airline industry and then expanded to hotels and car-rental companies. Through GDS, the hotelier can get the customer or a travel agent to make bookings in his hotel. GDS offers more flexibility and instant reservation confirmation.

Computer in Travel Retailing

The profound changes over the years in travel services have made the use of computer technology in retail travel a necessity. The impact of computer technology on travel retailing made itself felt since the beginning of 1980 with the introduction of first-generation agency computer system. It was in the year 1983, that Thomas Holidays, a British company, first used computers. With the success of Thomas Holidays in introducing reservations via Prestel, several more leading tour operators introduced similar systems to sell their 1984 summer programmes. A Prestel set allows travel agents to make reservations with as many principals as agreed to it. The rganized technology which allows tour operators and travel agents to open reservations through Prestel sets is applied to airlines through British Telecom's Skytrack, an automated airline reservation system. This enabled travel agents to make bookings on several hundreds of the world's airlines, using the standard Prestel television set and a keyboard. Prestel was being used for the basics required in the travel industry like finding out airline schedules and fares, making reservations and getting information on a tour operator's holiday packages. The advantage of the system over the travel literature like brochures and books was that the information is automatically updated and only flights or packages that are available are shown.

New Systems-many new systems have been developed lately. There is an intense competition between various systems. Sometimes it becomes difficult for a tour operator or a travel agent to make a choice and decide about the merits and demerits of alternate systems. The new systems which are being used today are Sabre, Apollo, Dacoda, Trav Automation, Worldspan Galileo and Abacus. These systems allow travel agents to find the lowest costs for customers, identify promotions involving frequent flyer miles and free trips and tailormade trips to a customer's specific needs. All these services are available through a push button via the computer terminal.

Computer in Railways

In addition to use of computers by airlines retail agents, travel agents and tour operators, these are also being used directly by the railway systems.

The railway system in Europe and some other countries have now been using computers extensively. In countries like France, Germany, Switzerland and Belgium, to name a few, computers have been in use for over a decade. The most important use of computers in railways, however, is in the area of ticket reservation. The information regarding availability of seats is now available instantly in various networks. Railway systems now use computers for route planning, engineering, accounting, inventory planning and control, purchase and a host of other functions.

The most remarkable use of computer in railways has, however, been made by France. The metro system in Paris is one of the best in the world. France has been making great advances in the technology in its metro system. The latest technological marvel has been achieved beneath the surface of the earth through a concrete cylinder. No one on board is at the controls because there are no controls on board. Instead the sleek good looking aluminium and steel train is being guided by a computer from a distant command centre. Moving at 100 kilometres an hour the train suddenly stops as soon as bright lights appear ahead. Glass doors slide open and the passengers step on an immaculate platform awash in filtered daylight, tastefully decorated with mosaics and sculptures.

The train is the remarkable VAL (Vehicule Automatique Leger), the most ultra-modern futuristic subway system in the world inaugurated in the year 1983 in the Northern French city of Lille. Built by a French high technology giant Matra, the 20-mile network links Lille to the nearby cities. This is considered to be the most advanced automatic subway line in the world. VAL is distinguished from most conventional subway systems by its compact size, speed and rganized d operating system. Each car is only 6.75 feet wide and 42.6 feet long as compared to 8 feet by 49.2 feet for a Paris metro car. Each train with two cars carries a normal capacity load of 124 passengers in clean, well-lighted comfort.

The system is operated from a control complex on the outskirts of Lille city. Two rows of television screens form an electronic tableau of the entire system. Four operators can call up images on the video monitors from 250 cameras installed in stations, tunnels and garages. The system's computer is programmed to run the trains at a rate of one train every minute during peak hours and every five minutes at other times. The computer is linked to about 200 microprocessors located in the stations and on board the train. In case of any mishap or accident, VAL operators can stop a train, slow it down or give any of the over 2,000 possible electronic commands.

The trains are equipped with telephones that enable passengers to report any crimes and summon the system's 20-member security force. The driverless system is almost foolproof as is claimed. Indeed, during one of the trial runs, a pigeon alighted on an elevated section of the line, tripping automatic detectors and stopping a train for only ten seconds before its on-board computer ascertained that it was safe to proceed. Railway systems, however, may not be able to indulge in such luxuries for a very long time. However, the importance of computers in railways has been more than rganized .

TECHNOLOGY ROLE

Role of Communication

In the field of travel and tourism, communication plays an impertant role as it is through this that a potential customer obtains information about a produce which in the final explanation is a destination which he proposes to visit. Travel being a service industry the require for not only proper but fast information about a destination becomes paramount for the satisfaction of the consumer. The significance of communication in diverse fields including travel and tourism has been well recognised. World renowned space scientist, Arthur C. Clarke, addressing the first meeting of the inter-government council of the International Programme for the Development of Communication held in Paris in the year 1981, said, "In several ways and for several purposes, printed matter, books, newspapers and wallpapers will forever be the best and the cheapest form of communication. But now electronics have provided us tools that can perform miracles not possible to the printed word and which, of course, can reach millions who are unable to read. The newest and most powerful of these communication devices rely upon space technology, a reality that is not usually recognised."

In the period between 1981 (when Arthur Clarke spoke about the newest and most powerful communication devices) and today, with a gap of fifteen years, there has been virtually a revolution in the diverse techniques in the field of communication and information. The diverse changes that have taken place since then have greatly benefited everyone. The electronics have performed similar miracles in the last two decades that today we find ourselves in the middle of a new world, a world of information revolution.

The developments have greatly facilitated rational management of the concern world. Newer techniques of data processing, mainly transmission of data and telecommunication, have even now formed a new field of activity, characterised by an enormous potential for development and development. Telecommunication devices are in utilize today in all but all fields of economy.

The new means of public telecommunication systems like teletext, telecopy or videotex have provided a very tough competition to previous pioneer public communication means like newspapers, magazines, etc. However, the new means of communication also offer great probabilities for improvement, rationalisation and the expansion of the existing facilities for data collection and transmission. Today the mass media world over has immensely benefited from the new technology and information techniques.

Modern Mass Media Techniques

Understanding of the modern mass media techniques as also the mass media means are essential for a person working in the travel and tourism field as knowledge of these will assist in keeping pace with rapid changing scenario in the concern of travel. The modern mass media techniques can be grouped as under :

(a) Satellite television
(b) Cable television networks
(c) Videotext
(d) Internet

All the four modern mass media techniques are widespread in the world and are considered to be decisive for concern and industry. These mass media techniques however have some limitations as far as their utilize for a peculiar person or an individual is concerned. Because of their widespread coverage and their technical methods of transmission these cannot be directed for the utilize of a peculiar person. Besides, the receiver of the information through these techniques cannot begin a dialogue or communicate with different person. The communication, therefore, is limited to one way.

For the direct transmission of information, there are dissimilar modern refers to which have been developed and are rather widespread. The inter flow of information through these means is possible. These means are as follows:

- Teletex
- Telecopy
- Telebox
- Videotex
- Telefax
- E-mail

Telecopy : Telecopy provides the feasibility of exchanging photocopies through a data network. Information in the form of either written document or technical drawing is remote copied. This means that two facilities for copying are connected, one at the sender's end and the other at the receiver's end. Transmission time is only a few minutes.

Teletex : Teletex is an improvement over telex and has in reality developed from it. The receiver for teletex is an electronic "typewriter", which can send electronically enriched "letters" to owners of ordinary telex equipment. The transmission of message time is generally shorter in comparison with time taken with telex. Besides, it is also possible to transmit more office typewriter symbols. A normal electronic typewriter can be used as a receiver for teletex.

Videotex : Videotex Occupies a Special position Among

the "new media". It plays a key role in the link between telecommunication and the computer sciences. Its benifits lie in the feasibility it provides for linking computers, and also in its interactive dialogue capabilities. Using a videotex, information and communication systems can be converted into interactive systems capable of communicating with one another. In fact, the videotex is a multipurpose instrument with multiplicity of uses. It serves as:

- A communication system; and
- A marketing instrument.
- An instrument for data processing;
- An information medium;
- An organisational aid;

This comparatively new service connects diverse forms of utilize of the above-mentioned facilities and at the same time offers some other possibilities. To operate the service, a television set with a decoder and telephone is essential without which the service cannot operate. In Europe, about all households have television sets and a telephone and with the assist of videotex separate households can be arrived in large areas. Members of

German BTX service as well as Members of France Telecom Service can now obtain all kinds of information from external computers or utilize data bank, all through their television sets. In several other countries in Europe, USA, etc., similar systems are in use.

The utilize of videotex (VTX) is prevalent today in several fields. In addition to its utilize in the field of concern as it allows rapid message transmission, rapid and inexpensive data collection and up-to-date information which are decisive for advertising, the system is also used by specialised groups of users for collecting orders in the field. It is also used in the field of tourism as a oneway system, for receiving bookings. Because of its low unit costs, it is used extensively mainly in connection with personal computers. It has been found that videotex (VTX) is the most beneficial means of communication, taking into account its low cost and the wider range of its application.

Telebox : Telebox is an electronic post office box system. Each member of the system has his or her "post office box" in the computer, where other members can leave their message. The owner of each box can electrically contact the others.

Networking : All the more than means discussed allow the exchange of information electronically through a data "network". The exchange of information between the members with the assistance of electronic transmission is very fast. The data are also competent in written form in printouts. "Network" is a system of transmission linking facilities for mechanical data processing. In this way dissimilar computers are connected, permitting data exchange and processing over long distances. Telecommunication is possible only when there is similar a network available.

Telephone is the simplest and the best known network. In addition, there is also a separate clear data network for the exchange of data which works digitally. In this source a high transmission speed is achieved and there is a very low ratio of errors during transmission. There are dissimilar types of networks which can be used for telecommunication motive either separately or combined. The text on the screen is given by a telephone network or any other network. Communication with other members or computers in any place by anyone can be achieved by combining the telephone network with additional facilities provided.

A large number of enterprises as well as individuals are extensively using the communication techniques discussed above. In the field of tourism, in addition to travel agents, tour operators, hoteliers, airlines, travel journalists, etc., utilize these techniques. Travel journalists who especially travel extensively utilize the following facilities:

- Telecopy (sending previously prepared texts as originals)

- Teletex (for collecting and sending texts),
- Data banks (for collecting information).

The utilize of telecommunication techniques offers fundamental facilities and benifits in the following areas of work:

- Collection of information,
- Processing of information, and
- Transmission of information.

Collection of Information

The collection of information is the main part of work carried out by the journalists in connection with their work. A journalist, therefore, has to find most reliable data in as short a time as possible. Besides, the data must be the latest and up-to-date. New means of communication enable journalists to acquire the data in a short time. The data can also be obtained at any time regardless of restrictions of working hours. Hundreds of thousands of pages are stored in computers to which the journalist can have access. The data can be obtained through data banks which can be arrived directly through a network that is used for most data banks.

A data bank is like a "master book" in which a mass of books, newspapers, substances from dissimilar meetings and all kinds of published work is stored. All the relevant information can be collected in no time by means of an electronic data bank. Collecting the same information from a book and a visit to a library would be time consuming and specially expensive. A journalist, seeking information on any subject for an article on tourism, can order the articles which are of interest to him, through the record room of his own editorial office, or directly through the data bank, and these are recorded on the screen. He can also acquire a written article through a directly connected printing machine. In this way, in a matter of minutes, he can finish his search and the collection of data for his article.

Processing of Information

Information processing is an original and most importent part of a journalist's work. A journalist has to evaluate collected information, combine the same with his new ideas and summarise the same in a compact form of an article. All this can be done only to a limited extent by means of telecommunication devices. For collecting data, the personal computer can offer new applications in absence of much difficulty, as a journalist can process articles collected with the assist of electronic devices. The wording of an article or the get-up can be changed as often as a journalist desires and it can be transmitted easily.

Transmission of Information

When the article is prepared on the basis of collected data, the same is to be transmitted to the editorial office or directly to the printers in their office. A journalist can do this personally by a telephone call or in a written form. But the quickest and simplest method is to transmit the information with the assistance of telecommunication devices. If the article is written in the normal source on a typewriter, then it can reach the editorial office in no time, given the journalist uses telecopy facilities. The process of writing can be speeded up if the article is written using a personal computer, as this will not need additional printing. The article then can be transmitted directly to the computer competent in the printing office.

Computer Technology

In the field of tourism, the computer has made entry in a big way. A computer is a managerial tool capable of processing large volumes of data rapidly. It can perform fundamental arithmetic functions (addition, subtraction, division and multiplication) and logical operations (sorting, ranking and assembling) in a fraction of a second. A computer dispenses conclusions in a large variety of formats. These are capable of repeating programmed instructions all but endlessly in absence of an error, and maintaining a vast database of stored information for possible future use. Today a computer can be put to a variety of uses in the day to day activities.

Although the computers were in utilize in some source or other in diverse branches of tourism industry since the early Sixties, today these are considered as indispensable. These are extensively used in all but all branches of the travel industry. They are part and parcel of a travel agency and are playing a key role in making the task of providing travel services an easy affair. Computers lately are undertaking among other jobs, the planning of vacations for an individual and his family through home terminals. The principal users of computers in the travel industry are:

(1) Airline Companies
(2) Hotel Companies
(3) Railways
(4) Shipping & Cruise Lines
(5) Travel Agents
(6) Tour Operators

USE OF COMPUTERS

Today all but all the airlines utilize computers for their entire reservation work. The sudden development about thirty five years ago in the universal travel put a big pressure on the handling of air traffic, especially the passenger traffic for the airlines, both international as well as domestic.

Growth patterns in passenger traffic had begun to point out that handling reservation manually could not be sustained long in absence of effecting efficiency in the customer service. It was then that a require to computerise passenger reservation systems was felt by the major airlines of the world.

IBM took the initiative and developed a computerised reservation system known as Programmed Airlines Reservation System (PARS). This system was developed in the early 1960s. However, PARS was not developed exclusively for or with any one certain airline. The system was designed as an all purpose software package that would fit the requirements of any domestic airline. It was designed around IBM's new hardware range system 360, which was subsequently to revolutionise the entire computer industry.

The first airline to utilize PARS was the United States based continental airlines in the year 1967. This was followed by most major US airlines which used the system making PARS the most famous and successful software product of the time. This was a major achievement for IBM. The system subsequent expanded to meet the requires of many other airlines outside the United States of America resulting in the creation of International Programmed Airlines Reservation System (IPARS). Initially this system was a joint venture between IBM and British Overseas Airways Corporation (BOAC) and aimed at adapting PARS to the requires of airlines that had mainly international operations.

The international package became all but as much of a standard as PARS. Although several airlines altered the system extensively, IPARS was at the base of most international airlines system. By the late 1960s, the system developed was known as CPARS (C for Compact). This system was followed by a system known as Univac Standard Airline System, USA. With the passing of the years more and more systems developed, incorporating more functions to enable the airlines to have more transactions and instructions. The functions of diverse systems are infact identical across all airline reservation systems. The differences between them are in areas not apparent to the passengers, like the flexibility with which they can handle control of space of flights, particularly where multiple classes and multiple sectors are involved.

The popularity of any system to a large extent relies on its coverage and on-line reservation network. The number of terminals which a system has is also an significant consideration. The more the terminals a system has, the larger will be the on-line reservation network. The number of reservation transactions carried out by a system in a provided time is different important aspect. However, it became obvious that the system was too costly, for smaller international airlines developed their own IBM oriented reservation systems in the early 1970s to be considered by an airline privious using a system. To sum up, the following main aspects are significant to make a system perfect and universally acceptable:

- Number of reservation transactions to be handled.
- Data links with other airlines.
- Number of terminals.
- Information processing capacity.
- Data volume capacity.

In recent years a major advance has been made in the airline reservation system in Germany. A computer system capable of carrying out as several as 1,000 reservation transactions every second, involving data links with 28 airlines, a host of car hire agencies and hotels and approximately 20,000 travel agencies in Europe alone has been set up at Erding in the Southern part of Germany. The system, known as "Amadeus", has been developed jointly at a cost of DM 350 million by four airlines-Air France, Iberia, SAS and Lufthansa. The information processing capacity of the mainframe IBM and Unisys computers installed at Erding, the world's biggest computer centre, involves a data volume equivalent to a library of 3,50,000 books.

Computers in Air Cargo : Most of the airlines are now using computers for cargo handling operations as well. The handling of cargo shipments on ground is a costly affair and the cost has been increasing over the years. Almost 50 per cent of the handling of cargo shipment reflect the cost of manual information processing. Freight rate increases have not kept pace with cost increase, so airlines had either to accept reduced margins or take steps to reduce overheads. Computerisation of cargo has helped reducing costs as this speeds up the handling of information concerned to consignments and also reduces the time the cargo spends on the ground. The pioneer in cargo computerisation was Alitalia, whose PO 4-cargo system was adopted and altered by several major airlines, like Swissair, TWA and British Airways. Univac's USAS has a completely developed cargo module. Almost all the major airlines in the world have now adopted one or different system of cargo computerisation.

The Advantages

Today many airlines have developed and adopted sophisticated computer systems for their use. The airlines also make competent their system to their appointed sales agents. The sales agents are equipped with an proper terminal and receive the essential instructions and procedures. Airlines have hence greatly benefited from the utilize and adaptation of computers. Some of the major benifits of utilize of computers by airlines are following-

(a) Revenue accounting;

(b) Fare quotations and construction;

(c) Ticket printing;

(d) Crew scheduling;
(e) Crew management; and
(f) Yield optimisation.
(g) High profile applications like passenger reservations;
(h) Applications of departure, control and cargo;
(i) Accounting, budgeting, forecasting and planning;
(j) Engineering management;
(k) Cargo management;

Role of SITA : The role of SITA, 'Societe International de Tele Communications Aeronautiques' in airlines automation has been very crucial. Automation is the key to achieving a higher level of productivity in any industry, especially in the airlines industry, and automation of airline functions will continue with more emphasis being put towards achieving short-term benefits.

SITA is liable for providing Data Processing Services. of course it is the major supplier of information handling services for the airline industry. Its aims are to encourage efficient telecommunications, data processing and transmission means for all categories of information required in the operation of air transport enterprises with the peculiar aim of promoting safe and regular air transport in all countries.

There has forever been a continued high development of demand for the services offered by SITA. It provides data processing services in the following sectors:

- Passenger Reservations.
- Credit Authorisation and Document Verification.
- Baggage Tracing (BAGTRAC).
- Share Cargo Service.
- Departure Control.
- Meteorological Data.
- Shared Flight Operations data base.
- Flight Planning.
- Baggage Handling and Management Service.
- Common Customs Interface System.
- Fuel Management.
- Airline Schedules and Flight Availability database.
- IATA Passenger Tariff Conference Support.

SITA is providing a valuable service to the airlines. Almost all the information required in the operation of air transport in the world is being given to the airlines industry. The range of services offered by SITA is very extensive and new services are being added as and when these are required.

Computers in Hotels : Like in airlines, the computer technology has entered the hotel industry in a big way. A hotel's most decisive internal resource is information and with the utilize of computers the information is competent in a source that saves labour and finally increases the profits.

Although computers in the hotel industry started being used as far back as in the late 1960s, it was only in the 1970s that the technological advances in the computer technology made possible the right combination of compactness and versatility for dissimilar sizes of hotels. The lower cost encouraged several individual hotels to install the system. Today computers are installed in large numbers and are widely recognised in the hotel industry. One of the most significant factors or its large scale acceptance in the industry has been its reliability. The computer system has been found to be very reliable in the dissemination of the right type of information at the push of a button.

Today, the hotel industry is a major market for the computer manufacturers and the software vendors. It has been increasingly realised that the hotel computer systems achieve better internal and external control and, through the utilize of explanation methods, give the opportunity to improve the overall profitability of the unit. Like in the airlines, the computers offer substantial benifits for reservation systems regarding speed and accuracy. The errors are all but negligible.

Application Areas : Hotel systems all over the world have traditionally been divided into the following two main areas:

(1) Front Office Application Areas.

(2) Back Office Application Areas.

Front Office Application Areas incorporate the following:

- Guest accounting
- Night auditing
- Reservations
- Registration
- Communication operations (telephones, telex, fax).

Back Office Application Areas incorporate the following:

- General ledger
- Credit card verifications
- Financial management
- Inventory control systems accounts
- Profit/loss accounts

The computer system streamlines the functioning of all the more than areas in a hotel set-up. It helps in the smooth functioning of the hotel, better guest relations, increased efficiency of staff and the overall profitability of the hotel. The key to successful operation of a hotel lies in the operation of an efficient information system. With the introduction of computers in the hotel the information system has become more proper and efficient. The guest has an approach to the required information with a push button convenience. Since the computer is used as a communication medium, there is better coordination between diverse departments. The computer has relieved the staff of several routine jobs enabling them to devote more time and attention to the requires of the guests.

The computers have made guest accounting systems more sophisticated and reliable. It automatically collects and calculates agents, receipts and payments and consolidates and verifies credit card payments and cash controls. The sales outlets, like restaurants, automatically record the guest's expenditure at the point of sale, while direct electronic links to the telephone system in the guest rooms can monitor guest calls for instant charging to their accounts. The computers have eliminated cumbersome accounting machines generally seen at the cashier's desk giving a front office system a modern and sophisticated look, resulting in greater guest satisfaction and adding to the prestige of a hotel.

Back office systems have a large number of areas having great potential for cost control where computers are used to a great benifit for the hotel. With the utilize of computers, management can monitor the progress of individual restaurants and other sales outlets against targets and budgets which may be set for differnt items. Daily reports on inventory usage become competent by source of organising input from each centre collected at regular intervals throughout the day.

Computer Terminals : Modern day concern traveller is increasingly obtaining used to having a computer in his hotel room. In fact, many similar business travellers in countries like USA, Belgium, Holland, France, Switzerland, Germany, Japan, Canada and several other countries are inquiring privious booking a room as to whether guest rooms where they are planning to stay have an in-room computer terminal. The computer has hence entered the guest room of several hotels in the west and have become the latest novelty of a luxury hotel. A number of individual hotels as well as hotel chains have introduced in-room terminals that are hooked by television and telephone into a data system that includes official airline guides, news agencies, stock market agencies, weather bureau, shopping services, travel, club, entertainment guide, electronic games and even job listing features. approach to the computer terminal is gained by the guest by source of punching a credit card number which is charged for their time at the terminals on sliding rates roughly equivalent to those for long distance telephone calls.

Computers in Travel Retailing : The utilize of computer in travel retailing as compared to in airlines have specially been slow. However, the profound changes over the years in travel services made the utilize of computerisation by travel agents a necessity. The impact of computer technology on travel retailing made itself felt since the starting of the 1980s with the introduction of the first generation agency computer system.

It was in the year 1983 that Thomas Holidays, a British company, first used computers. With the success of Thomson's TOP (Thomson open line programme) in introducing reservations via Prestel, many more leading tour operators introduced similar systems to sell their 1984 summer programmes. A Prestel set allows travel agents to formulate reservations with as several principals as agree to it. The videotex technology which allows tour operators and travel agents to open reservations through Prestel sets is applied to airlines through British telecom's Skytrack, an automated airline reservation system. This enabled travel agents to make booking on many hundreds of world's airlines, using the standard Prestel television set and a keyboard. Prestel was being used for the basics required in the travel industry, like finding out airline schedules and fares, making reservations and obtaining information on a tour operators' holiday packages. The benifit of the system over travel books and brochures is that the information is automatically updated and only flights or packages that are competent are shown.

New Systems : several new systems have been developed lately. There is an intense competition between diverse systems. Sometimes it becomes problem for a tour operator or a travel agent to make a choice and finalise about the merits and demerits of alternate systems. The new systems which are being used today are Sabre, Apollo, Dacoda, Trav Automation, Worldspan Galileo and Abacus. These systems permit travel agents to find the lowest costs for customers, identify promotions involving frequent flyer miles and free trips and tailor-made trips to customers special needs. All these services are competent through a push button via the computer terminal.

Computers in Railway : In addition to utilize of nations by airlines retail agents, travel agents and tour operators, these are also being used directly by the railway systems.

The railway system in Europe and some other countries have now been using computers extensively. In countries like France, Germany, Switzerland and Belgium, to name a few, computers have been in utilize for over a decade. The most significant use of computers in railways, however, is in the area of ticket reservation. The information in terms of availability of seats is now competent instantly in diverse networks. Railway systems now utilize the computers for route planning, engineering, accounting, inventory planning and control, purchase and a host of other functions.

The most significant use of computer in railways has, however, been made by France. The metro system in Paris is one of the best in the world. France has been making great advances in the technology in its metro system. The latest technological marvel has been achieved beneath the surface of the earth through a concrete cylinder. No one on board is at the controls because there are no controls on board. Instead the sleek good-looking aluminium and steel train is being guided by a computer from a distant command centre. Moving at 100 kilometers an hour the train suddenly stops as immediately as bright lights seem ahead. Glass doors slide open and the passengers step on an immaculate platform awash in filtered daylight, tastefully decorated with mosaics and sculptures.

The train is the remarkable VAL (Vehicle Automatique Leger), the most ultra-modern futuristic subway system in the world inaugurated in the year 1983 in the Northern French city of Lille. Built by a French high technology giant Matra, the 20-mile network links Lille to the nearby cities. This is considered to be the most advanced selfmoving subway line in the world. VAL is distinguished from most traditional subway systems by its compact size, speed and computerised operating system. Each car is only 6.75 feet wide and 42.6 feet long as compared to 8 feet by 49.2 feet for a Paris metro car. Each train with two cars carries a normal capacity load of 124 passengers in clean, well-lighted comfort.

The system is operated from a remarkable control complicanted on the outskirts of Lille city. Two rows of television screens form an electronic tableau of the entire system. Four operators can call up images on the video monitors from 250 cameras installed in stations, tunnels and garages. The systems' computer is programmed to run the trains at a rate of one train every minute during peak hours and every five minutes at other times. The computer is linked to approximately 200 microprocessors located in the stations and on board the train. In case of any mishap or accident, VAL operators can stop a train, slow it down or make any of the over 2,000 possible electronic commands.

The trains are equipped with telephones that enable passengers to report any crimes and summon the system's 20-member security force. The driverless system is all but foolproof as is claimed. Indeed, during one of the trial runs, a pigeon alighted on an elevated segment of the line, tripping mechanical detectors and stopping a train for only ten seconds privious its on-board computer ascertained that it was safe to proceed. Railway systems, however, may not be able to indulge in similar luxuries for a very long time. However, the significance of computers in railways has been above emphasised.

VIDEOTEX SYSTEM

This system discovered by British Telecom is a source of providing computerised information in absence of the expense of supplying a computer terminal. All that is required is a telephone line and a standard colour television receiver with an adapter to link it to a keyboard and a decoder. The videotex system has been a great assist to travel agents and tour operators in their day to day functioning.

Videotex provides efficient, low cost information and reservation facilities which allows direct communications between agents and principals throughout the industry. Information is transmitted quickly and properly via ordinary telephone lines to be visually displayed on a television kind screen. At the touch of a button it displays information on holiday packages, airfares, accommodations, cruises, car rentals, insurance, and several other travel-related services. The videotex system provides the following services to the travel agents/tour operators-

- Fast and efficient means of getting accurate, update information on every aspect of the travel industry with excellent visual capacity;
- Information on new product developments, fare changes, special offers and any other significant information put into the system; and
- Direct approach to the information supplied by industry principals, thereby speeding up transactions and increasing both the efficiency of selling and the characteristic of customer service;
- Display of tour itineraries, graphic illustrations of hotels, resorts and tourist attractions by selling staff. Some other videotex system advantages to users include:
  (a) key word-immediate approach to a peculiar piece of information;
  (b) up-to-date information-continued approach to an entire library of travel-related information.
  (c) increased sales-more sale conversations due to immediate approach of information;
  (d) increased productivity-more efficient customer servicing;
  (e) cost efficient-reduced costs due to greater efficiency of communication

Diverse technological advances discussed have allowed travel agents and tour operators to expand their roles and service their clients more efficiently and comprehensively than ever before. The benifits which the utilize of computers have provided to agents are far above the investments made for installing and using the system. Computers have become an necessary part of travel agency operations.

The Problems and Issues

The problems and issues concerning information technology applications in tourism are the following:

1. Tourism in India is relatively young and is not well rganized to absorb the advances in information technology. They generally lack technical and financial resources and their scale of operation it too limited to take advantage of information technology.
2. There has not been any specific policy or co-ordinated approach so far for the development of information products on tourism at the national level. It is yet to be evolved and implemented.

3. The information industry in India presently consists of a few software development firms, and some information centres in the Government sector. However, there are no database vendors in India who prepare their own databases and market them. In the absence of such units, all efforts are Government dominated and the products are generally not available in the market. It is, therefore, essential to provide adequate Government support and incentives for the development of such industries in India.

CHANNELS OF E-MARKETING

A marketing channel is a set of practices or activities necessary to transfer the ownership of goods, and to move goods, from the point of production to the point of consumption and, as such, which consists of all the institutions and all the marketing activities in the marketing process. A marketing channel is a useful tool for management.

Roles of marketing channel in marketing strategies:

- Links producers to buyers.
- Performs sales, advertising and promotion.
- Influences the firm's pricing strategy.
- Affecting product strategy through branding, policies, willingness to stock.
- Customizes profits, install, maintain, offer credit, etc.

An example of this is an apple orchard: Apple orchard > Transport > Processing factory > Packaging > Final product to be sold > Apple pie eaten

An alternative term is distribution channel or 'route-to-market'. It is a 'path' or 'pipeline' through which goods and services flow in one direction (from vendor to the consumer), and the payments generated by them flow in the opposite direction (from consumer to the vendor). A marketing channel can be as short as being direct from the vendor to the consumer or may include several inter-connected (usually independent but mutually dependent) intermediaries such as wholesalers, distributors, agents, retailers. Each intermediary receives the item at one pricing point and moves it to the next higher pricing point until it reaches the final buyer.

Marketing Channels can be long term or short term.

Short term channels are influenced by market factors such as: business users, geographically concentrated, extensive technical knowledge and regular servicing required, and large orders. Short term product are influenced by factors such as: perishable, complex, and expensive. Short term producer factors include whether the manufacturer has adequate resources to perform channel functions, Broad product line, and channel control is important. Short term competitive factors include: manufacturing feels satisfied with marketing intermediaries' performance in promoting products.

Long term market factors include consumers, geographically dispersed, little technical knowledge and regular servicing is not required, and small orders. Product factors for long term marketing channels are: durable, standardized, and inexpensive. Producer factors are manufacturer lacks adequate resources to perform channel functions, limited product line, and channel control not important. The competitive factors are: manufacturer feels dissatisfied with marketing intermediaries' performance in promoting products.

Marketing channels refers to the ways in which products move from the manufacturer to the distributor to the end user. Also called distribution channels, the number and efficiency of a company's marketing channel can have a strong impact on the company's success. If a company does not have enough channels through which to market their goods, or if thechannels are inefficient and expensive, it can be difficult for a company to locate customers for its products and/or to make a profit on sales of its products.

Some companies, often referred to as direct marketing companies, sell the product directly from the manufacturer to the end user, or consumer. In such cases, the companies do not create or establish marketing channels. Instead, the consumer orders directly and the item is shipped to him, reducing costs for marketing and distribution. It can be difficult, however, for a manufacturer to locate customers using this form of marketing, since it may be less convenient if there is no storefront for a customer to go to or no local retailer a customer can interface with; the Internet, however has reduced this problem somewhat and given rise to more direct selling.

Most often, however, products do not go directly from the manufacturer to the end user. Instead, the products are first sent to a distributor or retail outlet. The retail outlets and distributors that a product is sent to can be referred to marketing channels. For example, a company that produces clothing may have multiple marketing channels: it may send its clothing to boutique stores throughout the country and to large chain stores and department stores as well.

The manner in which the product gets from the manufacturer to the distributor or store selling its product is a part of the marketing channel. The clothing may move from the clothing designer to the plant that creates the design to the shipping company that moves the design to all of the boutiques to the boutiques themselves. This is one particularmarketing channel. A different channel may be used to send the items to the department stores; for example, perhaps a different shipping company is used or a different manufacturer to produce the items sold to the larger stores.

Usually, the more steps in the marketing channels, the higher the end cost is to the consumer. This phenomenon occurs because each of the people involved in the channel, or each of the "middle men," must be paid a premium, or fee. Thus an item sold in a direct sale may cost far less than the same item which had to be sent through several distribution steps before it reached the consumer.

PRODUCT PRODUCERS

They are the airlines, hotels, airlines, cruise lines, coach operators, taxis, ferries, resorts, museums, forts, palaces, heritage hotels, zoos, wildlife parks, bird sanctuaries etc that are the attractions for tourists. Because of a fascination for these, the tourist undertakes tours. These producers give products and services of various kinds to the tourist. But most of these are services. Items placed in the shops of shopping malls (of a tourist spot) are products. Food items, liquor, wines and water and also products. Attraction, research, exploration, social reasons (like marriages and meetings with friends) could be the reasons to undertake tours. Producer of these products and services sign tie-up agreements with channels of distribution so that they could sell their (products and services). They cannot go to the targeted marketers every now and then. They call use high-end magazines and newspapers to build nice images in the minds of prospective customers. But they normally depend upon the wholesalers (tour operators) and retailers (travel agencies) to actually sell these products and services. Airlines (producers of transport services) also sell their tickets directly to customers.

Wholesalers of Products

They buy various services of producers, or get reservations done for these services. They buy in bulk (allow prices) and that is why, they earn a lot (because they sell these services at much higher prices). They are normally called Tour Operators. They remain in touch with airlines, hotels, resort owners, discotheques, private spot owners and people involved in special sports (like parasailing, bungee jumping, kayaking, paragliding etc). They also buy tickets for State-operated tourist spots or sites. In this context, tickets for forts, museums, rope way transport systems, palaces and other ancient monuments can be considered. But if the government does not sell these tickets in advance, the executives of tour operators, buy these tickets for travel agents at such spots. Customers do not have to pay for these tickets because they have already paid for the same while buying their tour packages. Tour operators seldom deal with customers; they interact with travel agents most of the times. One tour operator can have many travel agents in its fold. These travel agents are not owned by the tour operator and their business dealings with the tour operator are based on commission percentages. In many countries, specialty chancellors buy the services of producers in bulk and sell them to other wholesalers, who operate at much lower levels.

Retailers of Products

They are the travel agents that buy services from wholesalers (tour operators). One travel agent may be associated with many tour operators simply because different tour operators may be catering to different tourism sectors. Travel agencies interact with customers on a day-to-day basis. They also send their executives to the homes and offices of clients or prospective clients. These executives undertake the real selling jobs, unlike the executives of tour operators who sell only to travel agencies. Services form a major part of any tourism package. Customers are free to buy products' when they are on tour. Some of the products (like breakfast, welcome drinks, dinner, complementary lunch etc.) are included in tour packages. Some travel agents are known for their excellent services. Thus, they grow because of their brand names. Some travel agencies also buy the services of producers in bulk. Thus, at times, they also act as tour operators (wholesalers). Not all travel agencies try to become tour operators because the risk involved in buying services (from producers).

The physical distribution channel in tourism is somewhat similar to the one in conventional marketing. However, actual goods and services are not provided to customers in their offices, homes, or at the retail stores (as is the case in conventional marketing). The tourist buys the services from travel agents that plan the entire programme for him. The bookings for airlines, hotels, resorts, fun parks, zoos, lakes, wildlife parks etc., are done in advance. The tourist also pays for these in advance. Then, on the stipulated day, he leaves his home (station of origin). He arrives at the destination station according to the terms mentioned in the tour itinerary. The agents of the travel agency or tour operator help him arrive at the hotel or spot where he is supposed to arrive. The tour itinerary is strictly followed (by the agents of the travel agency or tour operator). The producers of various goods and services provide these goods and services according to the itinerary. Such arrangements (bookings) are made even before the tourist leaves the station of origin. He can move from one destination station to another but according to the itinerary. He has no choice of changing the itinerary once he has finalised it (in most of the cases). At the end of the itinerary, the tourist is taken back to the station of origin according to the details mentioned in the itinerary.

Further, note that some tourists may not like to come back to the station of origin. Foreigners quite often plan their tours in this manner. They buy one-way tickets and move to the destination station. From the destination station, they can be on their own or associated with another travel agency. Such tour combinations are clearly planned and made known to all the staff members of the concerned travel agencies or tour operators. Finally, producers of tourism services are not liable to provide any other service that is beyond the gamut of their operations. Examples: A hotel would not take a tourist to a tourist spot within the city because it is not the duty of the hotel staff to do so. The travel agency must appoint a man (guide or coach driver) to take the tourist to that spot (according to the itinerary). Hotels are also not responsible for half-day sight seeing tours; such tours are the exclusive responsibilities of travel agencies that are running the entire show. Travel agencies also buy tickets for zoos, forts, lakes, palaces, historical monuments for their clients (tourists). If this is not possible, then the tourist is informed (at the station of origin) that he would be required to buy such tickets from his own pocket.

Emanation of Marketing Environment : The concept of marketing environment emanates from the broader concept of business environment.

Macro-environment

Marketing environment of a firm consists of the external factors and forces that affect the company's ability to develop and maintain successful transactions and relationships with its target markets. This definition was given by Phillip Kotler in his famous book Marketing Management: Analysis, Implementation and Control, 6th Ed, 1989, Prentice Hall. There are two parts of this environment, according to Kotler-internal environment and external environment.

Micro-environment : The microenvironment of the firm comprises the following.

The Firm: It is a part of the microenvironment. Its human resource, plant, machines, offices, retail outlets and equipment are a part of its microenvironment; so are its procedures, policies and strategies.

Suppliers: These are vendors who supply goods, services and professional advice to the firm in the context of its operations.

Marketing Intermediaries: These include middlemen, physical distribution channels and financial intermediaries.

Customers: These are the most important component of the microenvironment. The firm earns profits by selling its products and services to them. Consumer Behaviour has been discussed in detail in this section.

Competitors: There are 4 types of competitors-Desire Competitors (based on the desire to be satisfied), Generic competitors (depending upon the product the clients would like to consume), Form Competitors (depending upon the form or format of the product offered) and Brand competitors (depending upon the preference of clients for particular brands).

Public: A public is a group that has an actual or potential interest or impact on the ability of a firm to achieve its objectives. There are many types of public, namely, financial publics (like banks, investment houses and financial institutions), media public (like newspapers and TV channels), government publics (like government departments, commissions and ministries), citizen action publics (like NGOs, environmental action groups and minority associations), local publics (like neighbourhood associations), internal publics (like blue collar workers, white collar managers, the top brass and managers) of the firm and general public (people at large in a society or nation).

BEHAVIOUR OF CONSUMER

Before we delve deeply into the realms of buying behavioural let us study consumer characteristics.

Characteristics of Consumer

The following characteristics are associated with consumers of all categories.

Geographic Features

Geographic Situation and Terrain : Geographic data can often provide clues for an effective segmentation strategy. The geographical terrain of a market segment would decide the type of products or services to be sold in that area. Problems related to logistics would also have to be sorted out before the firm starts its marathon run in a market. Hills and mountains are a pretty tough terrain for all types of marketers. Snow-clad mountains and regions also need many products and services like liquor, woolens, shoes, trekking gear, radio paging systems, medicines, high-calorie foods etc. Deserts need different kind of treatment; so do marshes, plains of the rivers and plateaus of the world. The marketer has to collect the geographical data of the targeted region first. Then, he must find out how this data affects the buying habits and motives of the targeted (or prospective) clients living in that very region. And he must remember that Mother Nature can be very harsh at some places. Mountains and an uneven terrain may not be the cup of tea of many a tourist.

Size of Country : This is also a vital factor in determining the associated with buyers.

Size of City : Large city sizes would force consumers to buy more items of necessity. Luxury needs would also increase in terms of quantity and quality.

Determination of Products by Climate and Weather : It is obvious that weather and climate would also determine the types of products that would be demanded by customers. Rainfall, snowfall, heat etc., would determine he types of products that the customers may ask for.

DENSITY OF POPULATION

A higher population density would warrant the consumption of more products of a particular category. Climate would also play an important part in this context.

Natural Calamities

Natural calamities like deluge, draught, thunderstorm, typhoon, excessive snowfall etc., would lead to the demand of such products as would help people survive during the tenures of those calamities.

Demographic Features

The senior citizen market is growing around the world and a host of their needs and wants are not being fulfilled by existing products and services. These grey markets need special attention, products, services. In the West, these people are the privileged ones. But they are not looked after in countries like India where their population is on the rise. Another important market niche is that of young adults. They are the most eligible candidates for undertaking activities related to tourism. They are not keen to undertake religious tours. Nowadays, they are more keen to undertake foreign tours, albeit only for a few days. Little children and infants are the candidates for diapers, toys, chocolates and all things entertaining and glossy. But their parents take decisions at many occasions. Instance : They may refuse to buy chocolates and potato chips for their 7-year-old daughter who needs it badly while the family is on a tour. So, the marketer may have to target his advertising campaigns and pricing strategies towards the parents (decision makers) and not children (ultimate consumers). That is because the former may be taking most of the purchase decisions on behalf of the latter.

Veterans are keen to undertake religious tours. They may also show interest in archeological sites, forts, palaces, museums and ancient excavation sites. The youth may not show keen interest in the rich historical relics of the tourist spot being visited by them.

Income : Another useful demographic criterion is income. The table below gives the latest data on income classes of the world.

It is obvious that people in the higher income brackets would be tempted to undertake tours of foreign countries. People of lower income brackets would like to travel within the regions of their residence. They may take extra pains' to undertake religious tours to far off places, however. Instance: A resident of Jammu may take his parents to Puri and let them visit jagannath temple. His parents may have requested their son to help them complete the journey of char dhamas (Puri, Dwarka, Badrinath and Rameshwaram). People of middle income groups use trains to travel while rich people prefer aircraft and their own four-wheelers. Local taxis and auto-rickshaws are used by all the categories' of people because they are not well versed with the environs of the place visited. They do not mind Paying for this luxury because:

(a) they know that they are not going to visit that spot time and again and thus, spending on taxis and auto-rickshaws is justified at least at the tourist spot/city; and

(b) they are more keen to ensure the comfort of the family members who may be travelling along with them.

Instance: A tourist family from Gujarat may visit Goa and see the important churches, beaches and temples. It may use the services of a taxi/ van so that it could complete the tour in time.

Foreign tourists prefer coaches and taxis to move about in a city. They can afford the high costs of travel; moreover, they are dependent upon tour operators and travel agencies in respect of local sightseeing tours and excursions to wildlife sanctuaries.

Gender : There are two types of customer, if gender is the sole criterion of segregation-male and female. Ladies and girls may have special requirements like privacy, pleasant behaviour, respect, special clothes, medicines, escort, security in the hotel, company of kith and kin etc. Men and boys, on the other hand, are independent, ego-stricken, go-getters, explorers, willing and able to take risks; ready to take risks and above all, rough and tough. But in the new millennium, the differentiating line between men and women has been erased to a great extent. Instance: Women, like men, like bungee jumping. We have found many men avoiding this sport but women have willing volunteered to undertake the fall! SD, the modern-day woman must not be taken lightly, especially when she is on a tour.

Occupation : The type of occupation creates a distinct psyche in the mind of the customer. His decisions are moulded according to, the job he is doing. Example: An executive would buy the finest of perfumes but a labourer may never show interest in them.

Educated People : Highly educated people are demanding and quality conscious. Illiterate people may not give consideration to quality and hence, are eligible to be given cheap low-quality products and services.

People of Different Religion : The religion of a person bars him from consuming some products and forces him to follow a unique life-style. The buyer would act according to his religious influences in the Third World countries, especially India.

People of Different Race : People of different races have different orientations toward products and services. Their attitudes may have been gelled by their religious thoughts as well.

Life Cycle of Family : The stage in the Family life cycle would persuade the customer to buy different products and services.

Size of Family : The number of persons living in a family (on a permanent basis) would affect the buying patterns of the family as a whole.

People of Different Nations : People of different nations would prefer different types of products and services.

PSYCHOGRAPHIC NATURE

There are 5 major characteristics in this category, as follows.

Cultural Factors

Factors deeply associated with culture are vital when multinational firms attempt to develop a segmentation strategy with the world as large market. Differences among cultures can affect important processes such as product acceptance and post-purchase behaviour. Example: Tourists cannot eat pork in a Muslim country like Malaysia, the UAE, Kuwait and Saudi Arabia. In Europe, it is customary to attend a burial in black clothes (which signify death and mourning) and not white ones (which signify peace and prosperity).

Style of Living : A person's interests, opinions and activities combine to represent his or her life-style. Knowledge of life-styles of the targeted customers can provide vital data about a person or group of persons. It can indicate whether the person is keen to take part in outdoor sports, shopping, theatre or parasailing. It can also include information concerning attitudes and personality traits of the person being studied. Life-style affects the buying behavior of the person in the sense that the person in question wants to have at least the same level of comfort as he had been enjoying in the past. He may long for higher levels of comfort and luxury. But he would certainly not like to do away with his existing set of gadgets, luxury goods, clothes and habits. This is a good clue for all the tourism marketers. A direct outcome of this analysis is-give your customer what he already has (or prefers) but do not forget to show him what he doesn't have (or may prefer).

Factors of Whims and Fancies

Here we are! We know that these are the most important indicators of buyers' motives. Some women hate red socks but some others keep on wearing them even in the bed! Man is a strange creature. His behaviour is unpredictable at many moments. If the marketer can somehow understand how he would behave at particular occasions, he can give the products and services of the finest quality to him. And in this process, he would satisfy the most hidden desires of man, thus earning for himself fortunes beyond imagination. But judging the whims of humans is very difficult process. Many firms have failed in the past in this task.

This brings us to a vital question-how can hotel staff learn about the whims and fancies of a guest who has just checked in ? In such cases, when it is not possible to judge the preferences of the guest or customer, it is imperative to get an idea from that customer as soon as he arrives at the scene. The hotel staff can talk to the customer when he checks in.

His preferences for vegetarian and non-vegetarian food can be noted. His tour programme can also be jotted down so that the staff is aware when he would check out of the hotel. If the guest prefers blue colour, then, the staff can provide him a bed with a blue bedspread. This has to be done despite the fact that all the hotels use white linen in their rooms. If the guest is given sops like these, he feels important as his whims are satiated. And he is ready to pay for these extras.

Diverse Personality

Different types of personality would lead to different types of behaviours. The person could be an autocrat, gregarious, ambition or compulsive. Accordingly, his motivations for purchasing goods and/or services would defined.

Different Social Classes

People belonging to the lower-lower class would demand different products than those belonging to the upper-upper class. Class conflict would also play a major role while the customer buys products or services. Instance: A tourists belonging to the upper crust would travel by luxury class in an aircraft but a person of the middle income class would prefer the economy class.

Characteristics of Behavioural Consumer : This category of consumer characteristics is more closely associated with the purchasing process itself. The following characteristics are noteworthy.

Rate of Usage

A powerful segmentation variable is the usage rate of product or service. The marketer must find out who are the heavy users of his products or services and who are the light users of the same. The most interesting of all the targeted customers are the non-users. The challenge is to get them to try the product and ultimately, make them heavy users. Table below Gives the profile of all the types of users according to the degree of usage of a product or service.

The marketing manager must address at least two problems in this context :

- Development of such programs as attract members of targeted groups, or niches to try the product for the first time.
- Develop products or services that this group would like to buy regularly.
- Motivate non-users to trap in his marketing net.
- Try to pluck customers from the trees of customers in a sophisticated decent manner so that the latter do not cry 'foul.'
- Convert light users into medium users and medium users into heavy users.

Loyalty Status

There are 4 categories in the parlance of loyalty status-None, Medium, Strong, Absolute. This classification was done by Phillip Kotler. The loyalty status has many iminuations, which can be explained in the context of an example from the tourism industry. Example: When a brand such as Cox & Kings is competing in a well-defined class such as package tours, it is useful to consider brand loyalty as a basis for segmentation. The customers of Cox & Kings can be divided into two distinct classes-those who are loyal buyers of the brand and those who are not.

The disloyal buyer tends to buy several brands, selecting, for example, the least expensive or the most convenient brand at the moment of purchase. Similarly, non-users of Cox & Kings can also be divided into two classes-those, who are loyal only to particular brands and those, who buy several other brands at random. The marketer has to increase brand loyalty to his own brand by persuading brand loyalists of other brands. He has also to target the marketing campaigns to those fickle-minded customers who do not have a well-defined pattern of purchase. We have observed that tourists go to a different travel agency for purchasing air tickets.

They want to find out whether rates given by the previous travel agent were correct or not. Once they find a particular travel agency that gives them the best prices, they stick to it (an example of absolute loyalty). The same is true for holiday packages as well. Once the customer is convinced about the rates, efficient planning, courtesy and picture-perfect execution of a travel agency, he goes to it for undertaking another tom. Over a period of years, brand loyalists identify themselves with these travel agencies or hotels. They stay only at those hotels with which, their experiences in the past had been pretty good. Rarely, if ever, they change their preferences, they come back to the original set of hotels, travel agents etc. The marketer has to build brand loyalty among its corporate clientele by sending them mailers and letters on a regular basis. He can tell them about special discounts that he can offer to them. He can also give them extra sops like free accommodation for children, cold drinks, liquor, welcome breakfast, gifts in lieu of the brand loyalty that he gets from such customers. Many corporate clients are being served by reputed travel agencies of India in this manner.

Tourism products are perishable in nature. Customers are aware of this fact. They do not want to take risk while they select tour packages for themselves and their families. They want to get the best out of the package tour selected by them. That is because they cannot retrace their steps back to square one, once they have committed to undertake such tours. The task of the marketer is to convince the customer that the package being bought by him would give him the full value of money. It is, however, not an easy task. Customers withdraw their bookings many times, even if they have to forego some booking amount that is already with the travel agent. In our view, if the customer is an old one, he should be given the booking amount even if he does not undertake the tour due to one reason or the other. This would help the marketer get another order from him in the future.

The buyer wants reliability of the marketer (travel agency or hotel) because he knows that the product is perishable. Finally, if the advance amount cannot be returned to him, as is true in the cases of foreign tours, the marketer should give the customer some additional facilities so that the customer does not feel that he has been fleeced due to a wrong decision taken by him. He can be convinced that he would do well to undertake the tour that he has planned to cancel and that he would be given additional discount in the next tour. The travel agent can help the customer book the air ticket and hold seat for him for 14 days without paying a penny. But if the customer has not been able to change the departure schedule even after this limit, the travel agent must convince him that it is better to fly on the same ticket, lest he should lose money by way of cancellation charges.

SOCIAL CONSIDERATIONS

Social considerations are important when we discuss tourism as an activity for intermingling of various types of people. Every tourist in a group belongs to a different social set-up. These different social set-ups are able to create sets of beliefs in the minds of individuals. They cannot do away with these beliefs simply because they are visiting a foreign country. Even within a country like India, we can witness different societal forces acting at all the times on individuals.

Instance: A south Indian would love to wear a dhoti even if he has checked into a hotel of Shimla. For him, wearing a dhoti is a status symbol. His social beliefs have made him think that way. But the locals may not like his habit.

Instance: Some south Indians take food while sitting on the floor, without spoons and after some initial rituals like pula. But in a hotel of north India, they may seem to be out of place; it is not their native state, after all.

Instance: North Indians may not consume food or snacks prepared by Dallies.

The tourism marketer has to understand these beliefs of the targeted markets. Then, he must understand how these beliefs can be consolidated when the guest is making use of his services or consuming his products. He must address these problems and issues that are registered by his customer from time to time. Eventually, he would arrive at a set of beliefs or habits that a particular social group follows. This would be done over a period of time, after meeting lot many customers of a particular societal niche. Thus, the marketer would evolve a set of strategies to cater to the precise needs of that group. Similarly, he would define strategies for other groups that are his frequent or regular customers. Time would teach him these vital lessons.

Stage for Being Ready

The important parameters in this category ate-unaware, Aware, Informed, Interested, Desirous and Intending to Buy.

Consumer's Attitude's towards Product : : The important parameters in this category are-Enthusiastic, Positive, Indifferent, Negative and Hostile.

Users Status

The important parameters in this category are-Non-user, Ex-user, Potential User, First-time User and Regular User.

LEGAL FACTORS IN TRAVEL

These are the factors that govern the travel, stay, excursion, movements, purchases and other activities of a tourist in a foreign land. Even within a country, the rules of various state can differ from those of another state. The United States has 50 different Stales and each one of those has a different set of rules, though these are a part of the Big Apple. Rules related to octroi, entry and exit of foreigners, customs duties, airport taxes, rules for stay in a hotel, check out timings, rules for declaration of excess baggage, forms to be filled to declare special goods (while arriving at a new station or airport), halt at transit airports, entry into strategic places cantonments and rules for extradition of wily tourists or foreigners are different for different countries.

The marketer has to understand and imbibe the basic spirit of each and every rule that is associated with tourism. Then, he must communicate these rules to the targeted clients during the course of the marketing campaign. He may also have to communicate the same when the customer is being served by him.

That is because many tourists are not aware of the laws of the land and may commit mistakes during their tours. Safe hassle-free passage of the customer is the responsibility of the marketer; so, he must have a legal advisor/counsel to give him legal support. This would ensure that the customer does not face any problem during the itinerary. Legal factors are always in the back of the mind of every tourist. These control his actions and behaviour whenever he travels to a foreign land.

5
Digital Convergence in the Field of Tourism

Digital convergence refers to the convergence of four industries into one conglomerate, ITTCE (Information Technologies, Telecommunication, Consumer Electronics, and Entertainment). Previously separate technologies such as voice (and telephony features), data (and productivity applications), and video can now share resources and interact with each other synergistically.

Telecommunications convergence, network convergence or simply convergence are broad terms used to describe emerging telecommunications technologies, and network architecture used to migrate multiple communications services into a single network. Specifically this involves the converging of previously distinct media such as telephony and data communications into common interfaces on single devices, such as most smart phones can make phone calls and search the web.

The rise of digital communication in the late 20th century has made it possible for media organizations (or individuals) to deliver text, audio, and video material over the same wired, wireless, or fiber-optic connections. At the same time, it inspired some media organizations to explore multimedia delivery of information. This digital convergence of news media, in particular, was called "Mediamorphosis" by researcher Roger Fidler, in his 1997 book by that name. Today, we are surrounded by a multi-level convergent media world where all modes of communication and information are continually reforming to adapt to the enduring demands of technologies, "changing the way we create, consume, learn and interact with each other".

Convergence in this instance is defined as the interlinking of computing and other information technologies, media content, and communication networks that has arisen as the result of the evolution and popularization of the Internet as well as the activities, products and services that have emerged in the digital media space. Many experts view this as simply being the tip of the iceberg, as all facets of institutional activity and social life such as business, government, art, journalism, health, and education are increasingly being carried out in these digital media spaces across a growing network ofinformation and communication technology devices.

Also included in this topic is the basis of computer networks, wherein many different operating systems are able to communicate via different protocols. This could be a prelude to artificial intelligence networks on the Internet eventually leading to a powerful superintelligence via a technological singularity.

Convergent services, such as VoIP, IPTV, Mobile TV, Smart TV, and others, tend to replace the older technologies and thus can disrupt markets. IP-based convergence is inevitable and will result in new service and new demand in the market.

When the old technology converges into the public-owned common, IP based services become access-independent or less dependent. The old service is access-dependent.

DEFINITIONS

Siddhartha Menon defines convergence, in his *Policy initiative elemmas on Media Covergence: A Cross National Perspective*, as integration and digitalization. Integration, here, is defined as "a process of transformation measure by the degree to which diverse media such as phone, data broadcast and information technology infrastructures are combined into a single seamless all purpose network architecture platform".

Digitalization is not so much defined by its physical infrastructure, but by the content or the medium. Jan van Dijk suggests that "digitalization means breaking down signals into bytes consisting of ones and zeros".

Convergence is defined by Blackman, 1998, as a trend in the evolution of technology services and industry structures. Convergence is later defined more specifically as the coming together of telecommunications, computing and broadcasting into a single digital bit-stream. Mueller stands against the statement that convergence is really a takeover of all forms of media by one technology: digital computers.

History

Communication networks were designed to carry different types of information independently. Radio was designed for audio, and televisions were designed for video. The older media, such as television and radio, are broadcasting networks with passive audiences. Convergence of telecommunication technology permits the manipulation of all forms of information, voice, data, and video. Telecommunication has changed from a world of scarcity to one of seemingly limitless capacity. Consequently, the possibility of audience interactivity morphs the passive audience into an engaged audience.

The historical roots of convergence can be traced back to the emergence of mobile telephony and the Internet, although the term properly applies only from the point in marketing history when fixed and mobile telephony began to be offered by operators as joined products. Fixed and mobile operators were, for most of the 1990s, independent companies. Even when the same organization marketed both products, these were sold and serviced independently.

In the 1990s an implicit and often explicit assumption was that new media was going to replace the old media and Internet was going to replace broadcasting. In Nicholas Negroponte's *Being Digital*, Negroponte predicts the collapse of broadcast networks in favor of an era of narrow-casting. He also suggests that no government regulation can shatter the media conglomerate. "The monolithic empires of mass media are dissolving into an array of cottage industries.... Media barons of today will be grasping to hold onto their centralized empires tomorrow.... The combined forces of technology and human nature will ultimately take a stronger hand in plurality than any laws Congress can invent." The new media companies claimed that the old media would be absorbed fully and completely into the orbit of the emerging technologies.

George Gilder dismisses such claims saying,"The computer industry is converging with the television industry in the same sense that the automobile converged with the horse, the TV converged with the nickelodeon, the word-processing program converged with the typewriter, the CAD program converged with the drafting board, and digital desktop publishing converged with the Linotype machine and the letterpress." Gilder believes that computers had come not to transform mass culture but to destroy it.

Media companies put Media Convergence back to their agenda, after the dot-com bubble burst. Erstwhile Knight Ridder promulgated concept of portable magazines, newspaper, and books in 1994.

Technology Implications

Convergent solutions include both fixed-line and mobile technologies. Recent examples of new, convergent services include:

- Using the Internet for voice telephony
- Video on demand
- Fixed-mobile convergence
- Mobile-to-mobile convergence
- Location-based services
- Integrated products and bundles

Convergent technologies can integrate the fixed-line with mobile to deliver convergent solutions. Convergent technologies include:

- IP Multimedia Subsystem
- Session Initiation Protocol
- IPTV
- Voice over IP
- Voice call continuity
- Digital video broadcasting - handheld

Converging technological fields

NBIC, an acronym for **N**anotechnology, **B**iotechnology, **I**nformation technology and **C**ognitive science, was, in 2014, the most popular term for converging technologies. It was introduced into public discourse through the publication of*Converging Technologies for Improving Human Performance*, a report sponsored in part by the U. S. National Science Foundation.

Various other acronyms have been offered for the same concept such as GNR (Genetics, Nanotechnology and Robotics) (Bill Joy, 2000, Why the future doesn't need us). Journalist Joel Garreau in Radical Evolution: The Promise and Peril of Enhancing Our Minds, Our Bodies — and What It Means to Be Human uses "GRIN", for Genetic, Robotic, Information, andNano processes, while science journalist Douglas Mulhall in Our Molecular Future: How Nanotechnology, Robotics, Genetics and Artificial Intelligence Will Transform Our World uses "GRAIN", for Genetics, Robotics, Artificial Intelligence, and Nanotechnology. Another acronym coined by the appropriate technology organization ETC Group is "BANG" for "Bits, Atoms, Neurons, Genes".

Appliances

Some expect that we will eventually access all media content through one device, or "black box". As such, media business practice has been to identify the next "black box" to invest in and provide media for. This has caused a number of problems.

Firstly, as "black boxes" are invented and abandoned, the individual is left with numerous devices that can perform the same task, rather than one dedicated for each task. For example, one may own both a computer and a video games console, subsequently owning two DVD players. This is contrary to the streamlined goal of the "black box" theory, and instead creates clutter.

Secondly, technological convergence tends to be experimental in nature. This has led to consumers owning technologies with additional functions that are harder, if not impractical, to use rather than one specific device. For example, Intel has created a surfboard with an in-built laptop. Additionally, LG has created a microwave with a television screen. Many people would only watch the TV for the duration of the meal's cooking time, or whilst in the kitchen, but would not use the microwave as the household TV. These examples show that in many cases technological convergence is unnecessary or unneeded.

Furthermore, although consumers primarily use a specialized media device for their needs, other "black box" devices that perform the same task can be used to suit their current situation. As a 2002 Cheskin Research report explained:

... Your email needs and expectations are different whether you're at home, work, school, commuting, the airport, etc., and these different devices are designed to suit your needs for accessing content depending on where you are- your situated context. Despite the creation of "black boxes", intended to perform all of one's tasks, the trend is to use devices that can suit the consumer's physical position.

Due to the variable utility of portable technology, convergence occurs in high end mobile devices. They incorporate multimedia services, GPS, Internet access, and mobile telephony into a single device, heralding the rise of what has been termed the "smart phone," a device designed to remove the need to carry multiple devices.

Convergence of media occurs when multiple products come together to form one product with the advantages of all of them, also known as the black box. This idea of one technology, concocted by Henry Jenkins, has become known more as a fallacy because of the inability to actually put all technical pieces into one. For example, while people can have e-mail and Internet on their phone, they still want full computers with Internet and e-mail in addition.

For example, the Wii is not only a games console, but also a web browser and social networking tool. Mobile phones are another good example, in that they increasingly incorporate digital cameras, mp3 players, camcorders, voice recorders, and other devices. This type of convergence is popular. For the consumer, it means more features in less space; for media conglomerates it means remaining competitive.

However, convergence has a downside. Particularly in initial forms, converged devices are frequently less functional and reliable than their component parts (e. g., a mobile phone's web browser may not render some web pages correctly, due to not supporting certain rendering methods, such as the iPhone browser not supporting Flash content). As the number of functions in a single device escalates, the ability of that device to serve its original function decreases. For example, the iPhone (which by its name implies that its primary function is that of a mobile phone) can perform many different tasks, but does not feature a traditional numerical pad to make phone calls. Instead, the phone features a touchpad, which some users find more troublesome. As Rheingold asserts, technological convergence holds immense potential for the "improvement of life and liberty in some ways and (could) degrade it in others" He believes the same technology has the potential to be "used as both a weapon of social control and a means of resistance"

Since technology has evolved in the past ten years or so, companies are beginning to converge technologies to create demand for new products. This would include phone companies integrating 3G on their phones. In the mid 20th century, television converged the technologies of movies and radio, and television is now being converged with the mobile phone industry and the Internet. Phone calls are also being made with the use of personal computers.

Converging technologies combine multiple technologies into one. Newer mobile phones feature cameras, and can hold images, videos, music, and other media. Manufacturers now integrate more advanced features, such as video recording, GPS receivers, data storage, and security mechanisms into the traditional cellphone.

INTERNET

The role of the internet has changed from its original use as a communication tool to provide easier and faster access to information, mainly through a broadband connection. The television, radio and newspapers were the world's mediums for accessing news and entertainment; now, all three mediums have converged into one, and people all over the world can read and hear news and other information on the Internet. The convergence of the internet and conventional TV become popular in the 2010s, through smart TV, also sometimes referred to as "Connected TV" or "Hybrid TV", (not to be confused with IPTV, Internet TV, or with Web TV).

Smart TV is used to describe the current trend of integration of the internet and Web 2. 0 features into modern television sets and set-top boxes, as well as the technological convergence between computers and these television sets or set-top boxes. These new devices most often also have a much higher focus on online interactive media, Internet TV, over-the-top content, as well as on-demand streaming media, and less focus on traditional broadcast media like previous generations oftelevision sets and set-top boxes always have had.

Digital convergence

According to Harry Strasser, former CTO of Siemens" [digital convergence will substantially impact people's lifestyle and work style]". The next hot trend in digital convergence is converged content, mixing personal (user generated) content with professional (copyright protected) content. An example are personal music videos that combine user generated photos with chart music. The German startup Trivid GmbH has developed an award winning solution, Clipgenerator, that enables users to create personal music videos with popular chart music and to share them in social communities such as facebook, myspace and Bebo.

In the marketplace

Convergence is a global marketplace dynamic in which different companies and sectors are being brought together, both as competitors and collaborators, across traditional boundaries of industry and technology. In a world dominated by convergence, many traditional products, services and types of companies will become less relevant, but a stunning array of new ones are possible.

An array of technology developments act as accelerators of convergence, including mobility, analytics, cloud, digital and social networks. As a disruptive force, convergence is a threat to the unprepared, but a tremendous growth opportunity for companies that can out-innovate and out-execute their ever-expanding list of competitors under dramatically new marketplace rules.

With convergence, lines are blurred as companies diversify outside of their original markets. For instance, mobile services are increasingly an important part of the automobile; chemicals companies work with agribusiness; device manufacturers sell music, video and books; booksellers become consumer device companies; search and advertising companies become telcos; media companies act like telcos and vice versa; retailers act like financial services companies and vice versa; cosmetics companies work with pharmaceutical companies; and much, much more. Mobile phone usage broadens dramatically, becoming the means to do previously inconceivable things from making payments to watching videos to operating an intelligent home.

MEDIA

Generally, media convergence refers to the merging of both old and new media and can be seen as a product, a system or a process. Jenkins states that convergence is,

"the flow of content across multiple media platforms, the cooperation between multiple media industries, and the migratory behaviour of media audiences who would go almost anywhere in search of the kinds of entertainment experiences they wanted"

According to Jenkins, there are five areas of convergence: technological, economic, social or organic, cultural and global.

So media convergence is not just a technological shift or a technological process, it also includes shifts within the industrial, cultural, and social paradigms that encourage the consumer to seek out new information. Convergence, simply put, is how individual consumers interact with others on a social level and use various media platforms to create new experiences, new forms of media and content that connect us socially, and not just to other consumers, but to the corporate producers of media in ways that have not been as readily accessible in the past.

Advances in technology bring the ability for technological convergence that Rheingold believes can alter the "social-side effects," in that "the virtual, social and physical world are colliding, merging and coordinating."

It was predicted in the late 1980s, around the time that CD-ROM was becoming commonplace, that a digital revolutionwould take place, and that old media would be pushed to one side by new media. Broadcasting is increasingly being replaced by the Internet, enabling consumers all over the world the freedom to access their preferred media content more easily and at a more available rate than ever before.

However, when the dot com bubble of the 1990s suddenly popped, that poured cold water over the talk of such a digital revolution. In today's society, the idea of media convergence has once again emerged as a key point of reference as newer as well as established media companies attempt to visualize the future of the entertainment industry. If this revolutionary digital paradigm shift presumed that old media would be increasingly replaced by new media, the convergence paradigm that is currently emerging suggests that new and old media would interact in more complex ways than previously predicted. The paradigm shift that followed the digital revolution assumed that new media was going to change everything. When the dot com market crashed, there was a tendency to imagine that nothing had changed. The real truth lay somewhere in between as there were so many aspects of the current media environment to take into consideration. Many industry leaders are increasingly reverting to media convergence as a way of making sense in an era of disorientating change. In that respect, media convergence in theory is essentially an old concept taking on a new meaning.

Media convergence, in reality, is more than just a shift in technology. It alters relationships between industries, technologies, audiences, genres and markets. Media convergence changes the rationality media industries operate in, and the way that media consumers process news and entertainment. Media conver-gence is essentially a process and not an outcome, so no single black box controls the flow of media. With proliferation of different media channels and increasing portability of new telecommunications and computing technologies, we have entered into an era where media constantly surrounds us.

Media convergence requires that media companies rethink existing assumptions about media from the consumer's point of view, as these affect marketing and programming decisions. Media producers must respond to newly empowered consumers. Conversely, it would seem that hardware is instead diverging whilst media content is converging. Media has developed into brands that can offer content in a number of forms. Two examples of this are Star Wars and The Matrix. Both are films, but are also books, video games, cartoons, and action figures. Branding encourages expansion of one concept, rather than the creation of new ideas. In contrast, hardware has diversified to accommodate media convergence. Hardware must be specific to each function.

While most scholars argue that the flow of cross-media is accelerating, O'Donnell suggests, especially between films and video game, the semblance of media convergence is misunderstood by people outside of the media production industry. The conglomeration of media industry continues to sell the same story line in different media. For example, Batman is in comics, films, anime, and games. However, the data to create the image of batman in each media is created individually by different teams of creators. The same character and the same visual effect repetitively appear in different media is because of the synergy of media industry to make them similar as possible. In addition, convergence does not happen when the game of two different consoles is produced. No flows between two consoles because it is faster to create game from scratch for the industry.

One of the more interesting new media journalism forms is virtual reality. Reuters, a major international news service, has created and staffed a news "island" in the popular online virtual reality environment Second Life (www. secondlife. com, accessed January 3, 2008). Open to anyone, Second Life has emerged as a compelling 3D virtual reality for millions of citizens around the world who have created avatars (virtual representations of themselves) to populate and live in an altered state where personal flight is a reality, altered egos can flourish, and real money (US$1, 296, 257 were spent during the 24 hours concluding at 10:19 a. m. eastern time January 7, 2008) can be made without ever setting foot into the real world. The Reuters Island in Second Life is a virtual version of the Reuters real-world news service but covering the domain of Second Life for the citizens of Second Life (numbering 11, 807, 742 residents as of January 5, 2008).

Media Convergence in the Digital Era means the changes that are taking place in this current time with older forms of media and media companies. Media convergence has two roles, the first is the technological merging of different media channels – for example, magazines, radio programs, TV shows, and movies, now are available on the Internet through laptops, iPads, and smartphones. As discussed in Media Culture by Campbell, convergence of technology is not new. It has been going on since the late 1920s. An example is RCA the Radio Corporation of America purchased Victor Talking Machine Company and introduced machines that could play both radio and recorded music. Next came the TV, and radio lost some of its appeal as people started watching television which has both talking and music as well as visual. As technology advances, convergence of media's change to keep up with the time. The second definition of media convergence as Campbell discusses is, Cross- platform by media marketeer's, which means consolidating various media holdings, such as cable, phone, television and internet access under one corporate umbrella. This is not for the consumer to have more media choices, this is for the benefit of the company to cut down on costs and maximize its profits. As stated in the article, Convergence Culture and Media Work, by Mark Deuze, "the convergence of production and consumption of media across companies, channels, genres, and technologies is an expression of the convergence of all aspects of everyday life: work and play, the local and the global, self and social identity."

CONVERGENCE CULTURE

Henry Jenkins determines convergence culture to be the flow of content across multiple media platforms, the cooperation between multiple media industries, and the migratory behavior of media audiences who will go almost anywhere in search of the kinds of entertainment experiences they want. The convergence culture is an important factor in transmedia storytelling. Convergence culture introduces new stories and arguments from one form of media into many. Because of this culture a single piece of media content is represented in multiple forms of media. For instance, The Matrixstarts as a film, which is followed by two other installments, but in a convergence culture it is not constrained to that form. It becomes a story not only told in the movies but in animated shorts, video games and comic books, three different media platforms. Online, a wiki is created to keep track of the story's expanding canon. Fan films, discussion forums, and social media pages also form, expanding The Matrix to different online platforms. Convergence culture took what started as a film and expanded it across almost every type of media.

Convergence culture is a part of participatory culture. Because average people can now access their interests on many types of media they can also have more of a say. Fans and consumers are able to participate in the creation and circulation of new content. Some companies take advantage of this and search for feedback from their customers through social media and sharing sites such as YouTube. Besides marketing and entertainment, convergence culture has also affected the way we interact with news and information. We can access news on multiple levels of media from the radio, TV, newspapers, and the internet. The internet allows more people to be able to report the news through independent broadcasts and therefore allows a multitude of perspectives to be put forward and accessed by people in many different areas. Convergence allows news to be gathered on a much larger scale. For instance, photographs were taken of torture atAbu Ghraib. These photos were shared and eventually posted on the internet. This led to the breaking of a news story in newspapers, on TV, and the internet.

Media scholar Henry Jenkins has described the media convergence with participatory culture as:

... a "catalyst" for amateur digital film-making and what this case study suggests about the future directions popular culture may take. Star Wars fan films represent the intersection of two significant cultural trends—the corporate movement towards media convergence and the unleashing of significant new tools, which enable the grassroots archiving, annotation, appropriation, and recirculation of media content. These fan films build on long-standing practices of the fan community but they also reflect the influence of this changed technological environment that has dramatically lowered the costs of film production and distribution.

Cell phone convergence

The social function of the cell phone changes as the technology converges. Because of technological advancement, cell phones function more than just as a phone. They contain an internet connection, video players, Mp3 players, and a camera. Another example, Rok Sako To Rok Lo (2004) was screened in Delhi, Bangalore, Hyderabad, Mumbai, and other part of India through EDGE-enabled mobile phones with live video streaming facility.

Social movement

The integration of social movement in cyberspace is one of the potential strategies of social movement in the age of media convergence. Because of the neutrality of the internet and the end-to-end design, the power structure of the internet was designed to avoid discrimination between applications. Mexico's Zapatistas campaign for land rights was one of the most influential case in the information age; Manuel Castells defines the Zapatistas as "the first informational guerrilla movement". The Zapatista uprising had been marginalized by the popular press. The Zapatistas were able to construct a grassroots, decentralized social movement by using the internet. The Zapatistas Effect, observed by Cleaver, continues to organize social movements on a global scale. A sophisticated webmetric analysis, which maps the links between different websites and seeks to identify important nodal points in a network, demonstrates that the Zapatistas cause binds together hundreds of global NGOs. The majority of the social movement organized by Zapatistas targets their campaign especially against global neoliberalism. A successful social movement not only need online support but also protest on the street. Papic wrote, "Social Media Alone Do Not Instigate Revolutions", which discusses how the use of social media in social movements needs good organization both online and offline.

A study title, "Journalism in the age of media convergence: a survey of undergraduates' technology-related news habits", concluded that several focus group respondents reported they generally did not actively engage in media convergence, such as viewing slide shows or listening to podcast that accompanied an online story, as part of their Web-based news consumption, a significant number of students indicated the interactive features often associated with online news and media convergence were indeed appealing to them.

CONVERGENCE REGULATION

VoIP

The U. S. Federal Communications Commission (FCC) has not been able to decide how to regulate VoIP (Internet Telephony) because the convergent technology is still growing and changing. In addition to its growth, FCC is tentative to set regulation on VoIP in order to promote competition in the telecommunication industry. There is not a clear line between telecommunication service and the information service because of the growth of the new convergent media. Historically, telecommunication is subject to state regulation. The state of California concerned about the increasing popularity of internet telephony will eventually obliterate funding for the Universal Service Fund

Some States attempt to assert their traditional role of common carrier oversight onto this new technology. Meisel and Needles (2005) suggests that the FCC, federal courts, and state regulatory bodies on access line charges will directly impact the speed in which Internet telephony market grows. On one hand, the FCC is hesitant to regulate convergent technology because VoIP with different feature from the old Telecommunication; no fixed model to build legislature yet. On the other hand, the regulations is needed because Service over the internet might be quickly replaced telecommunication service, which will affect the entire economy.

Convergence has also raised several debates about classification of certain telecommunications services. As the lines between data transmission, and voice and media transmission are eroded, regulators are faced with the task of how best to classify the converging segments of the telecommunication sector. Traditionally, telecommunication regulation has focused on the operation of physical infrastructure, networks, and access to network. No content is regulated in the telecommunication because the content is considered private. In contrast, film and Television are regulated by contents. The rating system regulates its distribution to the audience.

Self-regulation is promoted by the industry. Bogle senior persuaded the entire industry to pay 0. 1 percent levy on all advertising and the money was used to give authority to the Advertising Standards Authority, which keeps the government away from setting legislature in the media industry.

The premises to regulate the new media, two-ways communications, concerns much about the change from old media to new media. Each medium has different features and characteristics. First, internet, the new medium, manipulates all form of information - voice, data and video. Second, the old regulation on the old media, such as radio and Television, emphasized its regulation on the scarcity of the channels. Internet, on the other hand, has the limitless capacity, due to the end-to-end design. Third, Two-ways communication encourages interactivity between the content producers and the audiences. "... Fundamental basis for classification, therefore, is to consider the need for regulation in terms of either market failure or in the public interests"(Blackman).

The Electronic Frontier Foundation (EFF), founded in 1990, is a non profit organization to defend free speech, privacy, innovation and consumer rights. DMCA, Digital Millennium Copyright Act regulates and protect the digital content producers and consumers.

Future

- Network Neutrality

Wu and Lessig (2004) explain two reasons to adapt neutral network. First, "a neutral network eliminates the risk of future discrimination, providing more incentive to invest in broadband application development." Second, "neutral network facilitates fair competition among application, no bias between applications." The two reasons also coincide with FCC's interest to stimulate investment and enhance innovation in broadband technology and services. Despite regulatory efforts of deregulation, privatization, and liberalization, the infrastructure barrier has been a negative factor in achieving effective competition. "Kim et al. argues that IP dissociates the telephony application from the infrastructure and Internet telephony is at the forefront of such dissociation." The neutrality of the network is very important for fair competition.

As the former FCC Charman Michael Powell puts it: "From its inception, the Internet was designed, as those present during the course of its creating will tell you, to prevent government or a corporation or anyone else from controlling it. It was designed to defeat discrimination against users, ideas and technologies" Because of these reasons, Shin concludes that regulator should make sure to regulate application and infrastructure separately.

- Layered Model

The layer Model is first proposed by Solum and Chug, Sicker, and Nakahata. Sicker, Warbach and Witt have supported using layered Model to regulate the telecommuni-cations industry with the emergence of convergence services. Many researchers have different layered approach, but they all agree that the emergence of convergent technology will create challenges and ambiguities for regulations. The key point of the layered model is that it reflects the reality of network architecture, and current business model. The layered Model consists of 1. Access Layer - where the physical infrastructure resides: copper wires, cable, or fiber optic. 2. transport layer - the provider of service. 3. Application layer - the interface between the data and the users. 4. content layer - the layer which users see. In *Convergence Technologies and the Layered Policy Model: Implication for Regulating Future*

Communications, Shin combines the Layered Model and Network Neutrality as the principle to regulate the future convergent Media Industry.

Messaging

Combination services include those that integrate SMS with voice, such as voice SMS. Providers include Bubble Motion, Jott, Kirusa, and SpinVox. Several operators have launched services that combine SMS with mobile instant messaging (MIM) and presence. Text-to-landline services also exist, where subscribers can send text messages to any landline phone and are charged at standard rates. This service has been popular in America, where fixed and mobile numbers are similar.

Inbound SMS has been converging to enable reception of different formats (SMS, voice, MMS, etc.). UK companies, including consumer goods companies and media giants, should soon be able to let consumers contact them via voice, SMS, MMS, IVR, or video using one five-digit number or long number. In April 2008, O2 UK launched voice-enabled shortcodes, adding voice functionality to the five-digit codes already used for SMS.

This type of convergence is particularly helpful for media companies, broadcasters, enterprises, call centres and help desks who need to develop a consistent contact strategy with the consumer. Because SMS is very popular today, it became relevant to include text messaging as a contact possibility for consumers. To avoid having multiple numbers (one for voice calls, another one for SMS), a simple way is to merge the reception of both formats under one number. This means that a consumer can text or call one number and be sure that the message will be received.

Mobile

"Mobile service provisions" refers not only to the ability to purchase mobile phone services, but the ability to wirelessly access everything: voice, Internet, audio, and video. Advancements in WiMAX and other leading edge technologies provide the ability to transfer information over a wireless link at a variety of speeds, distances, and non-line-of-sight conditions.

Multi-play

Multi-play is a marketing term describing the provision of different telecommunication services, such as Internet access, television, telephone, and mobile phone service, by organi-sations that traditionally only offered one or two of these services. Multi-play is a catch-all phrase; usually, the terms triple play (voice, video and data) or quadruple play (voice, video, data and wireless) are used to describe a more specific meaning.

A dual play service is a marketing term for the provisioning of the two services: it can be high-speed Internet (digital subscriber line) and telephone service over a single broadband connection in the case of phone companies, or high-speed Internet (cable modem) and TV service over a single broadband connection in the case of cable TV companies.

The convergence can also concern the underlying communication infrastructure. An example of this is a triple play service, where communication services are packaged allowing consumers to purchase TV, Internet, and telephony in one subscription.

A quadruple play service combines the triple play service of broadband Internet access, television, and telephone withwireless service provisions. This service set is also sometimes humorously referred to as "The Fantastic Four" or "Grand Slam".

The broadband cable market is transforming as pay-TV providers move aggressively into what was once considered the telco space. Meanwhile, customer expectations have risen as consumer and business customers alike seek rich content, multi-use devices, networked products and converged services including on-demand video, digital TV, high speed Internet, VoIP, and wireless applications. It's uncharted territory for most broadband companies.

A fundamental aspect of the quadruple play is not only the long awaited broadband convergence but also the players involved. Many of them, from the largest global service providers to whom we connect today via wires and cables to the smallest of startup service providers are interested. Opportunities are attractive: the big three telecom services – telephony, cable television, and wireless—could combine their industries.

In the UK, the recent merger of NTL:Telewest and Virgin Mobile resulted in a company offering a quadruple play of cable television, broadband Internet, home telephone, and mobile telephone services.

HOME NETWORK

Early in the 21st century, home LAN convergence so rapidly integrated home routers, wireless access points, and DSL modems that users were hard put to identify the resulting box they used to connect their computers to their Internet service. A general term for such a combined device is a residential gateway.

Modern wireless communication system

At the initial phase, mobile communication was restricted to certain official users and the cellular concept was never even dreamt of being made commercially available. Moreover, even the growth in the cellular networks was very slow. However, with the development of newer and better technologies starting from the 1970s and with the mobile users now connected to the PSTN, there has been a remarkable growth in the cellular radio. However, the spread of mobile communication was very fast in the 1990s when the government throughout the world provided radio spectrum licenses for Personal Communication Service (PCS) in 1. 8 - 2 GHz frequency band.

1G: First Generation Networks

The first mobile phone system in the market was AMPS. It was the first U. S. cellular telephone system, deployed in Chicago in 1983. The main technology of this first generation mobile system was FDMA/FDD and analog FM.

2G: Second Generation Networks

Digital modulation formats were introduced in this generation with the main technology as TDMA/FDD and CDMA/FDD. The 2G systems introduced three popular TDMA standards and one popular CDMA standard in the market. These are as follows:

TDMA/FDD Standards

(a) Global System for Mobile (GSM): The GSM standard, introduced by Groupe Special Mobile, was aimed at designing a uniform pan-European mobile system. It was the first fully digital system utilizing the 900 MHz frequency band. The initial GSM had 200 KHz radio channels, 8 full-rate or 16 half-rate TDMA channels per carrier, encryption of speech, low speed data services and support for SMS for which it gained quick popularity.

(b) Interim Standard 136 (IS-136): It was popularly known as North American Digital Cellular (NADC) system. In this system, there were 3 full-rate TDMA users over each 30 KHz channel. The need of this system was mainly to increase the capacity over the earlier analog (AMPS) system.

(c) Pacific Digital Cellular (PDC): This standard was developed as the counterpart of NADC in Japan. The main advantage of this standard was its low transmission bit rate which led to its better spectrum utilization.

CDMA/FDD Standard

Interim Standard 95 (IS-95): The IS-95 standard, also popularly known as CDMAOne, uses 64 orthogonally coded users and codewords are transmitted simultaneously on each of 1. 25 MHz channels. Certain services that have been standardized as a part of IS-95 standard are: short messaging service, slotted paging, over-the-air activation (meaning the mobile can be activated by the service provider without any third party intervention), enhanced mobile station identities etc.

2. 5G Mobile Networks

In an effort to retrofit the 2G standards for compatibility with increased throughput rates to support modern Internet application, the new data centric standards were developed to be overlaid on 2G standards and this is known as 2. 5G standard.

Here, the main upgradation techniques are:

- supporting higher data rate transmission for web browsing
- supporting e-mail traffic
- enabling location-based mobile service

2. 5G networks also brought into the market some popular application, a few of which are: Wireless Application Protocol (WAP), General Packet Radio Service (GPRS), High Speed Circuit Switched Dada (HSCSD), Enhanced Data rates for GSM Evolution (EDGE) etc.

3G: Third Generation Networks

3G is the third generation of mobile phone standards and technology, superseding 2. 5G. It is based on the International Telecommunication Union (ITU) family of standards under the International Mobile Telecommunications-2000 (IMT-2000). ITU launched IMT-2000 program, which, together with the main industry and standardization bodies worldwide, targets to implement a global frequency band that would support a single, ubiquitous wireless communication standard for all countries, to provide the framework for the definition of the 3G mobile systems. Several radio access technologies have been accepted by ITU as part of the IMT-2000 frame work.

3G networks enable network operators to offer users a wider range of more advanced services while achieving greater network capacity through improved spectral efficiency. Services include wide-area wireless voice telephony, video calls, and broadband wireless data, all in a mobile environment. Additional features also include HSPA data transmission capabilities able to deliver speeds up to 14. 4Mbit/s on the down link and 5. 8Mbit/s on the uplink.

3G networks are wide area cellular telephone networks which evolved to incorporate high-speed internet access and video telephony. IMT-2000 defines a set of technical requirements for the realization of such targets, which can be summarized as follows:

- high data rates: 144 kbps in all environments and 2 Mbps in low-mobility and indoor environments
- symmetrical and asymmetrical data transmission
- circuit-switched and packet-switched-based services
- speech quality comparable to wire-line quality
- improved spectral efficiency

- several simultaneous services to end users for multimedia services
- seamless incorporation of second-generation cellular systems
- global roaming
- open architecture for the rapid introduction of new services and technology.

3G Standards and Access Technologies

As mentioned before, there are several different radio access technologies defined within ITU, based on either CDMA or TDMA technology. An organization called 3rd Generation Partnership Project (3GPP) has continued that work by defining a mobile system that fulfills the IMT-2000 standard. This system is called Universal Mobile Telecommunications System (UMTS). After trying to establish a single 3G standard, ITU finally approved a family of five 3G standards, which are part of the 3G framework known as IMT-2000:

- W-CDMA
- CDMA2000
- TD-SCDMA

Europe, Japan, and Asia have agreed upon a 3G standard called the Universal Mobile Telecommunications System (UMTS), which is WCDMA operating at 2. 1 GHz. UMTS and WCDMA are often used as synonyms. In the USA and other parts of America, WCDMA will have to use another part of the radio spectrum.

3G W-CDMA (UMTS)

WCDMA is based on DS-CDMA (direct sequencecode division multiple access) technology in which user-information bits are spread over a wide bandwidth (much larger than the information signal bandwidth) by multiplying the user data with the spreading code. The chip (symbol rate) rate of the spreading sequence is 3. 84 Mcps, which, in the WCDMA system deployment is used together with the 5-MHz carrier spacing. The processing gain term refers to the relationship between the signal bandwidth and the information bandwidth. Thus, the name wideband is derived to differentiate it from the 2G CDMA (IS-95), which has a chip rate of 1. 2288 Mcps. In a CDMA system, all users are active at the same time on the same frequency and are separated from each other with the use of user specific spreading codes.

The wide carrier bandwidth of WCDMA allows supporting high user-data rates and also has certain performance benefits, such as increased multipath diversity. The actual carrier spacing to be used by the operator may vary on a 200-kHz grid between approximately 4. 4 and 5 MHz, depending on spectrum arrangement and the interference situation.

In WCDMA each user is allocated frames of 10 ms duration, during which the user-data rate is kept constant. However, the data rate among the users can change from frame to frame. This fast radio capacity allocation (or the limits for variation in the uplink) is controlled and coordinated by the radio resource management (RRM) functions in the network to achieve optimum throughput for packet data services and to ensure sufficient quality of service (QoS) for circuit-switched users. WCDMA supports two basic modes of operation: FDD and TDD. In the FDD mode, separate 5-MHz carrier frequencies with duplex spacing are used for the uplink and downlink, respectively, whereas in TDD only one 5-MHz carrier is time shared between the uplink and the downlink. WCDMA uses coherent detection based on the pilot symbols and/or common pilot. WCDMA allows many performance- enhancement methods to be used, such as transmit diversity or advanced CDMA receiver concepts.

The world's first commercial W-CDMA service, FoMA, was launched by NTT DoCoMo in Japan in 2001. FoMA is the short name for Freedom of Mobile Multimedia Access, is the brand name for the 3G services being offered by Japanese mobile phone operator NTT DoCoMo. Elsewhere, W-CDMA deployments have been exclusively UMTS based. UMTS or W-CDMA, assures backward compatibility with the second generation GSM, IS-136 and PDC TDMA technologies, as well as all 2. 5G TDMA technologies. The network structure and bit level packaging of GSM data is retained by W-CDMA, with additional capacity and bandwidth provided by a new CDMA air interface

3G CDMA2000

Code division multiple access 2000 is the natural evolution of IS-95 (cdmaOne). It includes additional functionality that increases its spectral efficiency and data rate capability. (code division multiple access) is a mobile digital radio technology where channels are defined with codes (PN sequences). CDMA permits many simultaneous transmitters on the same frequency channel. Since more phones can be served by

fewer cell sites, CDMA-based standards have a significant economic advantage over TDMA- or FDMA-based standards. This standard is being developed by Telecommunications Industry Association (TIA) of US and is is standardized by 3GPP2. The main CDMA2000 standards are: CDMA2000 1xRTT, CDMA2000 1xEV and CDMA2000 EV-DV. These are the approved radio interfaces for the ITU's IMT-2000 standard. In the following, a brief discussion about all these standards is given.

CDMA2000 1xRTT: RTT stands for Radio Transmission Technology and the designation "1x", meaning "1 times Radio Transmission Technology", indicates the same RF bandwidth as IS-95. The main features of CDMA2000 1X are as follows:

- Supports an instantaneous data rate upto 307kpbs for a user in packet mode and a typical throughput rates of 144kbps per user, depending on the number of user, the velociy of user and the propagating conditions.
- Provides the subscriber unit with upto two times the standby time for longer lasting battery life.

CDMA2000 EV: This is an evolutionary advancement of CDMA with the following characteristics:

- Provides CDMA carriers with the option of installing radio channels with data only (CDMA2000 EV-DO) and with data and voice (CDMA2000 EV-DV).
- The cdma2000 1xEV-DO supports greater than 2. 4Mbps of instantaneous high-speed packet throughput per user on a CDMA channel, although the user data rates are much lower and highly dependent on other factors.
- CDMA2000 EV-DV can offer data rates upto 144kbps with about twice as many voice channels as IS-95B.

CDMA2000 3x is (also known as EV-DO Rev B) is a multi-carrier evolution:

- It has higher rates per carrier (up to 4. 9 Mbit/s on the downlink per carrier). Typical deployments are expected to include 3 carriers for a peak rate of 14. 7 Mbit/s. Higher rates are possible by bundling multiple channels together. It enhances the user experience and enables new services such as high definition video streaming.
- Uses statistical multiplexing across channels to further reduce latency, enhancing the experience for latency-sensitive services such as gaming, video telephony, remote console sessions and web browsing
- It provides increased talk-time and standby time
- The interference from the adjacent sectors is reduced by hybrid frequency reuse and improves the rates that can be offered, especially to users at the edge of the cell.
- It has efficient support for services that have asymmetric download and upload requirements (i. e. different data rates required in each direction) such as file transfers, web browsing, and broadband multimedia content delivery.

3G TD-SCDMA

Time Division-Synchronous Code Division Multiple Access, or TD-SCDMA, is a 3G mobile telecommunications standard, being pursued in the People's Republic of China by the Chinese Academy of Telecommunications Technology (CATT). This proposal was adopted by ITU as one of the 3G options in late 1999. TD-SCDMA is based on spread spectrum technology. TD-SCDMA uses TDD, in contrast to the FDD scheme used by W-CDMA. By dynamically adjusting the number of timeslots used for downlink and uplink, the system can more easily accommodate asymmetric traffic with different data rate requirements on downlink and uplink than FDD schemes. Since it does not require paired spectrum for downlink and uplink, spectrum allocation flexibility is also increased. Also, using the same carrier frequency for uplink and downlink means that the channel condition is the same on both directions, and the base station can deduce the downlink channel information from uplink channel estimates, which is helpful to the application of beamforming techniques. TD-SCDMA also uses TDMA in addition to the CDMA used in WCDMA. This reduces the number of users in each timeslot, which reduces the implementation complexity of multiuser detection and beamforming schemes, but the non-continuous transmission also reduces coverage (because of the higher peak power needed), mobility (because of lower power control frequency) and complicates radio resource management algorithms. The "S" in TD-SCDMA stands for "synchronous", which means that uplink signals are synchronized at the base station receiver, achieved by continuous timing adjustments. This reduces the interference between users of the same timeslot using different codes by improving the orthogonality between the codes, therefore increasing system capacity, at the cost of some hardware complexity in achieving uplink synchronization.

WIRELESS TRANSMISSION PROTOCOLS

There are several transmission protocols in wireless manner to achieve different application oriented tasks. Below, some of these applications are given.

Wireless Local Loop (WLL) and LMDS

Microwave wireless links can be used to create a wireless local loop. The local loop can be thought of as the "last mile" of the telecommunication network that resides between the central office (CO) and the individual homes and business in close proximity to the CO. An advantage of WLL technology is that once the wireless equipment is paid for, there are no additional costs for transport between the CO and the customer premises equipment. Many new services have been proposed and this includes the concept of Local Multipoint Distribution Service (LMDS), which provides broadband telecommunication access in the local exchange.

Bluetooth

- Facilitates ad-hoc data transmission over short distances from fixed and mobile devices as shown in Figure 2. 1
- Uses a radio technology called frequency hopping spread spectrum. It chops up the data being sent and transmits chunks of it on up to 79 different frequencies.

In its basic mode, the modulation is Gaussian frequency shift keying (GFSK). It can achieve a gross data rate of 1 Mb/s

- Primarily designed for low power consumption, with a short range (powerclass-dependent: 1 meter, 10 meters, 100 meters) based on low-cost transceiver microchips in each device

Wireless Local Area Networks (W-LAN)

- IEEE 802. 11 WLAN uses ISM band (5. 275-5. 825GHz)
- Uses 11Mcps DS-SS spreading and 2Mbps user data rates (will fallback to 1Mbps in noisy conditions)
- IEEE 802. 11a stndard provides upto 54Mbps throughput in the 5GHz band. The DS-SS IEEE 802. 11b has been called Wi-Fi. Wi-Fi networks have limited range. A typical Wi-Fi home router using 802. 11b or 802. 11g with a stock antenna might have a range of 32 m (120 ft) indoors and 95 m (300 ft) outdoors. Range also varies with frequency band.
- IEEE 802. 11g uses Complementary Code Keying Orthogonal Frequency Division Multiplexing (CCK-OFDM) standards in both 2. 4GHz and 5GHz bands.

WiMax

- Provides upto 70 Mb/sec symmetric broadband speed without the need for cables. The technology is based on the IEEE 802. 16 standard (also called WirelessMAN)
- WiMAX can provide broadband wireless access (BWA) up to 30 miles (50 km) for fixed stations, and 3 - 10 miles (5 - 15 km) for mobile stations. In contrast, the WiFi/802. 11 wireless local area network standard is limited in most cases to only 100 - 300 feet (30 - 100m)
- The 802. 16 specification applies across a wide range of the RF spectrum, and WiMAX could function on any frequency below 66 GHz (higher frequencies would decrease the range of a Base Station to a few hundred meters in an urban environment).

Zigbee

- ZigBee is the specification for a suite of high level communication protocols using small, low-power digital radios based on the IEEE 802. 15. 4-2006 standard for wireless personal area networks (WPANs), such as wireless headphones connecting with cell phones via short-range radio.
- This technology is intended to be simpler and cheaper. ZigBee is targeted at radio-frequency (RF) applications that require a low data rate, long battery life, and secure networking.
- ZigBee operates in the industrial, scientific and medical (ISM) radio bands; 868 MHz in Europe, 915 MHz in countries such as USA and Australia, and 2. 4 GHz in most worldwide.

Wibree

- Wibree is a digital radio technology (intended to become an open standard of wireless communications) designed for ultra low power consumption (button cell batteries) within a short range (10 meters / 30 ft) based around low-cost transceiver microchips in each device. Wibree is known as Bluetooth with low energy technology.
- It operates in 2. 4 GHz ISM band with physical layer bit rate of 1 Mbps.

Conclusion: Beyond 3G Networks

Beyond 3G networks, or 4G (Fourth Generation), represent the next complete evolution in wireless communications. A 4G system will be able to provide a comprehensive IP solution where voice, data and streamed multimedia can be given to users at higher data rates than previous generations. There is no formal definition for 4G; however, there are certain objectives that are projected for 4G. It will be capable of providing between 100 Mbit/s and 1 Gbit/s speeds both indoors and outdoors, with premium quality and high security. It would also support systems like multicarrier communication, MIMO and UWB.

BIOMETRICS

Biometrics refers to metrics related to human characteristics. Biometrics authentication (or realistic authentication) is used in computer science as a form of identification and access control. It is also used to identify individuals in groups that are under surveillance.

Biometric identifiers are the distinctive, measurable characteristics used to label and describe individuals. Biometric identifiers are often categorized as physiological versus behavioral characteristics. Physiological characteristics are related to the shape of the body. Examples include, but are not limited tofingerprint, palm veins, face recognition, DNA, palm print, hand geometry, iris recognition, retina and odour/scent. Behavioral characteristics are related to the pattern of behavior of a person, including but not limited to typing rhythm, gait, and voice. Some researchers have coined the term behaviometrics to describe the latter class of biometrics.

More traditional means of access control include token-based identification systems, such as a driver's license or passport, and knowledge-based identification systems, such as a password orpersonal identification number. Since biometric identifiers are unique to individuals, they are more reliable in verifying identity than token and knowledge-based methods; however, the collection of biometric identifiers raises privacy concerns about the ultimate use of this information.

According to a CSO article the biometrics market will be worth US$13. 8 billion in 2015.

Biometric functionality

Many different aspects of human physiology, chemistry or behavior can be used for biometric authentication. The selection of a particular biometric for use in a specific application involves a weighting of several factors. Jain *et al.* (1999) identified seven such factors to be used when assessing the suitability of any trait for use in biometric authentication. Universality means that every person using a system should possess the trait. Uniqueness means the trait should be sufficiently different for individuals in the relevant population such that they can be distinguished from one another. Permanence relates to the manner in which a trait varies over time. More specifically, a trait with 'good' permanence will be reasonably invariant over time with respect to the specific matching algorithm. Measurability (collectability) relates to the ease of acquisition or measurement of the trait. In addition, acquired data should be in a form that permits subsequent processing and extraction of the relevant feature sets. Performance relates to the accuracy, speed, and robustness of technology used. Acceptability relates to how well individuals in the relevant population accept the technology such that they are willing to have their biometric trait captured and assessed. Circumvention relates to the ease with which a trait might be imitated using an artifact or substitute.

No single biometric will meet all the requirements of every possible application.

The block diagram illustrates the two basic modes of a biometric system. First, in verification (or authentication) mode the system performs a one-to-one comparison of a captured biometric with a specific template stored in a biometric database in order to verify the individual is the person they claim to be. Three steps are involved in the verification of a person. In the first step, reference models for all the users are generated and stored in the model database. In the second step, some samples are matched with reference models to generate the genuine and impostor scores and calculate the threshold. Third step is the testing step. This process may use a smart card, username or ID number (e. g. PIN) to indicate which template should be used for comparison.'Positive recognition' is a common use of the verification mode, "where the aim is to prevent multiple people from using same identity".

Second, in identification mode the system performs a one-to-many comparison against a biometric database in attempt to establish the identity of an unknown individual. The system will succeed in identifying the individual if the comparison of the biometric sample to a template in the database falls within a previously set threshold. Identification mode can be used either for 'positive recognition' (so that the user does not have to provide any information about the template to be used) or for 'negative recognition' of the person "where the system establishes whether the person is who she (implicitly or explicitly) denies to be". The latter function can only be achieved through biometrics since other methods of personal recognition such as passwords, PINs or keys are ineffective.

The first time an individual uses a biometric system is called *enrollment*. During the enrollment, biometric information from an individual is captured and stored. In subsequent uses, biometric information is detected and compared with the information stored at the time of enrollment. Note that it is crucial that storage and retrieval of such systems themselves be secure if the biometric system is to be robust. The first block (sensor) is the interface between the real world and the system; it has to acquire all the necessary data. Most of the times it is an image acquisition system, but it can change according to the characteristics desired. The second block performs all the necessary pre-processing: it has to removeartifacts from the sensor, to enhance the input (e. g. removing background noise), to use some kind of normalization, etc. In the third block necessary features are extracted. This step is an important step as the correct features need to be extracted in the optimal way. A vector of numbers or an image with particular properties is used to create a *template*. A template is a synthesis of the relevant characteristics extracted from the source. Elements of the biometric measurement that are not used in the comparison algorithm are discarded in the template to reduce the filesize and to protect the identity of the enrollee.

During the enrollment phase, the template is simply stored somewhere (on a card or within a database or both). During the matching phase, the obtained template is passed to a matcher that compares it with other existing templates, estimating the distance between them using any algorithm (e. g. Hamming distance). The matching program will analyze the template with the input. This will then be output for any specified use or purpose (e. g. entrance in a restricted area). Selection of biometrics in any practical application depending upon the characteristic measurements and user requirements. We should consider Performance, Acceptability, Circumvention, Robustness, Population coverage, Size, Identity theft deterrence in selecting a particular biometric. Selection of biometric based on user requirement considers Sensor availability, Device availability, Computational time and reliability, Cost, Sensor area and power consumption

MULTIMODAL BIOMETRIC SYSTEM

Multimodal biometric systems use multiple sensors or biometrics to overcome the limitations of unimodal biometric systems. For instance iris recognition systems can be compromised by aging irides and finger scanning systems by worn-out or cut fingerprints. While unimodal biometric systems are limited by the integrity of their identifier, it is unlikely that several unimodal systems will suffer from identical limitations. Multimodal biometric systems can obtain sets of information from the same marker (i. e., multiple images of an iris, or scans of the same finger) or information from different biometrics (requiring fingerprint scans and, using voice recognition, a spoken pass-code). Multimodal biometric systems can integrate these unimodal systems sequentially, simultaneously, a combination thereof, or in series, which refer to sequential, parallel, hierarchical and serial integration modes, respectively.

Broadly, the information fusion is divided into three parts, pre-mapping fusion, midst-mapping fusion, and post-mapping fusion/late fusion. In pre-mapping fusion information can be combined at sensor level or feature level. Sensor-level fusion can be mainly organized in three classes: (1) single sensor-multiple instances, (2) intra-class multiple sensors, and (3) inter-class multiple sensors. Feature-level fusion can be mainly organized in two categories: (1) intra-class and (2) inter-class. Intra-class is again classified into four subcategories: (a) Same sensor-same features, (b) Same sensor-different features, (c) Different sensors-same features, and (d) Different sensors-different features.

Spoof attacks consist in submitting fake biometric traits to biometric systems, and are a major threat that can curtail their security. Multi-modal biometric systems are commonly believed to be intrinsically more robust to spoof attacks, but recent studies have shown that they can be evaded by spoofing even a single biometric trait.

Performance

The following are used as performance metrics for biometric systems:

- False match rate (FMR): the probability that the system incorrectly matches the input pattern to a non-matching template in the database. It measures the percent of invalid inputs which are incorrectly accepted. In case of similarity scale, if the person is an imposter in reality, but the matching score is higher than the threshold, then he is treated as genuine. This increases the FAR, which thus also depends upon the threshold value.
- False non-match rate (FNMR): the probability that the system fails to detect a match between the input pattern and a matching template in the database. It measures the percent of valid inputs which are incorrectly rejected.
- Receiver operating characteristic or relative operating characteristic (ROC): The ROC plot is a visual characteri-zation of the trade-off between the FAR and the FRR. In general, the matching algorithm performs a

decision based on a threshold which determines how close to a template the input needs to be for it to be considered a match. If the threshold is reduced, there will be fewer false non-matches but more false accepts. Conversely, a higher threshold will reduce the FAR but increase the FRR. A common variation is the *Detection error trade-off (DET)*, which is obtained using normal deviation scales on both axes. This more linear graph illuminates the differences for higher performances (rarer errors).

- Equal error rate or crossover error rate (EER or CER): the rate at which both acceptance and rejection errors are equal. The value of the EER can be easily obtained from the ROC curve. The EER is a quick way to compare the accuracy of devices with different ROC curves. In general, the device with the lowest EER is the most accurate.
- Failure to enroll rate (FTE or FER): the rate at which attempts to create a template from an input is unsuccessful. This is most commonly caused by low quality inputs.
- Failure to capture rate (FTC): Within automatic systems, the probability that the system fails to detect a biometric input when presented correctly.
- Template capacity: the maximum number of sets of data which can be stored in the system.

History of biometrics

The earliest cataloging of fingerprints dates back to 1891 when Juan Vucetich started a collection of fingerprints of criminals in Argentina. The History of Fingerprints.

Adaptive biometric systems

Adaptive biometric Systems aim to auto-update the templates or model to the intra-class variation of the operational data. The two-fold advantages of these systems are solving the problem of limited training data and tracking the temporal variations of the input data through adaptation. Recently, adaptive biometrics have received a significant attention from the research community. This research direction is expected to gain momentum because of their key promulgated advantages. First, with an adaptive biometric system, one no longer needs to collect a large number of biometric samples during the enrollment process. Second, it is no longer necessary to re-enroll or retrain the system from scratch in order to cope with the changing environment. This convenience can significantly reduce the cost of maintaining a biometric system. Despite these advantages, there are several open issues involved with these systems. For mis-classification error (false acceptance) by the biometric system, cause adaptation using impostor sample. However, continuous research efforts are directed to resolve the open issues associated to the field of adaptive biometrics. More information about adaptive biometric systems can be found in the critical review by Rattani et al.

Current, emerging and future applications of biometrics

India's national ID program

India's national ID program called Aadhaar is the largest biometric database in the world. It is a biometrics-based digital identity assigned for a person's lifetime, verifiable online instantly in the public domain, at any time, from anywhere, in a paperless way. It is designed to enable government agencies to deliver a retail public service securely based on biometricdata (fingerprint, iris scan and face photo), along with demographic data (name, age, gender, address, parent/spouse name, mobile phone number) of a person. The data is transmitted in encrypted form over the internet for authentication, aiming to free it from the limitations of physical presence of a person at a given place.

About 550 million residents have been enrolled and assigned 480 million Aadhaar numbers as of 7 November 2013. It aims to cover the entire population of 1. 25 billion in a few years.

Recent advances in emerging biometrics

In recent times, biometrics based on brain (electroence phalogram) and heart (electrocardiogram) signals have emerged. The research group at University of Wolverhampton led by Ramaswamy Palaniappan has shown that people have certain distinct brain and heart patterns that are specific for each individual. The advantage of such 'futuristic' technology is that it is more fraud resistant compared to conventional biometrics like fingerprints. However, such technology is generally more cumbersome and still has issues such as lower accuracy and poor reproducibility over time.

Operator Signatures

An operator signature is a biometric mode where the manner in which a person using a device or complex system is recorded as a verification template. One potential use for this type of biometric signature is to distinguish between remote users of telerobotic surgery systems which utilize public networks for communication.

Proposal calls for biometric authentication to access certain public networks. John Michael (Mike) McConnell, a former vice admiral in the United States Navy, a former Director of US National Intelligence, and Senior Vice President of Booz Allen Hamilton promoted the development of a future capability to require biometric authentication to access certain public networks in his keynote speech at the 2009 Biometric Consortium Conference.

A basic premise in the above proposal is that the person that has uniquely authenticated themselves using biometrics with the computer is in fact also the agent performing potentially malicious actions from that computer. However, if control of the computer has been subverted, for example in which the computer is part of a botnet controlled by a hacker, then knowledge of the identity of the user at the terminal does not materially improve network security or aid law enforcement activities.

Recently, another approach to biometric security was developed, this method scans the entire body of prospects to guarantee a better identification of this prospect. This method is not globally accepted because it is very complex and prospects are concerned about their privacy.

Issues and Concerns

Privacy and Discrimination

It is possible that data obtained during biometric enrollment may be used in ways for which the enrolled individual has not consented. For example, biometric security that utilizes an employee's DNA profile could also be used to screen for various genetic diseases or other 'undesirable' traits.

There are three categories of privacy concerns:

1. Unintended functional scope: The authentication goes further than authentication, such as finding a tumor.
2. Unintended application scope: The authentication process correctly identifies the subject when the subject did not wish to be identified.
3. Covert identification: The subject is identified without seeking identification or authentication, i. e. a subject's face is identified in a crowd.

Danger to Owners of Secured Items

When thieves cannot get access to secure properties, there is a chance that the thieves will stalk and assault the property owner to gain access. If the item is secured with a biometric device, the damage to the owner could be irreversible, and potentially cost more than the secured property. For example, in 2005, Malaysian car thieves cut off the finger of aMercedes-Benz S-Class owner when attempting to steal the car.

Cancelable Biometrics

One advantage of passwords over biometrics is that they can be re-issued. If a token or a password is lost or stolen, it can be cancelled and replaced by a newer version. This is not naturally available in biometrics. If someone's face is compromised from a database, they cannot cancel or reissue it. Cancelable biometrics is a way in which to incorporate protection and the replacement features into biometrics. It was first proposed by Ratha et al.

Several methods for generating new exclusive biometrics have been proposed. The first fingerprint-based cancelable biometric system was designed and developed by Tulyakov et al. Essentially, cancelable biometrics perform a distortion of the biometric image or features before matching. The variability in the distortion parameters provides the cancelable nature of the scheme. Some of the proposed techniques operate using their own recognition engines, such as Teoh et al. and Savvides et al., whereas other methods, such as Dabbah et al., take the advantage of the advancement of the well-established biometric research for their recognition front-end to conduct recognition. Although this increases the restrictions on the protection system, it makes the cancellable templates more accessible for available biometric technologies

Soft Biometrics

Soft biometrics traits are physical, behavioural or adhered human characteristics, which have been derived from the way human beings normally distinguish their peers (e. g. height, gender, hair color). Those attributes have a low discriminating power, thus not capable of identification performance; additionally they are fully available to everyone which makes them privacy-safe.

International Sharing of Biometric Data

Many countries, including the United States, are planning to share biometric data with other nations.

In testimony before the US House Appropriations Committee, Subcommittee on Homeland Security on "biometric identification" in 2009, Kathleen Kraninger and Robert A Mocny commented on international cooperation and collaboration with respect to biometric data, as follows:

To ensure we can shut down terrorist networks before they ever get to the United States, we must also take the lead in driving international biometric standards. By developing compatible systems, we will be able to securely share terrorist information internationally to bolster our defenses. Just as we are improving the way we collaborate within the U. S. Government to identify and weed out terrorists and other dangerous people, we have the same obligation to work with our partners abroad to prevent terrorists from making any move undetected. Biometrics provide a new way to bring terrorists' true identities to light, stripping them of their greatest advantage—remaining unknown.

According to an article written in 2009 by S. Magnuson in the National Defense Magazine entitled "Defense Department Under Pressure to Share Biometric Data" the United States has bi-lateral agreements with other nations aimed at sharing biometric data. To quote that article:

Miller [a consultant to the Office of Homeland Defense and America's security affairs] said the United States has bi-lateral agreements to share biometric data with about 25 countries. Every time a foreign leader has visited Washington during the last few years, the State Department has made sure they sign such an agreement. Governments are unlikely to disclose full capabilities of biometric deployments.

Certain members of the civilian community are worried about how biometric data is used but full disclosure may not be forthcoming. In particular, the Unclassified Report of the Defense Science Board Task Force on Defense Biometrics states that it is wise to protect, and sometimes even to disguise, the true and total extent of national capabilities in areas related directly to the conduct of security-related activities. This also potentially applies to Biometrics. It goes on to say that this is a classic feature of intelligence and military operations. In short, the goal is to preserve the security of 'sources and methods'.

Countries Applying Biometrics

Countries using biometrics include Australia, Brazil, Canada, China, Gambia, Germany, India, Iraq, Israel, Italy, Netherlands, New Zealand, Norway, Ukraine, United Kingdom, and United States. Among low-middle income countries, roughly 1. 2 billion people have already received identification through a biometric identification program.

In Popular Culture

- In the movie *Happy New Year (2014)* one method of entering the Shalimar vault is via a biometric lock.
- Sneakers, a 1992 film starring Robert Redford. "My voice is my passport."
- In the movie, 21, the police officer catches the protagonist with the help of facial recognition technology.
- RED (film), a 2010 American action-comedy film based on the comic book mini-series. Using a photocopy of a fingerprint
- The 2002 film *Minority Report* features extensive use of casual Iris/Retina scanning techniques for both personal Identification and Point Of Sale transaction purposes. The main character changes his official Identity by having his eyes transplanted, and later accesses a security system using one of the removed eyes.
- The movie *Gattaca* portrays a society in which there are two classes of people: those genetically engineered to be superior (termed "Valid") and the inferior natural humans ("Invalid"). People considered "Valid" have greater privileges, and access to areas restricted to such persons is controlled by automated biometric scanners similar in appearance to fingerprint scanners, but which prick the finger and sample DNA from the resulting blood droplet

- The Disney, Pixar 2004 film *The Incredibles* shows a scene where Mrs Incredible visits Edna Mode (a fashion designer for superhero costumes) at her mansion. Edna Mode enters her lab by biometrically identifying herself: she takes off her glasses, has her eyes scanned and uses her voice in order to get into the lab.
- The television program *MythBusters* attempted to break into a commercial security door equipped with fingerprint authentication as well as a personal laptop so equipped. While the laptop's system proved more difficult to bypass, the advanced commercial security door with "live" sensing was fooled with a printed scan of a fingerprint after it had been licked, as well as by a photocopy of a fingerprint.
- In *Demolition Man* the character Simon Phoenix cuts out a living victim's eye in order to open a locked door which is fitted with iris scanning. A similar plot element was used in *Angels & Demons* (2009) when an assassin gains access to a top secret CERN facility using a physicist's eye. However, both of these examples are misleading to the audience since the methods depicted for enucleation (removal of an eye) from a corpse would not be a viable way to defeat such a system.

Access Control

In the fields of physical security and information security, **access control** is the selective restriction of access to a place or other resource. The act of *accessing*may mean consuming, entering, or using. Permission to access a resource is called *authorization*.

Physical Security

Geographical access control may be enforced by personnel (e. g:, border guard, bouncer, ticket checker), or with a device such as a turnstile. There may be fencesto avoid circumventing this access control. An alternative of access control in the strict sense (physically controlling access itself) is a system of checking authorized presence, see e. g. Ticket controller (transportation). A variant is exit control, e. g. of a shop (checkout) or a country. The term access control refers to the practice of restricting entrance to a property, a building, or a room to authorized persons. Physical access control can be achieved by a human (a guard, bouncer, or receptionist), through mechanical means such as locks and keys, or through technological means such as access control systems like the mantrap. Within these environments, physical key management may also be employed as a means of further managing and monitoring access to mechanically keyed areas or access to certain small assets. Physical access control is a matter of who, where, and when. An access control system determines who is allowed to enter or exit, where they are allowed to exit or enter, and when they

are allowed to enter or exit. Historically, this was partially accomplished through keys and locks. When a door is locked, only someone with a key can enter through the door, depending on how the lock is configured. Mechanical locks and keys do not allow restriction of the key holder to specific times or dates. Mechanical locks and keys do not provide records of the key used on any specific door, and the keys can be easily copied or transferred to an unauthorized person. When a mechanical key is lost or the key holder is no longer authorized to use the protected area, the locks must be re-keyed.

Electronic access control uses computers to solve the limitations of mechanical locks and keys. A wide range of credentials can be used to replace mechanical keys. The electronic access control system grants access based on the credential presented. When access is granted, the door is unlocked for a predetermined time and the transaction is recorded. When access is refused, the door remains locked and the attempted access is recorded. The system will also monitor the door and alarm if the door is forced open or held open too long after being unlocked.

ACCESS CONTROL SYSTEM OPERATION

When a credential is presented to a reader, the reader sends the credential's information, usually a number, to a control panel, a highly reliable processor. The control panel compares the credential's number to an access control list, grants or denies the presented request, and sends a transaction log to a database. When access is denied based on the access control list, the door remains locked. If there is a match between the credential and the access control list, the control panel operates a relay that in turn unlocks the door. The control panel also ignores a door open signal to prevent an alarm. Often the reader provides feedback, such as a flashing red LED for an access denied and a flashing green LED for an access granted.

The above description illustrates a single factor transaction. Credentials can be passed around, thus subverting the access control list. For example, Alice has access rights to the server room, but Bob does not. Alice either gives Bob her credential, or Bob takes it; he now has access to the server room. To prevent this, two-factor authentication can be used. In a two factor transaction, the presented credential and a second factor are needed for access to be granted; another factor can be a PIN, a second credential, operator intervention, or a biometric input.

There are three types (factors) of authenticating information:

- something the user knows, e. g. a password, pass-phrase or PIN
- something the user has, such as smart card or a key fob
- something the user is, such as fingerprint, verified by biometric measurement

Passwords are a common means of verifying a user's identity before access is given to information systems. In addition, a fourth factor of authentication is now recognized: someone you know, whereby another person who knows you can provide a human element of authentication in situations where systems have been set up to allow for such scenarios. For example, a user may have their password, but have forgotten their smart card. In such a scenario, if the user is known to designated cohorts, the cohorts may provide their smart card and password, in combination with the extant factor of the user in question, and thus provide two factors for the user with the missing credential, giving three factors overall to allow access.

CREDENTIAL

A credential is a physical/tangible object, a piece of knowledge, or a facet of a person's physical being, that enables an individual access to a given physical facility or computer-based information system. Typically, credentials can be something a person knows (such as a number or PIN), something they have (such as an access badge), something they are (such as a biometric feature) or some combination of these items. This is known as multi-factor authentication. The typical credential is an access card or key-fob, and newer software can also turn users' smartphones into access devices.

There are many card technologies including magnetic stripe, bar code, Wiegand, 125 kHz proximity, 26-bit card-swipe, contact smart cards, and contactless smart cards. Also available are key-fobs, which are more compact than ID cards, and attach to a key ring. Biometric technologies include fingerprint, facial recognition, iris recognition, retinal scan, voice, and hand geometry. The built-in biometric technologies found on newer smartphones can also be used as credentials in conjunction with access software running on mobile devices. In addition to older more traditional card access technologies, newer technologies such as Near field communication (NFC) and Bluetooth low energy also have potential to communicate user credentials to readers for system or building access.

Access Control System Components

An access control point, which can be a door, turnstile, parking gate, elevator, or other physical barrier, where granting access can be electronically controlled. Typically, the access point is a door. An electronic access control door can contain several elements. At its most basic, there is a stand-alone electric lock. The lock is unlocked by an operator with a switch. To automate this, operator intervention is replaced by a reader. The reader could be a keypad where a code is entered, it could be a card reader, or it could be a biometric reader. Readers do not usually make an access decision, but send a card number to an access control panel that verifies the number against an access list. To monitor the door position a magnetic door switch can be used. In concept, the door switch is not unlike those on refrigerators or car doors. Generally only entry is controlled, and exit is uncontrolled. In cases where exit is also controlled, a second reader is used on the opposite side of the door. In cases where exit is not controlled, free exit, a device called a request-to-exit (REX) is used. Request-to-exit devices can be a push-button or a motion detector. When the button is pushed, or the motion detector detects motion at the door, the door alarm is temporarily ignored while the door is opened. Exiting a door without having to electrically unlock the door is called mechanical free egress. This is an important safety feature. In cases where the lock must be electrically unlocked on exit, the request-to-exit device also unlocks the door. Computer Security

In computer security, general access control includes authorization, authentication, access approval, and audit. A more narrow definition of access control would cover only access approval, whereby the system makes a decision to grant or reject an access request from an already authenticated subject, based on what the subject is authorized to access. Authentication and access control are often combined into a single operation, so that access is approved based on successful authentication, or based on an anonymous access token. Authentication methods and tokens includepasswords, biometric scans, physical keys, electronic keys and devices, hidden paths, social barriers, and monitoring by humans and automated systems.

In any access-control model, the entities that can perform actions on the system are called *subjects*, and the entities representing resources to which access may need to be controlled are called *objects*. Subjects and objects should both be considered as software entities, rather than as human users: any human users can only have an effect on the system via the software entities that they control.

Although some systems equate subjects with *user IDs*, so that all processes started by a user by default have the same authority, this level of control is not fine-grained enough to satisfy the principle of least privilege, and arguably is responsible for the prevalence of malware in such systems.

In some models, for example the object-capability model, any software entity can potentially act as both subject and object.

As of 2014, access-control models tend to fall into one of two classes: those based on capabilities and those based onaccess control lists (ACLs).

- In a capability-based model, holding an unforgettable reference or *capability* to an object provides access to the object (roughly analogous to how possession of one's house key grants one access to one's house); access is conveyed to another party by transmitting such a capability over a secure channel

- In an ACL-based model, a subject's access to an object depends on whether its identity appears on a list associated with the object (roughly analogous to how a bouncer at a private party would check an ID to see if a name appears on the guest list); access is conveyed by editing the list. (Different ACL systems have a variety of different conventions regarding who or what is responsible for editing the list and how it is edited.)

Both capability-based and ACL-based models have mechanisms to allow access rights to be granted to all members of a*group* of subjects (often the group is itself modeled as a subject).

Access control systems provide the essential services of *authorization, identification and authentication (I&A)*, *access approval*, and *accountability* where:

- authorization specifies what a subject can do
- identification and authentication ensure that only legitimate subjects can log on to a system
- access approval grants access during operations, by association of users with the resources that they are allowed to access, based on the authorization policy
- accountability identifies what a subject (or all subjects associated with a user) did

Biometric passport

A biometric passport, also known as an e-passport, ePassport or a digital passport, is a combined paper and electronic passport that contains biometricinformation that can be used to authenticate the identity of travelers. It usescon-tactless smart card technology, including a microprocessor chip (computer chip) and antenna (for both power to the chip and communication) embedded in the front or back cover, or center page, of the passport. Document and chip characteristics are documented in the International Civil Aviation Organization's (ICAO) Doc 9303. The passport's critical information is both printed on the data page of the passport and stored in the chip. Public Key Infrastructure (PKI) is used to authenticate the data stored electronically in the passport chip making it expensive and difficult to forge when all security mechanisms are fully and correctly implemented.

The currently standardized biometrics used for this type of identification system are facial recognition, fingerprint recognition, and iris recognition. These were adopted after assessment of several different kinds of biometrics including-retinal scan. The ICAO defines the biometric file formats and communication protocols to be used in passports. Only the digital image (usually in JPEG or JPEG2000 format) of each biometric feature is actually stored in the chip. The comparison of biometric features is performed outside the passport chip by electronic border control systems (e-borders). To store biometric data on the contactless chip, it includes a minimum of 32 kilobytes of EEPROM storage memory, and runs on an interface in accordance with the ISO/IEC 14443 international standard, amongst others. These standards intend interopera-bility between different countries and different manufacturers of passport books.

Some national identity cards (e. g. in the Netherlands, Albania and Brazil) are fully ICAO9303 compliant biometric travel documents. However others, such as the USA passport card, are not.

Data protection

Biometric passports are equipped with protection mechanisms to avoid and/or detect attacks:

- Non-traceable chip characteristics. Random chip identifiers reply to each request with a different chip number. This prevents tracing of passport chips. Using random identification numbers is optional.
- Basic Access Control (BAC). BAC protects the communi-cation channel between the chip and the reader by encrypting transmitted information. Before data can be read from a chip, the reader needs to provide a key which is derived from the Machine Readable Zone: the date of birth, the date of expiry and the document number. If BAC is used, an attacker cannot (easily) eavesdrop transferred information without knowing the correct key. Using BAC is optional.
- Passive Authentication (PA). PA is aimed at identifying modification of passport chip data. The chip contains a file (SOD) that stores hash values of all files stored in the chip (picture, fingerprint, etc.) and a digital signature of these hashes. The digital signature is made using a document signing key which itself is signed by a country signing key. If a file in the chip (e. g. the picture) is changed, this can be detected since the hash value is incorrect. Readers need access to all used public country keys to check whether the digital signature is generated by a trusted country. Using PA is mandatory. According to a September 2011 United States Central Intelligence Agency document released by Wikileaks in December 2014, "Although falsified e-passports will not have the correct digital signature, inspectors may not detect the fraud if the passports are from countries that do not participate in the International Civil Aviation Organization's Public Key Directory (ICAO PKD). Only 15 of over 60 e-passport-issuing countries belong to the PKD program, as of December 2010"
- Active Authentication (AA). AA prevents cloning of passport chips. The chip contains a private key that cannot be read or copied, but its existence can easily be proven. Using AA is optional.

- Extended Access Control (EAC). EAC adds functionality to check the authenticity of both the chip (chip authentication) and the reader (terminal authentication). Furthermore it uses stronger encryption than BAC. EAC is typically used to protect fingerprints and iris scans. Using EAC is optional. In the European Union, using EAC is mandatory for all documents issued starting 28 June 2009.
- Supplemental Access Control (SAC) was introduced by ICAO in 2009 for addressing BAC weaknesses. It was introduced as a supplement to BAC (for keeping compatibility), but will replace it in the future.
- Shielding the chip. This prevents unauthorized reading. Some countries – including at least the US – have integrated a very thin metal mesh into the passport's cover to act as a shield when the passport cover is closed. The use of shielding is optional.

INTERNET AND WORLD WIDE WEB

The World Wide Web (www, W3) is an information space where documents and other web resources are identified byURIs, interlinked by hypertext links, and can be accessed via the Internet. It has become known simply as the Web. Hypertext documents are commonly called web pages, which are primarily text documents formatted and annotated with the Hypertext Markup Language (HTML). Webpages may contain links to images, video, and software components that are rendered to users of a web browser application, running on the user's computer, as coherent pages of multimedia content. Embedded hyperlinks permit users to navigate between web pages. When multiple web pages are published with a common theme or within a common domain name, the collection is usually called a *web site.*

British computer scientist Tim Berners-Lee is the inventor of the Web. As a CERN employee, Berners-Lee distributed a proposal on 12 March 1989 for what would eventually become the World Wide Web. The initial proposal intended a more effective CERN communication system, but Berners-Lee also realized the concept could be implemented throughout the world. Berners-Lee and Belgian computer scientist Robert Cailliau proposed in 1990 to use hypertext "to link and access information of various kinds as a web of nodes in which the user can browse at will", and Berners-Lee finished the first website in December of that year. The first test was completed around 20 December 1990 and Berners-Lee reported about the project on the newsgroup *alt. hypertext* on 7 August 1991.

HISTORY

On March 12, 1989, Tim Berners-Lee issued a proposal to the management at CERN that referenced ENQUIRE, a database and software project he had built in 1980, and described a more elaborate information management system based on links embedded in readable text: "Imagine, then, the references in this document all being associated with the network address of the thing to which they referred, so that while reading this document you could skip to them with a click of the mouse." Such a system, he explained, could be referred to using one of the existing meanings of the word *hypertext*, a term that he says was coined in the 1950s. There is no reason, the proposal continues, why such hypertext links could not encompass multimedia documents including graphics, speech and video, so that Berners-Lee goes on to propose the term *hypermedia*.

With help from Robert Cailliau, he published a more formal proposal (on 12 November 1990) to build a "Hypertext project" called "WorldWideWeb" (one word, also "W3") as a "web" of "hypertext documents" to be viewed by "browsers" using aclient–server architecture. This proposal estimated that a read-only web would be developed within three months and that it would take six months to achieve "the creation of new links and new material by readers, [so that] authorship becomes universal" as well as "the automatic notification of a reader when new material of interest to him/her has become available." While the read-only goal was met, accessible authorship of web content took longer to mature, with the wiki concept, WebDAV, blogs, Web 2. 0 and RSS/Atom.

The proposal was modeled after the SGML reader Dynatext by Electronic Book Technology, a spin-off from the Institute for Research in Information and Scholarship at Brown University. The Dynatext system, licensed by CERN, was a key player in the extension of SGML ISO 8879:1986 to Hypermedia within HyTime, but it was considered too expensive and had an inappropriate licensing policy for use in the general high energy physics community, namely a fee for each document and each document alteration.

A NeXT Computer was used by Berners-Lee as the world's first web server and also to write the first web browser, WorldWideWeb, in 1990. By Christmas 1990, Berners-Lee had built all the tools necessary for a working Web: the first web browser (which was a web editor as well); the first web server; and the first web pages, which described the project itself.

The first web page may be lost, but Paul Jones of UNC-Chapel Hill in North Carolina announced in May 2013 that Berners-Lee gave him what he says is the oldest known web page during a 1991 visit to UNC. Jones stored it on a magneto-optical drive and on his NeXT computer.

On 6 August 1991, Berners-Lee published a short summary of the World Wide Web project on the newsgroup *alt. hypertext*. This date also marked the debut of the Web as a publicly available service on the Internet, although new users only accessed it after 23 August. For this reason this is considered the internaut's day. Several newsmedia have reported that the first photo on the Web was published by Berners-Lee in 1992, an image of the CERN house band Les Horribles Cernettes taken by Silvano de Gennaro; Gennaro has disclaimed this story, writing that media were "totally distorting our words for the sake of cheap sensationalism."

The first server outside Europe was installed at the Stanford Linear Accelerator Center (SLAC) in Palo Alto, California, to host the SPIRES-HEP database. Accounts differ substantially as to the date of this event. The World Wide Web Consortium says December 1992, whereas SLAC itself claims 1991. This is supported by a W3C document titled *A Little History of the World Wide Web.*

The underlying concept of hypertext originated in previous projects from the 1960s, such as the Hypertext Editing System(HES) at Brown University, Ted Nelson's Project Xanadu, and Douglas Engelbart's oN-Line System (NLS). Both Nelson and Engelbart were in turn inspired by Vannevar Bush's microfilm-based *memex*, which was described in the 1945 essay "As We May Think".

Berners-Lee's breakthrough was to marry hypertext to the Internet. In his book *Weaving The Web*, he explains that he had repeatedly suggested that a marriage between the two technologies was possible to members of *both* technical communities, but when no one took up his invitation, he finally assumed the project himself. In the process, he developed three essential technologies:

- a system of globally unique identifiers for resources on the Web and elsewhere, the universal document identifier (UDI), later known as uniform resource locator (URL) and uniform resource identifier (URI);
- the publishing language HyperText Markup Language (HTML);
- the Hypertext Transfer Protocol (HTTP).

The World Wide Web had a number of differences from other hypertext systems available at the time. The Web required only unidirectional links rather than bidirectional ones, making it possible for someone to link to another resource without action by the owner of that resource. It also significantly reduced the difficulty of implementing web servers and browsers (in comparison to earlier systems), but in turn presented the chronic problem of *link rot*. Unlike predecessors such asHyperCard, the World Wide Web was non-proprietary, making it possible to develop servers and clients independently and to add extensions without licensing restrictions. On 30 April 1993, CERN announced that the World Wide Web would be free to anyone, with no fees due. Coming two months after the announcement that the server implementation of the Gopherprotocol was no longer free to use, this produced a rapid shift away from Gopher and towards the Web. An early popular web browser was ViolaWWW for Unix and the X Windowing System.

Scholars generally agree that a turning point for the World Wide Web began with the introduction of the Mosaic web browser in 1993, a graphical browser developed by a team at the National Center for Supercomputing Applications at theUniversity of Illinois at Urbana-Champaign (NCSA-UIUC), led by Marc Andreessen. Funding for Mosaic came from the U. S. *High-Performance Computing and Communications Initiative* and the *High Performance Computing and Communication Act of 1991*, one of several computing developments initiated by U. S. Senator Al Gore. Prior to the release of Mosaic, graphics were not commonly mixed with text in web pages and the web's popularity was less than older protocols in use over the Internet, such as Gopher and Wide Area Information Servers (WAIS). Mosaic's graphical user interface allowed the Web to become, by far, the most popular Internet protocol.

The World Wide Web Consortium (W3C) was founded by Tim Berners-Lee after he left the European Organization for Nuclear Research (CERN) in October 1994. It was founded at the Massachusetts Institute of Technology Laboratory for Computer Science (MIT/LCS) with support from the Defense Advanced Research Projects Agency (DARPA), which had pioneered the Internet; a year later, a second site was founded at INRIA (a French national computer research lab) with support from the European Commission DG InfSo; and in 1996, a third continental site was created in Japan at Keio University. By the end of 1994, the total number of websites was still relatively small, but manynotable websites were already active that foreshadowed or inspired today's most popular services.

Connected by the existing Internet, other websites were created around the world, adding international standards fordomain names and HTML. Since then, Berners-Lee has played an active role in guiding the development of web standards (such as the markup languages to compose web pages in), and has advocated his vision of a Semantic Web. The World Wide Web enabled the spread of information over the Internet through an easy-to-use and flexible format. It thus played an important role in popularizing use of the Internet. Although the two terms are sometimes conflated in popular use, *World Wide Web* is not synonymous with *Internet*. The Web is an information space containing hyperlinked documents and other resources, identified by their URIs. It is implemented as both client and server software using Internet protocols such as TCP/IP and HTTP.

Tim Berners-Lee was knighted in 2004 by Queen Elizabeth II for "services to the global development of the Internet".

Function

The terms *Internet* and *World Wide Web* are often used without much distinction. However, the two things are not the same. The Internet is a global system of interconnected computer networks. In contrast, the World Wide Web is one of the services transferred over these networks. It is a collection of text documents and other resources, linked by hyperlinks and URLs, usually accessed by web browsers, from web servers.

Viewing a web page on the World Wide Web normally begins either by typing theURL of the page into a web browser, or by following a hyperlink to that page or resource. The web browser then initiates a series of background communication messages to fetch and display the requested page. In the 1990s, using a browser to view web pages—and to move from one web page to another through hyperlinks—came to be known as 'browsing,' 'web surfing,' (after channel surfing), or 'navigating the Web'. Early studies of this new behavior investigated user patterns in using web browsers. One study, for example, found five user patterns: exploratory surfing, window surfing, evolved surfing, bounded navigation and targeted navigation.

The following example demonstrates the functioning of a web browser when accessing a page at the URL http: / /example. org / wiki / World_Wide_Web. The browser resolves the server name of the URL (*example. org*) into an Internet Protocol address using the globally distributed Domain Name System (DNS). This lookup returns an IP address such as*203. 0. 113. 4*. The browser then requests the resource by sending an HTTP request across the Internet to the computer at that address. It requests service from a specific TCP port number that is well known for the HTTP service, so that the receiving host can distinguish an HTTP request from other network protocols it may be servicing. The HTTP protocol normally uses port number 80. The content of the HTTP request can be as simple as two lines of text:

GET */wiki/World_Wide_Web* HTTP/1. 1

Host: *example. org*

The computer receiving the HTTP request delivers it to web server software listening for requests on port 80. If the web server can fulfill the request it sends an HTTP response back to the browser indicating success:

`HTTP/1. 0 200 OK`

Content-Type: text/html; charset=UTF-8

followed by the content of the requested page. The Hypertext Markup Language for a basic web page looks like <html> <head> <title>Example. org – The World Wide Web</ title> </head> <body> <p>The World Wide Web, abbreviated as WWW and commonly known... </ p> </body> </html>

The web browser parses the HTML and interprets the markup (<title>, <p> for paragraph, and such) that surrounds the words to format the text on the screen. Many web pages use HTML to reference the URLs of other resources such as images, other embedded media, scripts that affect page behavior, and Cascading Style Sheets that affect page layout. The browser makes additional HTTP requests to the web server for these other Internet media types. As it receives their content from the web server, the browser progressively renders the page onto the screen as specified by its HTML and these additional resources.

Linking

Most web pages contain hyperlinks to other related pages and perhaps to downloadable files, source documents, definitions and other web resources. In the underlying HTML, a hyperlink looks like <a href="*http://example. org/wiki/Main_Page*">*Example. org, a free encyclopedia*</a>

Such a collection of useful, related resources, interconnected via hypertext links is dubbed a *web* of information. Publication on the Internet created what Tim Berners-Lee first called the *WorldWideWeb* (in its original CamelCase, which was subsequently discarded) in November 1990.

The hyperlink structure of the WWW is described by the webgraph: the nodes of the webgraph correspond to the web pages (or URLs) the directed edges between them to the hyperlinks.

Over time, many web resources pointed to by hyperlinks disappear, relocate, or are replaced with different content. This makes hyperlinks obsolete, a phenomenon referred to in some circles as link rot, and the hyperlinks affected by it are often called dead links. The ephemeral nature of the Web has prompted many efforts to archive web sites. The Internet Archive, active since 1996, is the best known of such efforts.

Dynamic Updates of Web Pages

JavaScript is a scripting language that was initially developed in 1995 by Brendan Eich, then of Netscape, for use within web pages. The standardised version is ECMAScript. To make web pages more interactive, some web applications also use JavaScript techniques such as Ajax (asynchronous JavaScript and XML). Client-side script is delivered with the page that can make additional HTTP requests to the server, either in response to user actions such as mouse movements or clicks, or based on elapsed time. The server's responses are used to modify the current page rather than creating a new page with each response, so the server needs only to provide limited, incremental information. Multiple Ajax requests can be handled at the same time, and users can interact with the page while data is retrieved. Web pages may also regularlypoll the server to check whether new information is available.

WWW Prefix

Many hostnames used for the World Wide Web begin with *www* because of the long-standing practice of naming Internet hosts according to the services they provide. The hostname of a web server is often *www*, in the same way that it may be*ftp* for an FTP server, and *news* or *nntp* for a USENET news server. These host names appear as Domain Name System (DNS) or subdomain names, as in *www. example. com*. The use of *www* is not required by any technical or policy standard and many web sites do not use it; indeed, the first ever web server was called *nxoc01. cern. ch*. According to Paolo Palazzi, who worked at CERN along with Tim Berners-Lee, the popular use of *www* as subdomain was accidental; the World Wide Web project page was intended to be published at www. cern. ch while info. cern. ch was intended to be the CERN home page, however the DNS records were never switched, and the practice of prepending *www* to an institution's website domain name was subsequently copied. Many established websites still use the prefix, or they employ other subdomain names such as *www2, secure* or *en* for special purposes. Many such web servers are set up so that both the main domain name (e. g., example. com) and the *www* subdomain (e. g., www. example. com) refer to the same site; others require one form or the other, or they may map to different web sites.

The use of a subdomain name is useful for load balancing incoming web traffic by creating a CNAME record that points to a cluster of web servers. Since, currently, only a subdomain can be used in a CNAME, the same result cannot be achieved by using the bare domain root.

When a user submits an incomplete domain name to a web browser in its address bar input field, some web browsers automatically try adding the prefix "www" to the beginning of it and possibly ". com", ". org" and ". net" at the end, depending on what might be missing. For example, entering 'microsoft' may be transformed to *http://www. microsoft. com/* and 'openoffice' to *http://www. openoffice. org*. This feature started appearing in early versions of Mozilla Firefox, when it still had the working title 'Firebird' in early 2003, from an earlier practice in browsers such as Lynx. It is reported that Microsoft was granted a US patent for the same idea in 2008, but only for mobile devices.

In English, *www* is usually read as *double-u double-u double-u*. Some users pronounce it *dub-dub-dub*, particularly in New Zealand. Stephen Fry, in his "Podgrammes" series of podcasts, pronounces it *wuh wuh wuh*. The English writer Douglas Adams once quipped in The Independent on Sunday (1999): "The World Wide Web is the only thing I know of whose shortened form takes three times longer to say than what it's short for". In Mandarin Chinese, *World Wide Web*is commonly translated via a phono-semantic matching to *wàn wéi wǐng* (Nô~Qn), which satisfies *www* and literally means "myriad dimensional net", a translation that reflects the design concept and proliferation of the World Wide Web. Tim Berners-Lee's web-space states that *World Wide Web* is officially spelled as three separate words, each capitalised, with no intervening hyphens.

Use of the www prefix is declining as Web 2. 0 web applications seek to brand their domain names and make them easily pronounceable. As the mobile web grows in popularity, services like Gmail. com, MySpace. com, Facebook. com andTwitter. com are most often mentioned without adding "www." (or, indeed, ". com") to the domain.

Scheme Specifiers

The scheme specifiers *http://* and *https://* at the start of a web URI refer to Hypertext Transfer Protocol or HTTP Secure, respectively. They specify the communication protocol to use for the request and response. The HTTP protocol is fundamental to the operation of the World Wide Web, and the added encryption layer in HTTPS is essential when browsers send or retrieve confidential data, such as passwords or banking information. Web browsers usually automatically prepend http:// to user-entered URIs, if omitted.

Web Security

For criminals, the web has become the preferred way to spread malware. Cybercrime on the web can include identity theft, fraud, espionage and intelligence gathering. Web-based vulnerabilities now outnumber traditional computer security concerns, and as measured by Google, about one in ten web pages may contain malicious code. Most web-basedattacks take place on legitimate websites, and most, as measured by Sophos, are hosted in the United States, China and Russia. The most common of all malware threats is SQL injection attacks against websites. Through HTML and URIs, the Web was vulnerable to attacks like cross-site scripting (XSS) that came with the introduction of JavaScript and were exacerbated to some degree by Web 2. 0 and Ajax web design that favors the use of scripts. Today by one estimate, 70% of all websites are open to XSS attacks on their users. phishing is another common threat to the Web. "SA, the Security Division of EMC, today announced the findings of its January 2013 Fraud Report, estimating the global losses from phishing at $1. 5 Billion in 2012". Two of the well-known phishing methods are Covert Redirect and Open Redirect.

Proposed solutions vary to extremes. Large security vendors like McAfee already design governance and compliance suites to meet post-9/11 regulations, and some, like Finjan have recommended active real-time inspection of code and all content regardless of its source. Some have argued that for enterprise to see security as a business opportunity rather than a cost center,"ubiquitous, always-on digital rights management" enforced in the infrastructure by a handful of organizations must replace the hundreds of companies that today secure data and networks. Jonathan Zittrain has said users sharing responsibility for computing safety is far preferable to locking down the Internet.

Privacy

Every time a client requests a web page, the server can identify the request's IP address and usually logs it. Also, unless set not to do so, most web browsers record requested web pages in a viewable *history* feature, and usually cache much of the content locally. Unless the server-browser communication uses HTTPS encryption, web requests and responses travel in plain text across the internet and can be viewed, recorded, and cached by intermediate systems.

When a web page asks for, and the user supplies, personally identifiable information—such as their real name, address, e-mail address, etc. —web-based entities can associate current web traffic with that individual. If the website uses HTTP cookies, username and password authentication, or other tracking techniques, it can relate other web visits, before and after, to the identifiable information provided. In this way it is possible for a web-based organisation to develop and build a profile of the individual people who use its site or sites. It may be able to build a record for an individual that includes information about their leisure activities, their shopping interests, their profession, and other aspects of their demographic profile. These profiles are obviously of potential interest to marketeers, advertisers and others. Depending on the website'sterms and conditions and the local laws that apply information from these profiles may be sold, shared, or passed to other organisations without the user being informed. For many ordinary people, this means little more than some unexpected e-mails in their in-box, or some uncannily relevant advertising on a future web page. For others, it can mean that time spent indulging an unusual interest can result in a deluge of further targeted marketing that may be unwelcome. Law enforcement, counter terrorism and espionage agencies can also identify, target and track individuals based on their interests or proclivities on the Web.

Social networking sites try to get users to use their real names, interests, and locations. They believe this makes the social networking experience more realistic, and therefore more engaging for all their users. On the other hand, uploaded photographs or unguarded statements can be identified to an individual, who may regret this exposure. Employers, schools, parents, and other relatives may be influenced by aspects of social networking profiles that the posting individual did not intend for these audiences. On-line bullies may make use of personal information to harass or stalk users. Modern social networking websites allow fine grained control of the privacy settings for each individual posting, but these can be complex and not easy to find or use, especially for beginners.

Photographs and videos posted onto websites have caused particular problems, as they can add a person's face to an on-line profile. With modern and potential facial recognition technology, it may then be possible to relate that face with other, previously anonymous, images, events and scenarios that have been imaged elsewhere. Because of image caching, mirroring and copying, it is difficult to remove an image from the World Wide Web.

Standards

Many formal standards and other technical specifications and software define the operation of different aspects of the World Wide Web, the Internet, and computer information exchange. Many of the documents are the work of the World Wide Web Consortium (W3C), headed by Berners-Lee, but some are produced by the Internet Engineering Task Force (IETF) and other organizations.

Usually, when web standards are discussed, the following publications are seen as foundational:

- Recommendations for markup languages, especially HTML and XHTML, from the W3C. These define the structure and interpretation of hypertext documents.
- Recommendations for stylesheets, especially CSS, from the W3C.
- Standards for ECMAScript (usually in the form of JavaScript), from Ecma International.
- Recommendations for the Document Object Model, from W3C.

Additional publications provide definitions of other essential technologies for the World Wide Web, including, but not limited to, the following:

- *Uniform Resource Identifier* (URI), which is a universal system for referencing resources on the Internet, such as hypertext documents and images. URIs, often called URLs, are defined by the IETF's RFC 3986 / STD 66: *Uniform Resource Identifier (URI): Generic Syntax,* as well as its predecessors and numerous URI scheme-defining RFCs;
- *HyperText Transfer Protocol (HTTP)*, especially as defined by RFC 2616: *HTTP/1. 1* and RFC 2617: *HTTP Authentication,* which specify how the browser and server authenticate each other.

Accessibility

There are methods for accessing the Web in alternative mediums and formats to facilitate use by individuals with disabilities. These disabilities may be visual, auditory, physical, speech related, cognitive, neurological, or some combination. Accessibility features also help people with temporary disabilities, like a broken arm, or aging users as their abilities change. The Web receives information as well as providing information and interacting with society. The World Wide Web Consortium claims it essential that the Web be accessible, so it can provide equal access and equal opportunityto people with disabilities. Tim Berners-Lee once noted, "The power of the Web is in its universality. Access by everyone regardless of disability is an essential aspect." Many countries regulate web accessibility as a requirement for websites. International cooperation in the W3C Web Accessibility Initiative led to simple guidelines that web content authors as well as software developers can use to make the Web accessible to persons who may or may not be usingassistive technology.

INTERNATIONALIZATION

The W3C Internationalization Activity assures that web technology works in all languages, scripts, and cultures. Beginning in 2004 or 2005, Unicode gained ground and eventually in December 2007 surpassed both ASCII and Western European as the Web's most frequently used character encoding. Originally RFC 3986 allowed resources to be identified by URI in a subset of US-ASCII. RFC 3987 allows more characters—any character in the Universal Character Set—and now a resource can be identified by IRI in any language.

Statistics

Between 2005 and 2010, the number of web users doubled, and was expected to surpass two billion in 2010. Early studies in 1998 and 1999 estimating the size of the Web using capture/recapture methods showed that much of the web was not indexed by search engines and the Web was much larger than expected. According to a 2001 study, there was a massive number, over 550 billion, of documents on the Web, mostly in the invisible Web, or Deep Web. A 2002 survey of 2, 024 million web pages determined that by far the most web content was in the English language: 56. 4%; next were pages in German (7. 7%), French (5. 6%), and Japanese (4. 9%). A more recent study, which used web searches in 75 different languages to sample the Web, determined that there were over 11. 5 billion web pages in the publicly indexable web as of the end of January 2005. As of March 2009, the indexable web contains at least 25. 21 billion pages. On 25 July 2008, Google software engineers Jesse Alpert and Nissan Hajaj announced that Google Search had discovered one trillion unique URLs. As of May 2009, over 109. 5 million domains operated. Of these, 74% were commercial or other domains operating in the generic top-level domain *com*.

Statistics measuring a website's popularity are usually based either on the number of page views or on associated server 'hits' (file requests) that it receives.

Speed Issues

Frustration over congestion issues in the Internet infrastructure and the high latency that results in slow browsing has led to a pejorative name for the World Wide Web: the *World Wide Wait*. Speeding up the Internet is an ongoing discussion over the use of peering and QoS technologies. Other solutions to reduce the congestion can be found at W3C. Guidelines for web response times are:

- 0. 1 second (one tenth of a second). Ideal response time. The user does not sense any interruption.
- 1 second. Highest acceptable response time. Download times above 1 second interrupt the user experience.
- 10 seconds. Unacceptable response time. The user experience is interrupted and the user is likely to leave the site or system.

Web Caching

A web cache is a server computer located either on the public Internet, or within an enterprise that stores recently accessed web pages to improve response time for users when the same content is requested within a certain time after the original request.

Most web browsers also implement a browser cache for recently obtained data, usually on the local disk drive. HTTP requests by a browser may ask only for data that has changed since the last access. Web pages and resources may contain expiration information to control caching to secure sensitive data, such as in online banking, or to facilitate frequently updated sites, such as news media. Even sites with highly dynamic content may permit basic resources to be refreshed only occasionally. Web site designers find it worthwhile to collate resources such as CSS data and JavaScript into a few site-wide files so that they can be cached efficiently.

Enterprise firewalls often cache Web resources requested by one user for the benefit of many. Some search engines store cached content of frequently accessed websites.

Email Fundamentals – Systems Architecture

This article describes the high-level "architecture" of systems for handling Internet mail, and does not discuss the protocols used in a message transfer [Klensin08], the format of the messages [Resnick08], or any of the protocols and services at the "relay-level" of a mail handling system [Crocker08]. The cited references offer a very complete discussion of these related topics. Good elementary discussions can be found in most texts on computer networks [PnD07].

Internet mail has evolved without much central planning to a collection of very diverse and astonishingly complex systems. Like the Internet itself, it is helpful to study these systems the way a biologist would study an organism, or a social scientist the behavior of a group. Who are the Actors in a typical email system? What are their roles and responsibilities in handling the mail? What are their relationships with each other and with users? What are their motivations? How can we build better security systems?

A typical mail handling system has a network of Relays, each temporarily storing the message, performing some specialized function, and passing it on to the next Relay using the SMTP protocol. You can tell how many Relays handled a message by looking at the Received lines in the message header. There should be one for each Relay.

Figure 1 shows a typical system with the Relays grouped into functional blocks. In this diagram, we have named the blocks by the role they play in processing a message, and assigned each role to a different Actor (User or Agent). However, each Actor can have multiple blocks, each block can have multiple hosts, and each host can have multiple Relays running as independent daemon processes. A Transmitter might have a dozen Relays, operating in parallel to handle a large mailflow, or widely dispersed to serve users all over the world. An MDA might have a process dedicated to managing a large mailstore, another running a POP/IMAP server, and another providing a webmail interface.

Figure 1: Actors (Users and Agents) and roles (functional blocks) in a typical email system.

To understand a mail handling system, including its security vulnerabilities, we need to focus on the roles and responsibilities of each Actor and the relationships between them. Figure 1 is a simplified model of just one system. There are many other possibilities. We might add a Forwarder between the Receiver and the MDA, or an Open Relay floating in the cloud. We might join two blocks under one Agent. We might add another layer of organization, showing a group of Actors organized as a Mail Receiving Network [Moore05], or an ADMD (Administrative Management Domain) [Crocker08]. Yet another layer could be shown by grouping the Relays according to who controls the equipment.

Border

If we wonder why email continues to be such an insecure system, we can study this last example. Authentication protocols that try to correlate the Transmitter's domain name to the connecting IP address can fail when a Forwarder is involved. We cannot just dismiss Forwarding as an "edge case", however. It is important for a user who changes jobs or ESPs, and would like to continue receiving mail at his old address.

Let's follow a message from start to finish. The scenario begins with an Author composing a message using his mail client. There are countless mail clients available, just like there are many web browsers to choose from. In fact, most web browsers now include a mail client, or at least a mechanism to invoke the user's preferred client when he clicks a mailto: link in a webpage.

When the Author clicks SEND, his mail client connects to an MSA at his ESP, and the message is transferred using SMTP. A key responsibility of the MSA is to authenticate the Author. This can be done with a password, by assigning the client a static IP address, or by having the client on the MSA's local network, not directly connected to the Internet.

Most large ESPs operate their own transmitter Relays, but smaller companies, and organizations with a lot of bulk mail, often subcontract this specialized role to another Agent. The Transmitter's responsibilities include prevention of outgoing spam, and providing some means to prove their identity to unrelated Receivers. It isn't enough to say "HELO, this is trustme. com". Any spammer can do that. The Transmitter must provide some "out-of-band" data using a service like DNS that is more trusted than email.

??? <delete> Email authentication methods fall into two categories. Methods like SPF, SenderID, and CSV rely on the fact that certain IP addresses are firmly under the control of a sender (an individual or organization identified by its domain name). Methods like DKIM rely on a digital signature applied to the entire message and most of its headers. Both depend on the security of DNS. Only the domain owner has access to the DNS records under his name. With IP-based methods, the sender publishes in DNS the IP addresses authorized to use his domain name. With signature-based methods, the sender publishes a public key. IP methods can be very efficient, rejecting an entire session without transferring any messages. End-to-end signature methods can be very secure, even with an un-trusted Forwarder in the middle. </delete>

The Receiver's responsibilities include a number of functions we might call "Border defense" – blocking a DoS attack, authenticating the sender, and various spam-blocking strategies, including whitelisting, blacklisting, statistical analysis of message content, and use of heuristic rulesets that have proven effective in separating spam from legitimate mail. Border defense should be done at the Border. Loss of mail due to violations of this principle is common. A forwarded message can look like a forgery, and then the MDA has a tough choice – drop the message with no notice to the alleged sender, or send the notice and risk being reported for "bounce spam".

The problems with mis-configured mailsystems can be avoided if all Actors understand how the system works. When a Recipient sets up forwarding from his old Receiver/Forwarder to his new MDA, he should make sure that the Forwarder is whitelisted by the MDA. Forwarders should make sure that Recipients (non-expert users) understand this. MDAs should understand that forwarding is a common need, and make it easy for Recipients to whitelist at the domain level. Simple models will help reduce the confusion.

WEBSITE

A **website**, also written as **web site**, or simply **site**, is a set of related web pages typically served from a single web domain. A website is hosted on at least one web server, accessible via a network such as the Internet or a private local area network through an Internet address known as a uniform resource locator(URL). All publicly accessible websites collectively constitute the World Wide Web.

Web pages, which are the building blocks of websites, are documents, typically written in plain text interspersed with formatting instructions of Hypertext Markup Language (HTML, XHTML). They may incorporate elements from other websites with suitable markup anchors. Webpages are accessed and transported with theHypertext Transfer Protocol (HTTP), which may optionally employ encryption (HTTP Secure, HTTPS) to provide security and privacy for the user of the webpage content. The user's application, often a web browser, renders the page content according to its HTML markup instructions onto a display terminal.

The pages of a website can usually be accessed from a simple Uniform Resource Locator (URL) called the web address. The URLs of the pages organize them into a hierarchy, although hyperlinking between them conveys the reader's perceived site structure and guides the reader's navigation of the site which generally includes a home page with most of the links to the site's web content, and a supplementary about, contact and link page. Some websites require a subscription to access some or all of their content. Examples of subscription websites include many business sites, parts of news websites, academic journal websites, gaming websites, file-sharing websites, message boards, web-based email, social networking websites, websites providing real-time stock market data, and websites providing various other services (e. g., websites offering storing and/or sharing of images, files and so forth).

History

The World Wide Web (WWW) was created in 1990 by the British CERN physicist Tim Berners-Lee. On 30 April 1993, CERN announced that the World Wide Web would be free to use for anyone.

Before the introduction of HTML and HTTP, other protocols such as File Transfer Protocol and the gopher protocol were used to retrieve individual files from a server. These protocols offer a simple directory structure which the user navigates and chooses files to download. Documents were most often presented as plain text files without formatting, or were encoded in word processor formats.

Overview

Websites have many functions and can be used in various fashions; a website can be a personal website, a commercial website, a government website or a non-profit organization website. Websites can be the work of an individual, a business or other organization, and are typically dedicated to a particular topic or purpose. Any website can contain a hyperlink to any other website, so the distinction between individual sites, as perceived by the user, can be blurred.

Websites are written in, or converted to, HTML (Hyper Text Markup Language) and are accessed using a softwareinterface classified as a user agent. Web pages can be viewed or otherwise accessed from a range of computer-based and Internet-enabled devices of various sizes, including desktop computers, laptops, PDAs and cell phones.

A website is hosted on a computer system known as a web server, also called an HTTP server. These terms can also refer to the software that runs on these systems which retrieves and delivers the web pages in response to requests from the website's users. Apache is the most commonly used web server software (according to Netcraft statistics) and Microsoft'sIIS is also commonly used. Some alternatives, such as Nginx, Lighttpd, Hiawatha or Cherokee, are fully functional and lightweight.

Static website

A static website is one that has web pages stored on the server in the format that is sent to a client web browser. It is primarily coded in Hypertext Markup Language (HTML); Cascading Style Sheets (CSS) are used to control appearance beyond basic HTML. Images are commonly used to effect the desired appearance and as part of the main content. Audio or video might also be considered "static" content if it plays automatically or is generally non-interactive.

This type of website usually displays the same information to all visitors. Similar to handing out a printed brochure to customers or clients, a static website will generally provide consistent, standard information for an extended period of time. Although the website owner may make updates periodically, it is a manual process to edit the text, photos and other content and may require basic website design skills and software. Simple forms or marketing examples of websites, such as *classic website*, a *five-page website* or a *brochure website* are often static websites, because they present pre-defined, static information to the user. This may include information about a company and its products and services through text, photos, animations, audio/video, and navigation menus.

Static web sites can be edited using four broad categories of software:

- Text editors, such as Notepad or TextEdit, where content and HTML markup are manipulated directly within the editor program

- WYSIWYG offline editors, such as Microsoft FrontPage and Adobe Dreamweaver (previously Macromedia Dreamweaver), with which the site is edited using a GUI and the final HTML markup is generated automatically by the editor software
- WYSIWYG online editors which create media rich online presentation like web pages, widgets, intro, blogs, and other documents.
- Template-based editors, such as RapidWeaver and iWeb, which allow users to quickly create and upload web pages to a web server without detailed HTML knowledge, as they pick a suitable template from a palette and add pictures and text to it in a desktop publishing fashion without direct manipulation of HTML code

Static websites may still use server side includes (SSI) as an editing convenience, such as sharing a common menu bar across many pages. As the site's behaviour *to the reader* is still static, this is not considered a dynamic site.

Dynamic Website

A dynamic website is one that changes or customizes itself frequently and automatically.

Server-side dynamic pages are generated "on the fly" by computer code that produces the HTML (CSS are responsible for appearance and thus, are static files). There are a wide range of software systems, such as CGI, Java Servlets and Java Server Pages (JSP), Active Server Pages and ColdFusion (CFML) that are available to generate dynamic web systems and dynamic sites. Various web application frameworks and web template systems are available for general-use programming languages like PHP, Perl, Python, and Ruby, to make it faster and easier to create complex dynamic web sites.

A site can display the current state of a dialogue between users, monitor a changing situation, or provide information in some way personalized to the requirements of the individual user. For example, when the front page of a news site is requested, the code running on the web server might combine stored HTML fragments with news stores retrieved from adatabase or another web site via RSS to produce a page that includes the latest information. Dynamic sites can be interactive by using HTML forms, storing and reading back browser cookies, or by creating a series of pages that reflect the previous history of clicks. Another example of dynamic content is when a retail website with a database of media products allows a user to input a search request, e. g. for the keyword Beatles. In response, the content of the web page will spontaneously change the way it looked before, and will then display a list of Beatles products like CDs, DVDs and books.

Dynamic HTML uses JavaScript code to instruct the web browser how to interactively modify the page contents.

One way to simulate a certain type of dynamic web site while avoiding the performance loss of initiating the dynamic engine on a per-user or per-connection basis, is to periodically automatically regenerate a large series of static pages.

Multimedia and Interactive Content

Early web sites had only text, and soon after, images. Web browser plug ins were then used to add audio, video, and interactivity (such as for a rich Internet application that mirrors the complexity of a desktop application like a word processor). Examples of such plug-ins are Microsoft Silverlight, Adobe Flash, Adobe Shockwave, and applets written inJava. HTML 5 includes provisions for audio and video without plugins. JavaScript is also built into most modern web browsers, and allows for web site creators to send code to the web browser that instructs it how to interactively modify page content and communicate with the web server if needed. (The browser's internal representation of the content is known as the Document Object Model (DOM) and the technique is known as Dynamic HTML.) A more recent trend in websites called "responsive design" has given the best of viewing experience as it provides with a device based layout for users. These websites change their layout according to the device or mobile platform thus giving a rich user experience.

Spelling

The form "website" has become the most common spelling, but "Web site" (capitalised) and "web site" are also widely used, though declining. Some in academia, some large book publishers, and some dictionaries still use "Web site", reflecting the origin of the term in the proper name World Wide Web. There has also been similar debate regarding related terms such asweb page, web server, and webcam.

Among leading style guides, the Reuters style guide, *The Chicago Manual of Style*, and the *AP Stylebook* (since April 2010) all recommend "website". Among leading dictionaries and encyclopedias, the *Canadian Oxford Dictionary* prefers "website", and the *Oxford English Dictionary* changed to "website" in 2004. Wikipedia also uses "website", but Encyclopædia Britannica uses both "Web site" and "Website". Britannica's Merriam-Webster subsidiary uses "Web site", recognising "website" as a variant.

Among leading language-usage commentators, *Garner's Modern American Usage* acknowledges that "website" is the standard form, but Bill Walsh, of *The Washington Post*, argues for using "Web site" in his books and on his website(however, *The Washington Post* itself uses "website").

Among major Internet technology companies and corporations, Google uses "website", as does Apple, thoughMicrosoft uses both "website" and "web site".

TYPES OF WEBSITE

Websites can be divided into two broad categories - static and interactive. Interactive sites are part of the Web 2. 0community of sites, and allow for interactivity between the site owner and site visitors. Static sites serve or capture information but do not allow engagement with the audience directly. Some web sites are informational or produced by enthusiasts or for personal use or entertainment. Many web sites do aim to make money, using one or more business models, including:

- Posting interesting content and selling contextual advertising either through direct sales or through an advertising network.
- E-commerce - products or services are purchased directly through the web site
- Advertising products or services available at a brick and mortar business
- Freemium - basic content is available for free but premium content is paid

There are many varieties of websites, each specializing in a particular type of content or use, and they may be arbitrarily classified in any number of ways. A few such classifications might include:

Some websites may be included in one or more of these categories. For example, a business website may promote the business's products, but may also host informative documents, such as white papers. There are also numerous sub-categories to the ones listed above. For example, a porn site is a specific type of e-commerce site or business site (that is, it is trying to sell memberships for access to its site) or have social networking capabilities. A fansite may be a dedication from the owner to a particular celebrity.

Websites are constrained by architectural limits (e. g., the computing power dedicated to the website). Very large websites, such as Facebook, Yahoo!, Microsoft, and Google employ many servers and load balancing equipment such as CiscoContent Services Switches to distribute visitor loads over multiple computers at multiple locations. As of early 2011, Facebook utilized 9 data centers with approximately 63, 000 servers. In February 2009, Netcraft, an Internet monitoring company that has tracked Web growth since 1995, reported that there were 215, 675, 903 websites with domain names and content on them in 2009, compared to just 19, 732 websites in August 1995. After reaching 1 billion websites in September 2014, a milestone confirmed by NetCraft in its October 2014 Web Server Survey and that Internet Live Stats was the first to announce - as attested by this tweet from the inventor of the World Wide Web himself, Tim Berners-Lee - the number of websites in the world has subsequently declined, reverting to a level below 1 billion. This is due to the monthly fluctuations in the count of inactive websites. We do expect, however, to exceed 1 billion websites again sometime in 2015 and to stabilize the count above this historic milestone in 2016.

Awards

The Webby Awards, Favourite Website Awards, Interactive Media Awards and WebAwards are prominent award organizations recognizing the world's best websites.

Web hosting service

A **web hosting service** is a type of Internet hosting service that allows individuals and organizations to make their website accessible via the World Wide Web. Web hosts are companies that provide space on a server owned or leased for use by clients, as well as providing Internet connectivity, typically in a data center. Web hosts can also provide data center space and connectivity to the Internet for other servers located in their data center, called colocation, also known as *Housing* in Latin America or France.

The scope of web hosting services varies greatly. The most basic is web page and small-scale file hosting, where files can be uploaded via File Transfer Protocol(FTP) or a Web interface. The files are usually delivered to the Web "as is" or with minimal processing. Many Internet service providers (ISPs) offer this service free to subscribers. Individuals and organizations may also obtain Web page hosting from alternative service providers. Personal web site hosting is typically free, advertisement-sponsored, or inexpensive. Business web site hosting often has a higher expense depending upon the size and type of the site.

Single page hosting is generally sufficient for personal web pages. A complex site calls for a more comprehensive package that provides database support and application development platforms (e. g. PHP, Java, Ruby on Rails, ColdFusion, or ASP. NET). These facilities allow customers to write or install scripts for applications like forums and content management. Also, Secure Sockets Layer (SSL) is typically used for e-commerce.

The host may also provide an interface or control panel for managing the Web server and installing scripts, as well as other modules and service applications like e-mail. Some hosts specialize in certain software or services (e. g. e-commerce), which are commonly used by larger companies that outsource network infrastructure.

Reliability and uptime

The availability of a website is measured by the percentage of a year in which the website is publicly accessible and reachable via the internet.

This is different from measuring the uptime of a system. Uptime refers to the system itself being online. Uptime does not take into account being able to reach it as in the event of a network outage. A hosting provider's SLAs may include a certain amount of scheduled downtime per year in order to perform maintenance on the systems. This scheduled downtime is often excluded from the SLA timeframe, and needs to be subtracted from the Total Time when availability is calculated. Depending on the wording of an SLA, if the availability of a system drops below that in the signed SLA, a hosting provider often will provide a partial refund for time lost. How downtime is determined changes from provider to provider, therefore reading the SLA is imperative. Not all providers release uptime statistics.

TYPES OF HOSTING

Internet hosting services can run Web servers.

Many large companies that are not internet service providers need to be permanently connected to the web to send email, files, etc. to other sites. The company may use the computer as a website host to provide details of their goods and services and facilities for online orders.

- Free web hosting service: offered by different companies with limited services, sometimes supported by advertisements, and often limited when compared to paid hosting.
- Shared web hosting service: one's website is placed on the same server as many other sites, ranging from a few to hundreds or thousands. Typically, all domains may share a common pool of server resources, such as RAM and theCPU. The features available with this type of service can be quite basic and not flexible in terms of software and updates. Resellers often sell shared web hosting and web companies often have reseller accounts to provide hosting for clients.
- Reseller web hosting: allows clients to become web hosts themselves. Resellers could function, for individual domains, under any combination of these listed types of hosting, depending on who they are affiliated with as a reseller. Resellers' accounts may vary tremendously in size: they may have their own virtual dedicated server to a colocated server. Many resellers provide a nearly identical service to their provider's shared hosting plan and provide the technical support themselves.
- Virtual Dedicated Server: also known as a Virtual Private Server (VPS), divides server resources into virtual servers, where resources can be allocated in a way that does not directly reflect the underlying hardware. VPS will often be allocated resources based on a one server to many VPSs relationship, however virtualisation may be done for a number of reasons, including the ability to move a VPS container between servers. The users may have root access to their own virtual space. Customers

are sometimes responsible for patching and maintaining the server.

- Dedicated hosting service: the user gets his or her own Web server and gains full control over it (user has root accessfor Linux/administrator access for Windows); however, the user typically does not own the server. One type of dedicated hosting is self-managed or unmanaged. This is usually the least expensive for dedicated plans. The user has full administrative access to the server, which means the client is responsible for the security and maintenance of his own dedicated server.
- Managed hosting service: the user gets his or her own Web server but is not allowed full control over it (user is denied root access for Linux/administrator access for Windows); however, they are allowed to manage their data via FTP or other remote management tools. The user is disallowed full control so that the provider can guarantee quality of service by not allowing the user to modify the server or potentially create configuration problems. The user typically does not own the server. The server is leased to the client.
- Colocation web hosting service: similar to the dedicated web hosting service, but the user owns the colo server; the hosting company provides physical space that the server takes up and takes care of the server. This is the most powerful and expensive type of web hosting service. In most cases, the colocation provider may provide little to no support directly for their client's machine, providing only the electrical, Internet access, and storage facilities for the server. In most cases for colo, the client would have his own administrator visit the data center on site to do any hardware upgrades or changes. Formerly, many colocation providers would accept any system configuration for hosting, even ones housed in desktop-style minitower cases, but most hosts now require rack mount enclosures and standard system configurations.
- Cloud hosting: is a new type of hosting platform that allows customers powerful, scalable and reliable hosting based on clustered load-balanced servers and utility billing. A cloud hosted website may be more reliable than alternatives since other computers in the cloud can compensate when a single piece of hardware goes down. Also, local power disruptions or even natural disasters are less problematic for cloud hosted sites, as cloud hosting is decentralized. Cloud hosting also allows providers to charge users only for resources consumed by the user, rather than a flat fee for the amount the user expects they will use, or a fixed cost upfront hardware investment. Alternatively, the lack of centralization may give users less control on where their data is located which could be a problem for users with data security or privacy concerns.
- Clustered hosting: having multiple servers hosting the same content for better resource utilization. Clustered servers are a perfect solution for

high-availability dedicated hosting, or creating a scalable web hosting solution. A cluster may separate web serving from database hosting capability. (Usually web hosts use clustered hosting for their shared hosting plans, as there are multiple benefits to the mass managing of clients).

- Grid hosting: this form of distributed hosting is when a server cluster acts like a grid and is composed of multiple nodes.
- Home server: usually a single machine placed in a private residence can be used to host one or more web sites from a usually consumer-grade broadband connection. These can be purpose-built machines or more commonly old PCs. Some ISPs actively attempt to block home servers by disallowing incoming requests to TCP port 80 of the user's connection and by refusing to provide static IP addresses. A common way to attain a reliable DNS host name is by creating an account with a dynamic DNS service. A dynamic DNS service will automatically change the IP address that aURL points to when the IP address changes.

Some specific types of hosting provided by web host service providers:

- File hosting service: hosts files, not web pages
- Image hosting service
- Video hosting service
- Blog hosting service
- Paste bin
- Shopping cart software
- E-mail hosting service

Obtaining hosting

Web hosting is often provided as part of a general Internet access plan from internet service providers. There are also many free and paid providers offering web hosting.

A customer needs to evaluate the requirements of the application to choose what kind of hosting to use. Such considerations include database server software, scripting software, and operating system. Most hosting providers provide Linux-based web hosting which offers a wide range of different software. A typical configuration for a Linux server is theLAMP platform: Linux, Apache, MySQL, and PHP/Perl/Python. The web hosting client may want to have other services, such as email for their business domain, databases or multimedia services. A customer may also choose Windows as the hosting platform. The customer still can choose from PHP, Perl, and Python but may also use ASP. Net or Classic ASP. Web hosting packages often include a Web Content Management System, so the end-user does not have to worry about the more technical aspects.

An overview of browser and servers

Web browser

A **web browser** (commonly referred to as a **browser**) is a software application for retrieving, presenting and traversing information resources on the World Wide Web. An *information resource* is identified by a Uniform Resource Identifier (URI/URL) and may be a web page, image, video or other piece of content. Hyperlinkspresent in resources enable users easily to navigate their browsers to related resources.

Although browsers are primarily intended to use the World Wide Web, they can also be used to access information provided by web servers in private networks or files in file systems.

The major web browsers are Firefox, Internet Explorer, Google Chrome, Opera, and Safari.

History

The first web browser was invented in 1990 by Sir Tim Berners-Lee. Berners-Lee is the director of the World Wide Web Consortium (W3C), which oversees the Web's continued development, and is also the founder of the World Wide Web Foundation. His browser was called WorldWideWeb and later renamed Nexus.

The first commonly available web browser with a graphical user interface was Erwise. The development of Erwise was initiated by Robert Cailliau.

In 1993, browser software was further innovated by Marc Andreessen with the release ofMosaic, "the world's first popular browser", which made the World Wide Web system easy to use and more accessible to the average person. Andreesen's browser sparked the internet boom of the 1990s. The introduction of Mosaic in 1993 – one of the first graphical web browsers – led to an explosion in web use. Andreessen, the leader of the Mosaic team at National Center for Supercomputing Applications (NCSA), soon started his own company, named Netscape, and released the Mosaic-influenced Netscape Navigator in 1994, which quickly became the world's most popular browser, accounting for 90% of all web use at its peak.

Microsoft responded with its Internet Explorer in 1995, also heavily influenced by Mosaic, initiating the industry's first browser war. Bundled with Windows, Internet Explorer gained dominance in the web browser market; Internet Explorer usage share peaked at over 95% by 2002.

Opera debuted in 1996; it has never achieved widespread use, having less than 2% browser usage share as of February 2012 according to Net Applications. Its Opera-mini version has an additive share, in April 2011 amounting to 1. 1% of overall browser use, but focused on the fast-growing mobile phone web browser market, being preinstalled on over 40 million phones. It is also available on several other embedded systems, including Nintendo's Wii video game console.

In 1998, Netscape launched what was to become the Mozilla Foundation in an attempt to produce a competitive browser using the open source software model. That browser would eventually evolve into Firefox, which developed a respectable following while still in the beta stage of development; shortly after the release of Firefox 1. 0 in late 2004, Firefox (all versions) accounted for 7% of browser use. As of August 2011, Firefox has a 28% usage share.

Apple's Safari had its first beta release in January 2003; as of April 2011, it had a dominant share of Apple-based web browsing, accounting for just over 7% of the entire browser market.

The most recent major entrant to the browser market is Chrome, first released in September 2008. Chrome's take-up has increased significantly year by year, by doubling its usage share from 8% to 16% by August 2011. This increase seems largely to be at the expense of Internet Explorer, whose share has tended to decrease from month to month. In December 2011, Chrome overtook Internet Explorer 8 as the most widely used web browser but still had lower usage than all versions of Internet Explorer combined. Chrome's user-base continued to grow and in May 2012, Chrome's usage passed the usage of all versions of Internet Explorer combined. By April 2014, Chrome's usage had hit 45%.

Internet Explorer will be deprecated in Windows 10, with Microsoft Edge replacing it as the default web browser.

Business models

The ways that web browser makers fund their development costs has changed over time. The first web browser, WorldWideWeb, was a research project.

Netscape Navigator was sold commercially, as was Opera.

Internet Explorer, on the other hand, was bundled free with the Windows operating system (and was also downloadable free), and therefore it was funded partly by the sales of Windows to computer manufacturers and direct to users. Internet Explorer also used to be available for the Mac. It is likely that releasing IE for the Mac was part of Microsoft's overall strategy to fight threats to its quasi-monopoly platform dominance - threats such as web standards and Java - by making some web developers, or at least their managers, assume that there was "no need" to develop for anything other than Internet Explorer. In this respect, IE may have contributed to Windows and Microsoft applications sales in another way, through "lock-in" to Microsoft's browser.

In January 2009, the European Commission announced it would investigate the bundling of Internet Explorer with Windows operating systems from Microsoft, saying "Microsoft's tying of Internet Explorer to the Windows operating system harms competition between web browsers, undermines product innovation and ultimately reduces consumer choice."Microsoft Corp v Commission

Safari and Mobile Safari were likewise always included with OS X and iOS respectively, so, similarly, they were originally funded by sales of Apple computers and mobile devices, and formed part of the overall Apple experience to customers.

Today, most commercial web browsers are paid by search engine companies to make their engine default, or to include them as another option. For example, Google pays Mozilla, the maker of Firefox, to make Google Search the default search engine in Firefox. Mozilla makes enough money from this deal that it does not need to charge users for Firefox. In addition, Google Search is also (as one would expect) the default search engine in Google Chrome. Users searching for websites or items on the Internet would be led to Google's search results page, increasing ad revenue and which funds development at Google and of Google Chrome.

Many less-well-known free software browsers, such as Konqueror, were hardly funded at all and were developed mostly by volunteers free of charge.

FUNCTION

The primary purpose of a web browser is to bring information resources to the user ("retrieval" or "fetching"), allowing them to view the information ("display", "rendering"), and then access other information ("navigation", "following links").

This process begins when the user inputs a Uniform Resource Locator (URL), for example *http://en. wikipedia. org/*, into the browser. The prefix of the URL, the Uniform Resource Identifier or URI, determines how the URL will be interpreted. The most commonly used kind of URI starts with *http:* and identifies a resource to be retrieved over the Hypertext Transfer Protocol (HTTP). Many browsers also support a variety of other prefixes, such as *https:* for HTTPS, *ftp:* for the File Transfer Protocol, and *file:* for local files. Prefixes that the web browser cannot directly handle are often handed off to another application entirely. For example, *mailto:* URIs are usually passed to the user's default e-mail application, and*news:* URIs are passed to the user's default newsgroup reader.

In the case of *http*, *https*, *file*, and others, once the resource has been retrieved the web browser will display it. HTML and associated content (image files, formatting information such as CSS, etc.) is passed to the browser's layout engine to be transformed from markup to an interactive document, a process known as "rendering". Aside from HTML, web browsers can generally display any kind of content that can be part of a web page. Most browsers can display images, audio, video, and XML files, and often have plug-ins to support Flash applications and Java applets. Upon encountering a file of an unsupported type or a file that is set up to be downloaded rather than displayed, the browser prompts the user to save the file to disk. Information resources may contain hyperlinks to other information resources. Each link contains the URI of a resource to go to. When a link is clicked, the browser navigates to the resource indicated by the link's target URI, and the process of bringing content to the user begins again.

Features

For more details on this topic, see Comparison of web browsers.

Available web browsers range in features from minimal, text-based user interfaces with bare-bones support for HTML to rich user interfaces supporting a wide variety of file formats and protocols. Browsers which include additional components to support e-mail, Usenet news, and Internet Relay Chat (IRC), are sometimes referred to as "Internet suites" rather than merely "web browsers".

All major web browsers allow the user to open multiple information resources at the same time, either in different browser windows or in different tabs of the same window. Major browsers also include pop-up blockers to prevent unwanted windows from "popping up" without the user's consent.

Most web browsers can display a list of web pages that the user has *bookmarked* so that the user can quickly return to them. Bookmarks are also called "Favorites" in Internet Explorer. In addition, all major web browsers have some form of built-in web feed aggregator. In Firefox, web feeds are formatted as "live bookmarks" and behave like a folder of bookmarks corresponding to recent entries in the feed. In Opera, a more traditional feed reader is included which stores and displays the contents of the feed.

Furthermore, most browsers can be extended via plug-ins, downloadable components that provide additional features.

User interface

Most major web browsers have these user interface elements in common:

- *Back* and *forward* buttons to go back to the previous resource and forward respectively.
- A *refresh* or *reload* button to reload the current resource.
- A *stop* button to cancel loading the resource. In some browsers, the stop button is merged with the reload button.
- A *home* button to return to the user's home page.
- An address bar to input the Uniform Resource Identifier (URI) of the desired resource and display it.
- A search bar to input terms into a search engine. In some browsers, the search bar is merged with the address bar.

- The *viewport*, the visible area of the webpage within the browser window.
- The ability to view the HTML source for a page.

Major browsers also possess incremental find features to search within a web page.

Privacy and security

Most browsers support HTTP Secure and offer quick and easy ways to delete the web cache, cookies, and browsing history. For a comparison of the current security vulnerabilities of browsers, see comparison of web browsers.

Standards support

Early web browsers supported only a very simple version of HTML. The rapid development of proprietary web browsers led to the development of non-standard dialects of HTML, leading to problems with interoperability. Modern web browsers support a combination of standards-based and *de facto* HTML and XHTML, which should be rendered in the same way by all browsers.

Extensibility

A browser extension is a computer program that extends the functionality of a web browser. Every major web browser supports the development of browser extensions.

Components

Web browsers consist of a user interface, layout engine, rendering engine, JavaScript interpreter, UI backend, networking component and data persistence component. These components achieve different functionalities of a web browser and together provide all capabilities of a web browser.

WEB SERVER

A web server is an information technology that processes requests via HTTP, the basic network protocol used to distribute information on the World Wide Web. The term can refer either to the entire computer system, an appliance, or specifically to the software that accepts and supervises the HTTP requests.

Overview

The primary function of a web server is to store, process and deliver web pages toclients. The communication between client and server takes place using theHypertext Transfer Protocol (HTTP). Pages delivered are most frequently HTML documents, which may include images, style sheets and scripts in addition to text content.

A user agent, commonly a web browser or web crawler, initiates communication by making a request for a specific resource using HTTP and the server responds with the content of that resource or an error message if unable to do so. The resource is typically a real file on the server's secondary storage, but this is not necessarily the case and depends on how the web server is implemented.

While the primary function is to serve content, a full implementation of HTTP also includes ways of receiving content from clients. This feature is used for submitting web forms, including uploading of files.

Many generic web servers also support server-side scripting using Active Server Pages (ASP), PHP, or other scripting languages. This means that the behaviour of the web server can be scripted in separate files, while the actual server software remains unchanged. Usually, this function is used to generate HTML documents dynamically ("on-the-fly") as opposed to returning static documents. The former is primarily used for retrieving and/or modifying information fromdatabases. The latter is typically much faster and more easily cached but cannot deliver dynamic content.

Web servers are not always used for serving the World Wide Web. They can also be found embedded in devices such asprinters, routers, webcams and serving only a local network. The web server may then be used as a part of a system for monitoring and/or administering the device in question. This usually means that no additional software has to be installed on the client computer, since only a web browser is required (which now is included with most operating systems).

History

In 1989 Tim Berners-Lee proposed a new project to his employer CERN, with the goal of easing the exchange of information between scientists by using a hypertextsystem. The project resulted in Berners-Lee writing two programs in 1990:

- A browser called WorldWideWeb.
- The world's first web server, later known as CERN httpd, which ran onNeXTSTEP

Between 1991 and 1994, the simplicity and effectiveness of early technologies used to surf and exchange data through the World Wide Web helped to port them to many different operating systems and spread their use among scientific organizations and universities, and then to industry.

In 1994 Tim Berners-Lee decided to constitute the World Wide Web Consortium(W3C) to regulate the further development of the many technologies involved (HTTP, HTML, etc.) through a standardization process.

Common features

- Large file support to be able to serve files whose size is greater than 2 GB on 32 bit OS
- Bandwidth throttling to limit the speed of responses in order to not saturate the network and to be able to serve more clients
- Server-side scripting to generate dynamic web pages, still keeping web server and website implementations separate from each other

Path translation

Web servers are able to map the path component of a Uniform Resource Locator (**URL**) into:

- A local file system resource (for static requests)
- An internal or external program name (for dynamic requests)

For a *static request* the URL path specified by the client is relative to the web server's root directory.

Consider the following URL as it would be requested by a client:

`http://www. example. com/path/file. html`

The client's user agent will translate it into a connection to www. example. com with the following HTTP 1. 1 request:

GET /path/file. html HTTP/1. 1

`Host: www. example. com`

The web server on www. example. com will append the given path to the path of its root directory. On an Apache server, this is commonly /home/www (On Unix machines, usually /var/www). The result is the local file system resource:

`/home/www`**`/path/file. htm`**

The web server then reads the file, if it exists and sends a response to the client's web browser. The response will describe the content of the file and contain the file itself or an error message will return saying that the file does not exist or is unavailable.

Kernel-mode and user-mode web servers

A web server can be either incorporated into the OS kernel, or in user space (like other regular applications).

An in-kernel web server (like Microsoft IIS on Windows or TUX on GNU/Linux) will usually work faster, because, as part of the system, it can directly use all the hardware resources it needs, such as non-paged memory, CPU time-slices, network adapters, or buffers.

Web servers that run in user-mode have to ask the system for permission to use more memory or more CPU resources. Not only do these requests to the kernel take time, but they are not always satisfied because the system reserves resources for its own usage and has the responsibility to share hardware resources with all the other running applications. Executing in user mode can also mean useless buffer copies which are another handicap for user-mode web servers.

LOAD LIMITS

A web server (program) has defined load limits, because it can handle only a limited number of concurrent client connections (usually between 2 and 80, 000, by default between 500 and 1, 000) per IP address (and TCP port) and it can serve only a certain maximum number of requests per second depending on:

- its own settings,
- the HTTP request type,
- whether the content is static or dynamic,
- whether the content is cached, and
- the hardware and software limitations of the OS of the computer on which the web server runs.

When a web server is near to or over its limit, it becomes unresponsive.

Causes of Overload

At any time web servers can be overloaded due to:

- Excess legitimate web traffic. Thousands or even millions of clients connecting to the web site in a short interval, e. g., Slashdot effect;
- Distributed Denial of Service attacks. A denial-of-service attack (DoS attack) or distributed denial-of-service attack (DDoS attack) is an attempt to make a computer or network resource unavailable to its intended users;
- Computer worms that sometimes cause abnormal traffic because of millions of infected computers (not coordinated among them);
- XSS viruses can cause high traffic because of millions of infected browsers and/or web servers;
- Internet bots Traffic not filtered/limited on large web sites with very few resources (bandwidth, etc.);
- Internet (network) slowdowns, so that client requests are served more slowly and the number of connections increases so much that server limits are reached;
- Web servers (computers) partial unavailability. This can happen because of required or urgent maintenance or upgrade, hardware or software failures, back-end (e. g., database) failures, etc.; in these cases the remaining web servers get too much traffic and become overloaded.

Symptoms of overload

The symptoms of an overloaded web server are:

- Requests are served with (possibly long) delays (from 1 second to a few hundred seconds).
- The web server returns an HTTP error code, such as 500, 502, 503, 504, 408, or even 404, which is inappropriate for an overload condition.
- The web server refuses or resets (interrupts) TCP connections before it returns any content.
- In very rare cases, the web server returns only a part of the requested content. This behavior can be considered a bug, even if it usually arises as a symptom of overload.

Anti-overload Techniques

To partially overcome above average load limits and to prevent overload, most popular web sites use common techniques like:

- Managing network traffic, by using:
- Firewalls to block unwanted traffic coming from bad IP sources or having bad patterns
- HTTP traffic managers to drop, redirect or rewrite requests having bad HTTP patterns
- Bandwidth management and traffic shaping, in order to smooth down peaks in network usage
- Deploying web cache techniques
- Using different domain names to serve different (static and dynamic) content by separate web servers, i. e. :
- http: / /images. example. com
- http: / /www. example. com
- Using different domain names and/or computers to separate big files from small and medium-sized files; the idea is to be able to fully cache small and medium-sized files and to efficiently serve big or huge (over 10 - 1000 MB) files by using different settings
- Using many internet servers (programs) per computer, each one bound to its own network card and IP address
- Using many internet servers (computers) that are grouped together behind a load balancer so that they act or are seen as one big web server
- Adding more hardware resources (i. e. RAM, disks) to each computer
- Tuning OS parameters for hardware capabilities and usage
- Using more efficient computer programs for web servers, etc.
- Using other workarounds, especially if dynamic content is involved

Internet Access Methods

Internet access connects individual computer terminals, computers, mobile devices, and computer networks to the Internet, enabling users to access Internet services, such as email and the World Wide Web. Internet service providers (ISPs) offer Internet access through various technologies that offer a wide range of data signalling rates (speeds).

Consumer use of the Internet first became popular through dial-up Internet access in the 1990s. By the first decade of the 21st century, many consumers in developed nations used faster, broadband Internet access technologies. As of 2014, broadband was ubiquitous around the world, with a global average connection speed exceeding 4 Mbit/s.

HISTORY

The Internet developed from the ARPANET, which was funded by the US government to support projects within the government and at universities and research laboratories in the US – but grew over time to include most of the world's large universities and the research arms of many technology companies. Use by a wider audience only came in 1995 when restrictions on the use of the Internet to carry commercial traffic were lifted.

In the early to mid-1980s, most Internet access was from personal computers and workstations directly connected to local area networks or from dial-up connections using modems and analog telephone lines. LANs typically operated at 10 Mbit/s and grew to support 100 and 1000 Mbit/s, while modem data-rates grew from 1200 and 2400 bit/s in the 1980s, to 28 and 56 kbit/s by the mid to late 1990s. Initially dial-up connections were made from terminals or computers running terminal emulation software to terminal servers on LANs. These dial-up connections did not support end-to-end use of the Internet protocols and only provided terminal to host connections. The introduction of network access servers (NASs) supporting theSerial Line Internet Protocol (SLIP) and later the point-to-point protocol (PPP) extended the Internet protocols and made the full range of Internet services available to dial-up users, subject only to limitations imposed by the lower data rates available using dial-up.

Broadband Internet access, often shortened to just broadband and also known as high-speed Internet access, are services that provide bit-rates considerably higher than that available using a 56 kbit/s modem. In the US National Broadband Planof 2009, the U. S. Federal Communications Commission (FCC) defined broadband access as "Internet access that is always on and faster than the traditional dial-up access", although the FCC has defined it differently through the years. The term broadband was originally a reference to multi-frequency communication, as opposed to narrowband or baseband. Broadband is now a marketing term that telephone, cable, and other companies use to sell their more expensive higher-data-rate products. Broadband connections are typically made using a computer's built in Ethernet networking capabilities, or by using a NIC expansion card.

Most broadband services provide a continuous "always on" connection; there is no dial-in process required, and it does not "hog" phone lines. Broadband provides improved access to Internet services such as:

- Faster world wide web browsing
- Faster downloading of documents, photographs, videos, and other large files
- Telephony, radio, television, and videoconferencing
- Virtual private networks and remote system administration
- Online gaming, especially massively multiplayer online role-playing games which are interaction-intensive

In the 1990s, the National Information Infrastructure initiative in the U. S. made broadband Internet access a public policy issue. In 2000, most Internet access to homes was provided using dial-up, while many businesses and schools were using broadband connections. In 2000 there were just under 150 million dial-up subscriptions in the 34 OECD countriesand fewer than 20 million broadband subscriptions. By 2004, broadband had grown and dial-up had declined so that the number of subscriptions were roughly equal at 130 million each. In 2010, in the OECD countries, over 90% of the Internet access subscriptions used broadband, broadband had grown to more than 300 million subscriptions, and dial-up subscriptions had declined to fewer than 30 million.

The broadband technologies in widest use are ADSL and cable Internet access. Newer technologies include VDSL andoptical fibre extended closer to the subscriber in both telephone and cable plants. Fibre-optic communication, while only recently being used in premises and to the curb schemes, has played a crucial role in enabling broadband Internet access by making transmission of information at very high data rates over longer distances much more cost-effective than copper wire technology. In areas not served by ADSL or cable, some community organizations and local governments are installing Wi-Fi networks. Wireless and satellite Internet are often used in rural, undeveloped, or other hard to serve areas where wired Internet is not readily available. Newer technologies being deployed for fixed (stationary) and mobile broadband access include WiMAX, LTE, and fixed wireless, e. g., Motorola Canopy.

Starting in roughly 2006, mobile broadband access is increasingly available at the consumer level using "3G" and "4G" technologies such as HSPA, EV-DO, HSPA+, and LTE.

INTERNET AS A KNOWLEDGE REPOSITORY

In the information age, lifelong learning and collaboration are essential aspects of most innovative work. Information technology is not only transforming our workplace but also our educational system. The information revolution is having a profound and permanent effect on the way we learn. Fortunately, the computer technology which drives the information explosion also has the potential to help individuals and teams to learn much of what they need to know on demand. In particular, computer-based systems on the Internet can be designed to capture knowledge as it is generated within a community of practice and to deliver relevant knowledge when it is useful.

In this internet world, we can search any kind of information. Just type the keyword in search engine and you can find a lot of information about it. The internet is recognized as a rich source of information, which can be easily tapped by any person who has the skills to use the internet. More than ever before online databases are easily accessible to all learners who have a computer and a telephone line.

The rapid development of Information and Communication Technology has yielded an almost unlimited variety of databases and multimedia platforms that are able to supply multifarious needs, including knowledge, edutainment, entertainment, leisure activities, consumer facilities, interpersonal interaction etc. there are many knowledge centers in the net like which can be accessed and used by all. There are virtual library and also on-line discussion boards which are useful tools for academic exchanges. Thus the use of internet by students and teachers is perceived as a vehicle to increase knowledge and skills necessary for successful negotiation of tasks presented by 21st century.

Knowledge repository means a place to store knowledge and retrieve knowledge. Hence internet is truly a knowledge repository.

6

Promotion and Advertising

In today's changing and competitive international marketplace, advertising is important. Advertising is an activity designed to spread information with a view to promoting the sales of marketable goods and services. As such, it operates in two ways: first, by spreading information amongst consumers about the possibilities of consumption, and second, by seeking to influence their judgement in favour of the particular goods which are the subject of the advertisement. Any organization which uses this promotional instrument has to use certain media space which is paid for. In other words, we can also define advertisement as "paid public messages designed to describe or praise a product". This product in tourism is any destination area which is visited by a tourist. The media space for advertisement can be bought in newspapers, general and specialized magazines, in the form of posters or billboards. Besides the use of paid media space in the form of newspapers, magazines, etc., use of media time is also made in radio and television in order to transmit a pre-determined message to a predetermined audience.

Advertising has several inherent advantages in this method. The biggest advantage is its wide coverage. Advertising is especially appropriate for communication with a large number of prospective purchasers of a commodity or a service. A uniform sales message is directed towards all prospective purchasers. An advertisement can be placed before a large number of prospective customers as compared with the efforts of a salesman. Frequency is another advantage. It can make its appeal more frequently, whereas the calls of salesmen are usually not so frequent. Another advantage is its accessibility. It may reach prospects whom salesmen would find difficult to interview, owing to lack of interest, or inaccessibility to salesmen. Advertisement may reach such prospects through many types of media and under a variety of circumstances, and may thus attract their attention and arouse their interest. Lower cost is another major advantage. Large numbers can be reached economically, i.e. at a lower cost per contact than in any other technique available.

Advertising may be used to do a variety of selling tasks. A great deal of advertising attempts to win acceptance for the product. Such advertising may produce few specific demands for the advertised brands, yet when retailers display or show advertised goods they sell more readily than non-advertised ones. Therefore, retailers often hesitate to handle non-advertised goods unless they are obtainable at low prices. Advertising thus directly stimulates sales to retailers. Advertising may at times be used to make the complete sale. Some direct mail and periodical advertising attempts to make sales by requesting readers to forward orders accompanied by the necessary payment. When the number of potential buyers is small and when they are widely scattered, it could be extremely costly to reach them through salesmen. Advertising then becomes the most economical means of doing the entire sales job.

Planning the Advertising : While planning the advertising, the agency must give careful consideration to the actual make-up of the advertisement. This headline copy, illustrations, colour scheme, size, layout, and method of printing or reproducing the advertisement must be planned very carefully. This is necessary in order to gain attention of the customer, maintain his interest in the message, and secure the action desired by the seller. Closely related is the question of periodicity of advertisement. How frequently to advertise? For instance, is it better to use a full-page advertisement once a month or a quarter-page weekly? A frequently presented thought is likely to force itself into our consciousness. People are inclined to believe statements they hear or see repeatedly and hence the logic of frequent repetition of advertisements. In starting a special campaign the advertisements should not be spaced regularly. Early in the campaign they should be used close together, while later on they can be issued at much longer intervals. This is desirable because consumers forget rapidly; at first and much more slowly later on. After the facts are retained; by the prospects, the advertisements can be presented at much longer intervals.

Media Selection : The advertiser should give careful attention in planning to the selection of the medium or media especially adopted to his needs. The selection will depend upon the factors like the area to be covered, the type of audience to be reached, the appeals to be used and upon the services and facilities of the particular medium in relation to costs. The important factors which influence the media selection are: (i) media habits of the target audience; (ii) product characteristics (for example, TV may be the appropriate medium for those products which may require a demonstration of their operation for effective impact on the target audience); and (iii) cost of the media.

Message Selection : The message selected for use in the advertisement should be such that it retains the interest in the minds of the customers about the product. The customer must maintain his interest in the message, and secure the action desired by the seller of the product. The objective is to present the advertiser's message in such a way that the illustration may lead the reader to favourable considerations of the advertisement. The important characteristics of an effective message are:

Information: It should be adequate for a decision;

Interest: It should be able to catch the attention of the target audience;

Authenticity : It should avoid exaggerated claims;

Persuasion: It should be capable of creating a favourable conviction in the target audience; and

Memory Value: It should have something in it which can help the target audience to remember it.

Cost of Advertising : The agency must relate the estimated cost of the objectives planned and the contribution expected from advertising. Can the advertiser carry on a campaign large enough to make it effective? Are the funds available or will they become available through the sale of the product. How much the agency spends for the advertising? The various methods commonly used are:

Affordable Method: Here, the advertising budget is set on the basis of what the agency can afford;

Percentage of Sales Method: In this case, the agency sets the advertising budget on the basis of specific percentage of sales;

Competitive Parity Method : Here the company sets its budget to match those of its major competitors;

Objective and Task Method : In this the advertising budget represents the outlay required to perform the various tasks which are necessary to achieve the properly defined advertising objectives of the company. This method is considered the most rational.

Defining Advertising Effectiveness : In today's world, advertisement through any medium has become extremely expensive. Hence, it is important for the agency to ensure that the money spent on it does bring returns by way of increased sales. This could be done by way of evaluating or testing the effectiveness of advertising. Testing methods may be used to evaluate the results of an advertising campaign. By evaluating and analysing the effectiveness of advertisements that have been used, future advertisements may be improved. In addition, tests may be applied before advertisements are run. Pre-testing of an advertisement prevents expenditure that would not be profitable and leads to expenditures that give the best results. In determining advertising effectiveness the commonly used methods are given below.

Inquiries: Answer-back coupons, with same inducement, are incorporated in many advertisements. The amount of response is an indication of the effectiveness of the concerned advertisement.

Recall Tests: Here the respondents are shown the magazine cover or any other medium in which the concerned advertisement has appeared. They are then asked to tell which advertisements in that publication they remember.

Recognition Tests: Here the respondents are shown the advertisements and asked if they have read them.

Sales Tests: Here the actual sales results before and after the concerned advertising are examined. The sales results in the selected 'test markets' are also compared to those in some chosen 'control markets', i.e., the markets where the concerned advertising is not done. This is done to eliminate certain factors, other than advertising, which may also have influenced the sales.

In tourism, advertising is used extensively for promotion of various tourist products. This is a far cry from the era when colourful folders and posters were the only apparent form of travel promotion. In the field of tourism, advertising is mainly used to create initial awareness and interest in the tourist service or destination to be promoted and motivates potential tourists to decide to make further enquiries about costs, bookings, facilities, etc. It implies indirect communication with selected target groups-the potential tourists-through paid messages designed to praise a particular destination or an area. For a country which is trying to attract tourists, there can be two principal forms of advertising: (i) consumer advertising and (ii) trade advertising. To reach a wide number of consumers, such media as newspaper advertisements, radio spots, TV prime-time advertising are used. However, this form of advertisement is very expensive. For a developing nation it is extremely difficult to afford such a type of advertisement because of financial constraints. Trade advertising, on the other hand, is an indirect form of advertising and an economical method.

A large number of people today travel in groups. A tourist for various reasons chooses to travel as a member of a group, as opposed to travelling individually. The result, therefore, has been that a number of large tour operators have established their offices in such market areas. While the tour operator puts together inclusive tour packages, the tourist merely pays one package price for all services and is assured of a holiday. Such packages are then sold in retail by numerous smaller travel agents located in various market areas, and the result is that a group is formed. For a country which is trying to market its product, the area towards which these efforts are aimed is thus narrowed down to the important tour operators/ wholesalers. The media used to achieve this is large-scale advertising in travel trade journals and newspapers of international repute having travel sections.

Advertising plays a crucial role in marketing a tourist product. If the right combination of conditions is present the effect of advertising would be to increase the demand for the particular country's tourist product. Among the factors favourable to the successful use of advertising are the rising trend of demand in the particular product and an opportunity to stimulate selective demand, i.e., preference for the particular product. This is most likely where, there is a possibility of product differentials, and where consumer satisfaction depends largely on hidden qualities that cannot easily be judged at the time of purchase, or where strong emotional buying motive exists as in the case of tourism.

The American Marketing Association has defined advertising as "any paid form of non-personal presentation and promotion of ideas, goods or services by an identified sponsor". However, there have been several other definitions of advertising. One definition that may be accepted as related to all kinds of advertising is "the planned and controlled communication of persuasive ideas to a defined audience". The question may arise as to the selling function of advertising. The answer to this question is that while advertising will certainly be contributing towards sales, it cannot and does not always complete the sale.

A variety of other factors contribute to this and include pricing, distribution, dealer cooperation, etc., and all these jointly with advertising make up what is today called marketing activity. Mail order advertising, where readers send in written orders in response to press advertisements or home-delivered catalogues, is perhaps the single instance of directly related advertising selling. In other cases advertising acts as the communication factor contributing to the total selling function. In the case of service products such as tourism, banking and insurance, the direct selling action of advertising is rather limited. It must, however, be stressed that this does not mean that advertising is less important for such products.

Advertising Campaign : Any organization, in order to promote its product, has to resort to advertising to achieve desired results. Tourism organizations all over the world resort to this communication tool. Launching an advertising compaign for promoting a product is very crucial and has to be done in a planned manner. The term 'product' in the larger sense includes not only tangible products like furniture or a motorcar but also service products such as tourism, insurance, etc. There are various stages through which any advertising campaign must evolve.

Defining the Product : Before one can develop any communication of advertising for a product it is essential to know what it is that the product offers to consumers. This is very important. When you advertise soap, you are not advertising a cake of compound of alkali and oil in an attractive printed pack, but you may be advertising beauty or deodorant protection or youthfulness. To assess, therefore, what the product means to the prospective users we have to first ascertain the benefits that the users will derive from the product. Here are a few examples of this kind of benefit derivation:

- Car tyre can offer confidence, security or safety;
- Household cleaning can offer convenience, pride or hygienic conditions;
- Cosmetics can offer romance, self-confidence or glamour;

- Cigarettes can offer social status, confidence;
- Travel can offer rest, relaxation glamour, confidence or status.

The above examples show that in most cases the user benefit is not always apparent as a product feature. But it must be remembered that people buy things for the benefits they derive when using them. We must look at the product through the mind and eyes of the user. To do this it is sometimes necessary to conduct research amongst users or prospective users to find out what it is that they get from particular products. One can, at the same time, assess their knowledge, attitude and usage of competitive or substitute products so that the strengths and weaknesses of one's own product are known. This study of consumer assessment is important as in any system of communication the idea existing in the mind of the receiver will affect the interpretation of the message being received. In some cases it may prevent the message from either being noticed or perceived, let alone being received or understood.

Once we have arrived at this product benefit definition, we must then study this in relation to other factors. First, relative importance to the consumer of the several product benefits-the more important the benefit the greater its motivating values. Second, the relative position of one's own brand and substitute brands in regard to these product benefits-to create a unique and memorable message, the main ideas or benefits should be as distinctive and different from others as possible. Let us now assume that we have studied our product and its users and potential users attitude towards the product and have arrived at a definition of product benefits which we feel are most important.

Defining the Market Segments : We have a product. We know what users expect or want from it. Now we must assess how many users we have and where they are located. Most of this information will have been collected through various sources and supplied by the organization marketing the product. The kind of information that should be available will relate to the following:

CONSUMER INFORMATION

- Type of Consumer : Number, sex, age, socio-economic profile;
- Location of the Consumer: Whether they will be found in cities, small towns or rural areas or in all and in what proportion in each;
- Geographic Distribution: Whether there are any regional variations in the market spread and if so, why;
- Shopping Habits: The amount or size of individual purchases, the frequency or number of times a product is brought during a month or a year, whether bought on a regular planned basis or through an impulse decision ,at point of sale.

Decision Making: Often the person who actually buys the product does not always make the decision. It, therefore, becomes important to find out who it is that makes the decision and also the extent of the actual buyer's role in changing or influencing this decision. The reason for finding this out is to get an idea as to whom the advertising message should be directed. The person who decides is very important and in the case of joint decisions it may well be necessary to direct the advertising to two or more decision makers.

Distribution Information : Types of outlets, number of such outlets and the importance of each type; the location of these outlets in different cities, towns and rural markets; the dealer's part in the selling activity.

Sales Information : The trends over the years and any significant shifts that may have occurred in different geographic areas and the reasons for these changes is very important information. Seasonal variations that may be related to weather, festivals and other local and national reasons are also very important. In giving us all this information the manufacturer will not merely be giving us information about his product but also of competitive and substitute product against which his product will compete. All this information will provide us with a knowledge of the dimension of the market so that we will be in a position to assess which particular markets are of greater importance. This will also assist in creating the media plan to reach each market and also in creating relevant messages for each. In terms of media selection, the statistical information that will be supplied will enable to plan a campaign using media which will provide cover, reach and frequency related to the market definition.

Attitude Segmentation : This relates to segmenting the market by user motivation. For example, it has been shown that certain types of people use certain products in larger quantities and more regularly than others. In the same way, some people travel more often than others. These groups are termed the heavy-user group. And, in most cases, it is not the usual socio-economic categorisation that distinguishes them. This may be termed as attitude segmentation or separation. The problem in such segmenting or separating into two groups is that unlike socio-economic segmentation it is difficult to physically isolate the group. This can, however, be achieved through segmenting as it were the advertising message. It is important to note, however, that this sort of segmentation should not be overdone. Social appeals or segmented campaigns should only be developed if it is found that there are large enough groups of consumers who have attitude which would respond to such appeals. Often, however, it is not only the advertising that is segmented but the product itself is separately produced for each of the segments. At this stage we will have progressed from product definition to a knowledge of the market, its size, location and, different segmentation patterns.

Interpreting the Marketing Objectives

What we have been discussing until now is information of the environment in which the advertising campaign will have to work. As we know, since advertising is only the communication aspect of the total marketing function we have to take into account the marketing plans of the both enterprises in the long-term and short-term, and relate the advertising to these. The marketing objectives that are given by the enterprise will detail the plans that the enterprise has for its product in the coming year and in some cases for a few years ahead. These plans would cover items such as:

- The sales targets for the coming years broken down into regional targets or others, as the case may be.
- The distribution, merchandising and sales promotion activities planned to support the sales increase;
- The role that advertising is expected to play in creating consumers;
- The inhibiting factors which will work to prevent the enterprises from achieving the target, competitive products and their advertising, consumer attitudes, etc.

It is important to note that in any marketing operation the product formulation, packaging and pricing, distribution and availability at point of sale are all of vital importance. All that advertising can do is to bring consumer to the point of sale. But if the product is not properly made, packaged or priced or is not well merchandised or promoted at point of sale and, therefore, is not visible, then it is quite possible that the sales effect of the advertising will not fructify. This brings out the importance of integrating these various activities.

Once we have got clearly the marketing objectives of the enterprise and their plans in relation to these objectives, we can see what advertising has to communicate and to whom with a view to provide the maximum relevant support to the agreed marketing plan.

PLANNING THE ADVERTISING CAMPAIGN

We now know what we have to sell, to whom we have to sell, where the prospective consumers are located and also how the product will be made available to them. Our object now is to create an advertising campaign which will reach target audience and motivate them to come to ask for and buy the product. We have now processed all the facts that the enterprise has given and have perhaps had a dialogue with the consumer, through research, to ascertain his knowledge, attitude and usage of the product and its competitors. As a result, we have found out the proposition that we feel would be most motivating. We have also found out where the consumer is located, how and when he buys the product. We are now in a position to get down to work on two aspects which make up an advertising plan. These aspects are: (i) the creative strategy and (ii) the media plan.

Creative Strategy: Creativity in advertising is very crucial as on this depends the comprehension of the customer to understand the product. We now have to transform proposition or statement into an idea which is to be communicated to the customer. In converting the proposition into an idea, use of creativity is of paramount importance. Creativity must take into consideration direction and relevance. For the bright idea to be useful, there must be a right idea. It is this idea which has to be communicated to target group. In order to communicate the idea, media personnel, production personnel as well as creative personnel will have to be involved in this area. Finally the idea will have to be channelised into various material that will be required for advertising campaign. This can range from press advertisements to film commercials, to radio spots and TV spots, to posters and other point-of-sale material. All these items will be creative interpretation of the idea.

The Media Plan: While creativity is perhaps most closely related in an agency with the development of an idea and its interpretation into advertising material, it also plays a role in the development of a media plan. Let us know briefly the way in which an agency constructs a media plan. Media may be defined as vehicles of mass communication which are used to carry advertising messages. Very rarely, except in the case of direct-mail advertising, are media developed solely as advertising communication vehicles.

One may broadly classify media into two groups:

(a) Media which are read, seen or heard by the consumer for their 'editorial' worth. These are the newspapers, magazines, the radio programmes cinema shows, TV programmes which are read or tuned into or watched by the consumer for the 'editorial' material which they offer. The advertising benefits from the editorial climate of this media.

(b) Media, usually more 'reminder' type of media such as outdoor media, hoarding, transportation signs, posters, kiosks, neon signs, etc., which are noticed in passing only. They obtain consumer exposure due to the fact that the consumer's living habits cause him to pass by them. For instance, commuters in trains and buses, motorists and pedestrians on roads are all exposed to such media.

The above group also includes point-of-sale items. In preparing media plans one has to study the behaviour and exposure of consumer groups with regard to both kinds of media. We have to study both kinds of media. We have to study what media our target consumer looks at for 'editorial' pleasure and when he does so and in what frame of mind. By studying consumers living habits and pattern of movement we can assess which of the second group of media he will be exposed to as a general rule. In the more advanced countries it is possible to get detailed statistics on the kind of audience that each medium has. In advanced countries this information is very detailed indeed and permits one to prepare accurate media plans. In other countries, however, this information is still very scanty and apart from basic circulation information it is rare that one gets much else.

INTERNATIONAL TOURISM ADVERTISING

International Tourism Advertising is tourism-related marketing on the part of a private or public entity directed towards audiences abroad, and might target potential travelers and non-travelers alike. Wholly private firms such as travel agencies, hotel chains, cruise agencies, non-governmental organizations (NGOs) often run their own advertising campaigns to market their existence, mission, or services and/or goods offered to the consumer, and these advertisements seldom carry intentional political messages. On the other hand, advertising distributed by governments themselves, such as through tourism ministries or government-owned private sector enterprises, is sometimes intended to convey more than simply the value of the product, service, or experience; governments can use tourism ads as a channel for communicating directly to the public of other countries because tourism is a common and internationally encouraged industry and the advertising of it is subject to minimal content regulation.

As the global travel market continues to expand with yearly increasing flights among international destinations, advertising efforts on the part of the major actors in this market are also increasing. Advertising campaigns to promote travel to destinations abroad are particularly prevalent in western countries where the general public's expenditures on tourism tend to be consistently high, even in light of the economic recession. Many advertisers, which include both private entities and foreign governments themselves, share the intended goal of increasing their own revenue by popularizing their service (e.g., airline or hotel chain) or destination to boost receipts from travelers; however, some travel campaigns have additional or alternative purposes, such as promoting good public sentiments or improving existing ones towards them among the target audience. Sometimes, states may use the branding of a product or service, itself, as a means of conveying a specific message without explicitly stating the message; this tactic is often used to soften the implied message itself, thus allowing the brander to sidestep or minimize controversy and/or opposition.

Types

Tourism advertising can take many forms, utilize a wide array of advertising tactics, and be driven by a scope of private or public intents. Destination advertising is designed to make a location itself seem more appealing, while travel services advertising seeks to gain an audience's buy-in for the tourism-related service or product. Below are some instances of international tourism advertising overlapping with states' political, economic, and/or social interests.

Destination advertising

A great degree of ads promoting foreign countries are produced and distributed by the tourism ministries of those countries, so these ads often serve as vehicles for political statements and/or depictions of the destination country's desired foreign public perception(s). Following are only a few of the many examples of government-produced tourism destination advertising that also serve political or social functions.

Bahamas

The Bahamas are commonly considered to be a focal point of leisure and recreational travel in the Caribbean and the island nation advertises itself as such. Television ads and website produced by the government of the Bahamas specifically foster the image of the islands providing a carefree, exciting, culturally rich, and even romantic experience for travelers; a recent slogan for the marketing campaign was "It's better in the Bahamas" to reinforce the contrast between the desired perception as a low-stress getaway and the hectic nature of whatever living environment tourists would be leaving behind. The Bahamas have, however, actually traditionally seen high violent crime rates, so the tourism marketing attempts to focus the audience's attention on the azure water and beaches and draw it away from any negative elements of life there. Managing perceptions is a common part of advertising of many consumer products and services, focusing the audience's mind solely on the desirable aspects of whatever is being sold and away from any possible drawbacks or consequences.

India

The common impression of India in the West has long been either negative-including perceptions of widespread poverty, lack of sophisticated hygiene, and violent ethnic and religious clashes-or ambivalent, so the Indian government's Ministry of Tourism began a marketing campaign, "Incredible !ndia," to emphasize the country's rich culture, historic sites, tourist attractions, and general sense of excitement and dynamism to western audiences. Tourism is an extremely lucrative and growing global industry so it is no surprise that India, a developing nation, is striving to capitalize on that market to boost its economy. In addition, India is also looking to strengthen its international security and diplomatic ties while broadening and deepening its trade relationships, especially with the U.S., so it is in India's interest to promote a positive light for itself among the American and western voting populations in order to garner future international support and aid.

Kazakhstan

After the 2006 release of the Sacha Baron Cohen comedy Borat, which depicts a politically incorrect and socially oblivious fictional Kazakhi reporter who travels throughout the United States interviewing and meeting Americans from various walks of life, the government of Kazakhstan was highly offended by the depiction of its less than two-decade-old country and criticized the film and its creator as being defamatory and slanderous. The issue of preserving Kazakhstan's public image in light of the movie was of such high importance that Kazakh President Nursultan Nazarbayev had it listed as a main issue when he traveled to the U.S. in September 2006 to meet with then-President George W. Bush. Coupled with Nazarbeyev's visit, according to Kazakhstan embassy spokesman Roman Vassilenko, the Kazakh government staged a large-scale public relations "blitz," including "running four-page ads in The New York Times and U.S. News and World Report and commercials on CNN and the local ABC affiliate in Washington, D.C.", as well as launching TV ads to promote tourism to Kazakhstan. These travel ads specifically featured cultural and historical features of the country as well as views of its developed infrastructure, specifically to counter the type of impression given by the Borat character to the West that Kazakhstan is socially and physically underdeveloped.

Mexico

Recently in 2010 the Tourism Board of Mexico, a public office that aggregates the resources and interests of the federal, state, and municipal governments, launched a tourism advertising campaign in the United States and Canada-Mexico's two North American Free Trade Agreement (NAFTA) partners-geared towards renovating common public political and social perceptions of Mexico, including impressions of poverty, government and law enforcement corruption, petty and organized crime and drug trading, and illegal immigration into the U.S.; the new campaign's purpose is expressly demonstrated by its marketing slogan, "Mexico, the place you thought you knew." The print and television ads feature views of Mexico's beaches, natural wonders, cultural festivities, and historical artifacts like Mayan pyramids and Spanish churches in order to provide a counterbalance to the less preferable popular preconceptions. The Tourism Board's stated goal of the advertising surge is to "generat[e] more than three [positive] impressions per person" among the North American audience. The eventual goal is likely to increase tourism revenue for the country, but, for now, the Tourism Board is focusing on managing perceptions among the general populations of Mexico's two major neighboring trade partners.

Travel Services Advertising

Additionally, a wide range of foreign airlines and travel-related services which also advertise separately from the destinations, themselves, are owned by their respective governments, such as the Emirates airline (Dubai), Qatar Airways (Qatar), China Airlines(Taiwan/Republic of China), and Air China (People's Republic of China).

China Air?ways and Air China

China Airlines is the official flag carrier airline of Taiwan. The Taiwanese government refers to its state as the Republic of China and considers itself to be the legitimate, non-Communist leadership-in-exile of all of China since the Communist overthrow in the mid-1950s. The name of the airline carries the message of the long-lasting and ongoing cultural and political conflict between Communist "mainland" China (PRC) and Taiwan, that the Republic of China is the "true" China and that the state commonly referred to as "China" is illegitimate and usurped control of the country from the rightful leadership. Similarly, the PRC counters this message by having named one of its largest international carriers "Air China" to reinforce the PRC's claim to be the legitimate of the "two Chinas." The implicit conflict between the two states is likely lost on the majority of the general public outside the immediate region, such as theUnited States and Europe, but the strategic use of using advertising and targeting the international community through tourism is apparent on both sides.

Emirates

Through advertising for the Emirates airline, one of the major themes that Dubai promotes is its evolving status as a key geographic and economic player in the Middle East. Emirates advertising describes Dubai as "the perfect hub for an expanding global network" and illustrates this claim in the airline's "Centre of the World" television ad. On the other hand, Dubai subtly promotes an official stance of multinationalism and a stated intent to cater to the comfort of travelers from abroad in the Emirates' "Multinational Cabin Crew" television ad. These positions, among others, are portrayed via visually and audibly appealing commercials which are designed to relate to the target audience(s) and make the ads' messages maximally amenable to global viewers. Emirates additionally adds to its effort to appeal to the West through its sponsorship of the Arsenal Football Club, including constructing the team's new venue,Emirates Stadium, which opened in July 2006 and prominently displays the Emirates branding on the exterior; in this way, any depictions of the stadium will result in de facto advertising and reinforce the public recognition of the Emirates company as one that is associated with western sports and culture.

Emirates, along with the aviation services company Dnata, is owned by the parent company The Emirates Group which, in turn, is wholly owned by the Government of Dubai. The chairman and CEO of The Emirates Group, HH Sheikh Ahmed Bin Saeed Al Maktoum, is the younger brother of the former ruler of Dubai, HH Sheikh Rashid Bin Saeed Al Maktoum, and uncle of the current ruler, HH SheikhMohammed Bin Rashid Al Maktoum. In 1985, Sheikh Ahmed was appointed President of the Dubai Department of Civil Aviation (DCA), the governing body for airline regulation and airport control and operation. The DCA was restructured and expanded in 2007, thus creating the Dubai Civil Aviation Authority (DCAA) which has since been the airline regulatory authority in the Emirate and the Dubai Airports company which owns and operates Dubai's airports, Dubai International and the currently under-construction Dubai World Central - Al Maktoum International. Dubai International (IATA: DXB) is a primary international hub in the Middle East, offering flights to every continent except Antarctica. As of November 2010, DXB is the 6th busiest airport in the world for cargo traffic, and the 14th highest passenger throughput of all international airports.

Sheikh Ahmed currently simultaneously holds the positions of Chairman and CEO of Emirates Airline & Group, which includes the Emirates airline and Dnata air services company, Chairman of the Dubai Airports company, and President of the Dubai Civil Aviation Authority. Because Dubai's government leadership is directly involved and intertwined with private-sector enterprises, including the Emirates airline and many other facets of the tourism industry, the government there necessarily has a vested interest in the public perception of Dubai.

7

Ethics

Cyberethics is the philosophic study of ethics pertaining to computers, encompassing user behavior and what computers are programmed to do, and how this affects individuals and society.

Privacy History

In the late 19th century, the invention of cameras spurred similar ethical debates as the internet does today. During aHarvard Law Review seminar in 1890, Warren and Brandeis defined privacy from an ethical and moral point of view to be "central to dignity and individuality and personhood. Privacy is also indispensable to a sense of autonomy — to 'a feeling that there is an area of an individual's life that is totally under his or her control, an area that is free from outside intrusion.' The deprivation of privacy can even endanger a person's health." Over 100 years later, the internet and proliferation of private data through governments and ecommerce is a phenomenon which requires a new round of ethical debate involving a person's privacy.

Privacy can be decomposed to the limitation of others' access to an individual with "three elements of secrecy, anonymity, and solitude." Anonymity refers to the individual's right to protection from undesired attention. Solitude refers to the lack of physical proximity of an individual to others. Secrecy refers to the protection of personalized information from being freely distributed.

Individuals surrender private information when conducting transactions and registering for services. Ethical business practice protects the privacy of their customers by securing information which may contribute to the loss of secrecy, anonymity, and solitude. Credit card information, social security numbers, phone numbers, mothers' maiden names, addresses and phone numbers freely collected and shared over the internet may lead to a loss of Privacy.

Fraud and impersonation are some of the malicious activities that occur due to the direct or indirect abuse of private information. Identity theft is rising rapidly due to the availability of private information in the internet. For instance, seven million Americans fell victim to identity theft in 2002, and nearly 12 million Americans were victims of identity theft in 2011 making it the fastest growing crime in the United States. Public records search engines and databases are the main culprits contributing to the rise of cybercrime. Listed below are a few recommendations to restrict online databases from proliferating sensitive personnel information.

1. Exclude sensitive unique identifiers from database records such as social security numbers, birth dates, hometown and mothers' maiden names.
2. Exclude phone numbers that are normally unlisted.
3. Clear provision of a method which allows people to have their names removed from a database.
4. Banning the reverse social security number lookup services.

Private Data Collection

Data warehouses are used today to collect and store huge amounts of personal data and consumer transactions. These facilities can preserve large volumes of consumer information for an indefinite amount of time. Some of the key architectures contributing to the erosion of privacy include databases, cookies and spyware.

Some may argue that data warehouses are supposed to stand alone and be protected. However, the fact is enough personal information can be gathered from corporate websites and social networking sites to initiate a reverse lookup. Therefore, is it not important to address some of the ethical issues regarding how protected data ends up in the public domain?

As a result, identity theft protection businesses are on the rise. Companies such as LifeLock and JPMorgan Chase have begun to capitalize on selling identity theft protection insurance.

Property

Ethical debate has long included the concept of property. This concept has created many clashes in the world of cyberethics. One philosophy of the internet is centered around the freedom of information. The controversy over ownership occurs when the property of information is infringed upon or uncertain.

Intellectual Property Rights

The ever-increasing speed of the internet and the emergence of compression technology, such as mp3 opened the doors to Peer-to-peer file sharing, a technology that allowed users to anonymously transfer files to each other, previously seen on programs such as Napster or now seen through communications protocol such as BitTorrent. Much of this, however, was copyrighted music and illegal to transfer to other users. Whether it is ethical to transfer copyrighted media is another question.

Proponents of unrestricted file sharing point out how file sharing has given people broader and faster access to media, has increased exposure to new artists, and has reduced the costs of transferring media (including less environmental damage). Supporters of restrictions on file sharing argue that we must protect the income of our artists and other people who work to create our media. This argument is partially answered by pointing to the small proportion of money artists receive from the legitimate sale of media.

We also see a similar debate over intellectual property rights in respect to software ownership. The two opposing views are for closed source software distributed under restrictive licenses or for free and open source software. The argument can be made that restrictions are required because companies would not invest weeks and months in development if there is no incentive for revenue generated from sales and licensing fees. A counter argument to this is that standing on shoulders of giants is far cheaper when the giants don't hold IP rights. Some proponents for open source believe that all programs should be available to anyone who wants to study them.

Digital Rights Management (DRM)

With the introduction of digital rights management software, new issues are raised over whether the subverting of DRM is ethical. Some champion the hackers of DRM as defenders of users' rights, allowing the blind to make audio books of PDFs they receive, allowing people to burn music they have legitimately bought to CD or to transfer it to a new computer. Others see this as nothing but simply a violation of the rights of the intellectual property holders, opening the door to uncompensated use of copyrighted media.

Security

Security has long been a topic of ethical debate. Is it better to protect the common good of the community or rather should we safeguard the rights of the individual? There is a continual dispute over the boundaries between the two and which compromises are right to make. As an ever increasing amount of people connect to the internet and more and more personal data is available online there is susceptibility to identity theft, cyber crimes and computer hacking. This also leads to the question of who has the right to regulate the internet in the interest of security?

Accuracy

Due to the ease of accessibility and sometimes collective nature of the internet we often come across issues of accuracy e. g. who is responsible for the authenticity and fidelity of the information available online? Ethically this includes debate over who should be allowed to contribute content and who should be held accountable if there are errors in the content or if it is false. This also brings up the question of how is the injured party, if any, to be made whole and under which jurisdicti-ondoes the offense lay?

Accessibility, Censorship and Filtering

Accessibility, censorship and filtering bring up many ethical issues that have several branches in cyberethics. Many questions have arisen which continue to challenge our understanding of privacy, security and our participation in society. Throughout the centuries mechanisms have been constructed in the name of protection and security. Today the applications are in the form of software that filters domains and content so that they may not be easily accessed or obtained without elaborate circumvention or on a personal and business level through free or content-control software. Internet censorship and filtering are used to control or suppress the publishing or accessing of information. The legal issues are similar to offline censorship and filtering. The same arguments that apply to offline censorship and filtering apply to online censorship and filtering; whether people are better off with free access to information or should be protected from what is considered by a governing body as harmful, indecent or illicit. The fear of access by minors drives much of the concern and many online advocate groups have sprung up to raise awareness and of controlling the accessibility of minors to the internet.

Censorship and filtering occurs on small to large scales, whether it be a company restricting their employees' access to cyberspace by blocking certain websites which are deemed as relevant only to personal usage and therefore damaging to productivity or on a larger scale where a government creates large firewalls which censor and filter access to certain information available online frequently from outside their country to their citizens and anyone within their borders. One of the most famous examples of a country controlling access is the Golden Shield Project, also referred to as the Great Firewall of China, a censorship and surveillance project set up and operated by the People's Republic of China. Another instance is the 2000 case of the League Against Racism and Antisemitism (LICRA), French Union of Jewish Students, vs. Yahoo! Inc (USA) and Yahoo! France, where the French Court declared that "access by French Internet users to the auction website containing Nazi objects constituted a contravention of French law and an offence to the 'collective memory' of the country and that the simple act of displaying such objects (e. g. exhibition of uniforms, insignia or emblems resembling those worn or displayed by the Nazis) in France constitutes a violation of the Article R645-1 of the Penal Code and is therefore considered as a threat to internal public order." Since the French judicial ruling many websites must abide by the rules of the countries in which they are accessible.

Freedom of Information

Freedom of information, that is the freedom of speech as well as the freedom to seek, obtain and impart information brings up the question of who or what, has the jurisdiction in cyberspace. The right of freedom of information is commonly subject to limitations dependent upon the country, society and culture concerned.

Generally there are three standpoints on the issue as it relates to the internet. First is the argument that the internet is a form of media, put out and accessed by citizens of governments and therefore should be regulated by each individual government within the borders of their respective jurisdictions. Second, is that, "Governments of the Industrial World... have no sovereignty [over the internet]... We have no elected government, nor are we likely to have one,... You have no moral right to rule us nor do you possess any methods of enforcement we have true reason to fear." A third party believes that the internet supersedes all tangible borders such as the borders of countries, authority should be given to an international body since what is legal in one country may be against the law in the other.

Digital divide

An issue specific to the ethical issues of the freedom of information is what is known as the digital divide. This refers to the unequal socio-economic divide between those who have access to digital and information technology such as cyberspace and those who have limited or no access at all. This gap of access between countries or regions of the world is called theglobal digital divide.

Sexuality and Pornography

Sexuality in terms of sexual orientation, infidelity, sex with or between minors, public display and pornography have always stirred ethical controversy. These issues are reflected online to varying degrees. In terms of its resonance, the historical development of the online pornography industry and user-generated content have been the studied by media academics. One of the largest cyberethical debates is over the regulation, distribution and accessibility of pornography online. Hardcore pornographic material is generally controlled by governments with laws regarding how old one has to be to obtain it and what forms are acceptable or not. The availability of pornography online calls into question jurisdiction as well as brings up the problem of regulation in particular over child pornography, which is illegal in most countries, as well as pornography involving violence or animals, which is restricted within most countries.

Gambling

Gambling is often a topic in ethical debate as some view it as inherently wrong and support prohibition while others support no legal interference at all. "Between these extremes lies a multitude of opinions on what types of gambling the government should permit and where it should be allowed to take place. Discussion of gambling forces public policy makers to deal with issues as diverse as addiction, tribal rights, taxation, senior living, professional and college sports, organized crime, neurobiology, suicide, divorce, and religion." Due to its controversy gambling is either banned or heavily controlled on local or national levels. The accessibility of the internet and its ability to cross geographic-borders have led to illegal online gambling, often offshore operations. Over the years online gambling, both legal and illegal, has grown exponentially which has led to difficulties in regulation. This enormous growth has even called into question by some the ethical place of gambling online.

Related organizations

The following organizations are of notable interest in the cyberethics debate:

- International Federation for Information Processing (IFIP)
- Association for Computing Machinery, Special Interest Group: Computers and Society (SIGCAS)
- Electronic Privacy Information Center (EPIC)
- Electronic Frontier Foundation (EFF)
- International Center for Information Ethics (ICIE)
- Directions and Implications in Advanced Computing (DIAC)
- The Centre for Computing and Social Responsibility (CCSR)
- Cyber-Rights and Cyber-liberties
- International Journal of Cyber Ethics in Education IJCEE (www. igi-global. com/ijcee)

Codes of ethics in computing

Four notable examples of ethics codes for IT professionals are listed below:

RFC 1087

In January 1989, the Internet Architecture Board (IAB) in RFC 1087 defines an activity as unethical and unacceptable if it:

1. Seeks to gain unauthorized access to the resources of the Internet.
2. Disrupts the intended use of the Internet.
3. Wastes resources (people, capacity, computer) through such actions.
4. Destroys the integrity of computer-based information, or
5. Compromises the privacy of users.

The Code of Fair Information Practices

The Code of Fair Information Practices is based on five principles outlining the requirements for records keeping systems. This requirement was implemented in 1973 by the U. S. Department of Health, Education and Welfare.

1. There must be no personal data record-keeping systems whose very existence is secret.
2. There must be a way for a person to find out what information about the person is in a record and how it is used.
3. There must be a way for a person to prevent information about the person that was obtained for one purpose from being used or made available for other purposes without the person's consent.
4. There must be a way for a person to correct or amend a record of identifiable information about the person.
5. Any organization creating, maintaining, using, or disseminating records of identifiable personal data must assure the reliability of the data for their intended use and must take precautions to prevent misuses of the data.

Ten Commandments of Computer Ethics

The ethical values as defined in 1992 by the Computer Ethics Institute; a nonprofit organization whose mission is to advance technology by ethical means, lists these rules as a guide to computer ethics:

1. Thou shalt not use a computer to harm other people.
2. Thou shalt not interfere with other people's computer work.
3. Thou shalt not snoop around in other people's computer files.
4. Thou shalt not use a computer to steal.
5. Thou shalt not use a computer to bear false witness.
6. Thou shalt not copy or use proprietary software for which you have not paid.
7. Thou shalt not use other people's computer resources without authorization or proper compensation.
8. Thou shalt not appropriate other people's intellectual output.
9. Thou shalt think about the social consequences of the program you are writing or the system you are designing.
10. Thou shalt always use a computer in ways that ensure consideration and respect for your fellow humans.

(ISC) code of ethics

(ISC) an organization committed to certification of computer security professional has further defined its own code of ethics generally as:

1. Act honestly, justly, responsibly, and legally, and protecting the commonwealth.
2. Work diligently and provide competent services and advance the security profession.
3. Encourage the growth of research – teach, mentor, and value the certification.

4. Discourage unsafe practices, and preserve and strengthen the integrity of public infrastructures.
5. Observe and abide by all contracts, expressed or implied, and give prudent advice.
6. Avoid any conflict of interest, respect the trust that others put in you, and take on only those jobs you are qualified to perform.
7. Stay current on skills, and do not become involved with activities that could injure the reputation of other security professionals.

What is Cyber Law?

In order to arrive at an acceptable definition of the term Cyber Law, we must first understand the meaning of the term law.

Simply put, law encompasses the rules of conduct:

1. that have been approved by the government, and
2. which are in force over a certain territory, and
3. which must be obeyed by all persons on that territory.

Violation of these rules will lead to government action such as imprisonment or fine or an order to pay compensation.

The term cyber or cyberspace has today come to signify everything related to computers, the Internet, websites, data, emails, networks, software, data storage devices (such as hard disks, USB disks etc) and even electronic devices such as cell phones, ATM machines etc. Thus a simplified definition of cyber law is that it is the "law governing cyber space". The issues addressed by cyber law include:

1. Cyber crime1
2. Electronic commerce2
3. Intellectual Property in as much as it applies to cyberspace3
4. Data protection & privacy4

For sake of convenience we shall briefly discuss the development of cyber law around the world under two heads – international measures and national measures.

International Measures

The first comprehensive international effort dealing with the criminal law problems of computer crime was initiated by the Organisation for Economic Co-operation and Development (OECD)6. From 1983 to 1985, an ad hoc committee of OECD discussed the possibilities of an international harmonization of criminal laws in order to fight computer-related economic crime. In September 1985, the committee recommended that member countries consider the extent to which knowingly committed acts in the field of computer-related abuse should be criminalized and covered by national penal legislation.

In 1986, based on a comparative analysis of substantive law, OECD suggested that the following list of acts could constitute a common denominator for the different approaches being taken by member countries:

1. The input, alteration, erasure and/or suppression of computer data and/or computer programs made willfully with the intent to commit an illegal transfer of funds or of another thing of value;
2. The input, alteration, erasure and/or suppression of computer data and/or computer programs made willfully with the intent to commit a forgery;
3. The input, alteration, erasure and/or suppression of computer data and/or computer programs, or other interference with computer systems, made willfully with the intent to hinder the functioning of a computer and/or telecommunication system;
4. The infringement of the exclusive right of the owner of a protected computer program with the intent to exploit commercially the program and put in on the market;
5. The access to or the interception of a computer and/or telecommunication system made knowingly and without the authorization of the person responsible for the system, either (i) by infringement of security measures or (ii) for other dishonest or harmful intentions."

From 1985 to 1989, the Select Committee of Experts on Computer-Related Crime of the Council of Europe discussed the legal problems of computer crime. The Select Committee and the European Committee on Crime Problems prepared Recommendation No. R(89)9, which was adopted by the Council on 13 September 1989.

This document "recommends the Governments of Member States to take into account, when reviewing their legislation or initiating new legislation, the report on computer-related crime... and in particular the guidelines for the national legislatures".

The guidelines for national legislatures include a minimum list, which reflects the general consensus of the Committee regarding certain computer-related abuses that should be dealt with by criminal law, as well as an optional list, which describes acts that have already been penalized in some States, but on which an international consensus for criminalization could not be reached.

The minimum list of offences for which uniform criminal policy on legislation concerning computer-related crime had been achieved enumerates the following offences:

1. Computer fraud. The input, alteration, erasure or suppression of computer data or computer programs, or other interference with the course of data processing that influences the result of data processing, thereby causing economic or possessory loss of property of another

person with the intent of procuring an unlawful economic gain for himself or for another person;

2. Computer forgery. The input, alteration, erasure or suppression of computer data or computer programs, or other interference with the course of data processing in a manner or under such conditions, as prescribed by national law, that it would constitute the offence of forgery if it had been committed with respect to a traditional object of such an offence;
3. Damage to computer data or computer programs. The erasure, damaging, deterioration or suppression of computer data or computer programs without right;
4. Computer sabotage. The input, alteration, erasure or suppression of computer data or computer programs, or other interference with computer systems, with the intent to hinder the functioning of a computer or a telecommuni-cations system;
5. Unauthorized access. The access without right to a computer system or network by infringing security measures;
6. Unauthorized interception. The interception, made without right and by technical means, of communications to, from and within a computer system or network;
7. Unauthorized reproduction of a protected computer program. The reproduction, distribution or communication to the public without right of a computer program which is protected by law;
8. Unauthorized reproduction of a topography. The reproduction without right of a topography protected by law, of a semiconductor product, or the commercial exploitation or the importation for that purpose, done without right, of a topography or of a semiconductor product manufactured by using the topography.

The optional list relates to the following:

1. Alteration of computer data or computer programs. The alteration of computer data or computer programs without right;
2. Computer espionage. The acquisition by improper means or the disclosure, transfer or use of a trade or commercial secret without right or any other legal justification, with intent either to cause economic loss to the person entitled to the secret or to obtain an unlawful economic advantage for oneself or a third person;
3. Unauthorized use of a computer. The use of a computer system or network without right, that either: (i) is made with the acceptance of significant risk of loss being caused to the person entitled to use the system or harm to the system or its functioning, or (ii) is made with the intent to cause loss to the person entitled to use the system or harm to the system or its functioning, or (iii) causes loss to the person entitled to use the system or harm to the system or its functioning;

4. Unauthorized use of a protected computer program. The use without right of a computer program which is protected by law and which has been reproduced without right, with the intent, either to procure an unlawful economic gain for himself or for another person or to cause harm to the holder of the right.

In 1990, the legal aspects of computer crime were also discussed by the United Nations, particularly at the Eighth United Nations Congress on the Prevention of Crime and the Treatment of Offenders, at Havana, as well as at the accompanying symposium on computer crime organized by the Foundation for Responsible Computing. The Eighth United Nations Congress adopted a resolution on computer-related crime. In its resolution 45/121, the General Assembly welcomed the instruments and resolutions adopted by the Eighth Congress and invited Governments to be guided by them in the formulation of appropriate legislation and policy directives in accordance with the economic, social, legal, cultural and political circumstances of each country. The United Nations Commission on International Trade Law (UNCITRAL) formulated the UNCITRAL Model Law on Electronic Commerce in 1996. The Model Law is intended to facilitate the use of modern means of communication and storage of information. It is based on the establishment of a functional equivalent in electronic media for paper-based concepts such as "writing", "signature" and "original".

The Convention on Cybercrime of the Council of Europe is currently the only binding international instrument on the issue of cyber crime. The convention serves as a guideline for countries developing a comprehensive national legislation against Cybercrime. It also serves as a framework for international cooperation between State Parties to the treaty7.

The Convention is supplemented by a Protocol on Xenophobia and Racism committed through computer systems.

NATIONAL MEASURES

Being at the forefront of computer technology, and being the country that developed what is today referred to as the Internet, the USA has been the global leader in developing laws relating to cyber crime.

In 1977, Senator Abraham Ribicoff introduced the first Federal Systems Protection Act Bill. This evolved into House Bill 5616 in 1986, which resulted in the Computer Fraud and Abuse Act of 1987 established as Article 1030, Chapter 47 of Title 18 of Criminal Code. The US states of Florida, Michigan, Colorado, Rhode Island and Arizona were the first to have computer crime laws based on the first Ribicoff bill8.

Some of the earlier relevant federal legislations include the Communications Fraud and Abuse Act of 1986, the Electronic Communications Privacy Act of 1986, the Credit Card Fraud Act of 1984, the Federal Copyright Act of 1976 and the Wire Fraud Act.

Also relevant are provisions of the Electronic Fund Transfer Act (Title XX of Financial Institutions Regulatory and Interest Rate Control Act of 1978) and the Federal Privacy Act of 1974 (codified in 5 USC Sect. 552a).

Some of the more recent US legislations relevant to cyber law are the 'No Electronic Theft' Act (1997), the Digital Millennium Copyright Act (1998), the Internet Tax Freedom Act (1998), the Child Online Protection Act (1998), the U. S. Trademark Cyberpiracy Prevention Act (1999), the Uniform Electronic Transactions Act (UETA) (1999), the Uniform Computer Information Transactions Act (UCITA) (2000), the Electronic Signatures in Global & National Commerce Act (E-Sign) (2000), the Children's Internet Protection Act (2001) and the USA Patriot Act (2001).

In China, the relevant laws are the Computer Information Network and Internet Security, Protection and Management Regulations (1997), the Regulations on Computer Software Protection (2002) and the Criminal Law of the People's Republic of China (1979) as revised in 1997.

In Australia the relevant law for cyber crime is the Cybercrime Act (2001) and the revised Criminal Code Act (1995). For electronic commerce, the relevant law is the Electronic Transactions Act 1999. Also relevant is The Commonwealth's Privacy Act (1988).

In Canada, the relevant law for cyber crime is the Criminal Code as amended to include computer crimes. For electronic commerce, the relevant law is the Electronic Transactions Act (2001).

In Malaysia, the relevant law for cyber crime is the Computer Crimes Act (1997). For electronic commerce, the relevant law is the Digital Signatures Act (1997).

In Singapore the relevant law for cyber crime is the Computer Misuse Act. For electronic commerce, the relevant law is the Electronic Transactions Act (1998).

In United Arab Emirates (UAE), the relevant law for cyber crime is the Federal Law No. 2 of 2006 Combating Information Technology Crimes. For electronic commerce, the relevant law is the Law No. 2 of 2002 of the Emirate of Dubai – Electronic Transactions and Commerce Law.

In the United Kingdom the relevant laws for cyber crime are the Forgery and Counterfeiting Act (1981), Computer Misuse Act (1990), Data Protection Act (1998), Terrorism Act (2000), Regulation of Investigatory Powers Act (2000), Anti-terrorism, Crime and Security Act (2001) and Fraud Act (2006). For electronic commerce, the relevant laws are the Electronic Communications Act (2000) and the Electronic Signatures Regulations (2002).

In Japan the relevant laws for cyber crime are the Unauthorized Computer Access Law (Law No. 128 of 1999) and the Online Dating Site Regulating Act (June 2008).

In India, the primary legislation for cyber crimes as well as electronic commerce is the Information Technology Act (2000) as amended by the

Information Technology (Amendment) Act, 2008. Also relevant for cyber crimes is the amended Indian Penal Code.

Legal aspects of Computing

Legal aspects of computing are related to the overlapping areas of law andcomputing.

The first one, historically, was **information technology law** (or **IT law**). *("IT law" should not be confused with the IT aspects of law itself, although there are overlapping issues.)* **IT law** consists of the law (statutes, regulations, and caselaw) which governs the digital dissemination of both (digitalized) information and software itself, and legal aspects of information technologymore broadly. IT law covers mainly the digital information (including information security and electronic commerce) aspects and it has been described as "paper laws" for a "paperless environment".

Cyberlaw or **Internet law** is a term that encapsulates the legal issues related to use of the Internet. It is less a distinct field of law than intellectual property or contract law, as it is a domain covering many areas of law and regulation. Some leading topics include internet access and usage, privacy, freedom of expression, and jurisdiction.

"Computer law" is a third term which tends to relate to issues including both Internet law and the patent and copyright aspects of computer technology and software.

Areas of Law

There are intellectual property in general, including copyright, rules on fair use, and special rules on copy protection for digital media, and circumvention of such schemes. The area of software patents is controversial, and still evolving in Europe and elsewhere.

The related topics of software licenses, end user license agreements, free software licenses and open-source licenses can involve discussion of product liability, professional liability of individual developers, warranties, contract law, trade secrets and intellectual property.

In various countries, areas of the computing and communi-cation industries are regulated – often strictly – by government bodies. There are rules on the uses to which computers and computer networks may be put, in particular there are rules onunauthorized access, data privacy and spamming. There are also limits on the use of encryption and of equipment which may be used to defeat copy protection schemes. The export of hardware and software between certain states within theUnited States is also controlled.

There are laws governing trade on the Internet, taxation, consumer protection, and advertising.

There are laws on censorship versus freedom of expression, rules on public access to government information, and individual access to information held on them by private bodies. There are laws on what data must be retained for law enforcement, and what may not be gathered or retained, for privacy reasons.

In certain circumstances and jurisdictions, computer communications may be used in evidence, and to establish contracts. New methods of tapping and surveillance made possible by computers have wildly differing rules on how they may be used by law enforcement bodies and as evidence in court.

Computerized voting technology, from polling machines to internet and mobile-phone voting, raise a host of legal issues.

Some states limit access to the Internet, by law as well as by technical means.

Jurisdiction

Issues of jurisdiction and sovereignty have quickly come to the fore in the era of the Internet.

Jurisdiction is an aspect of state sovereignty and it refers to judicial, legislative and administrative competence. Although jurisdiction is an aspect of sovereignty, it is not coextensive with it. The laws of a nation may have extraterritorial impact extending the jurisdiction beyond the sovereign and territorial limits of that nation. This is particularly problematic as the medium of the Internet does not explicitly recognize sovereignty and territorial limitations. There is no uniform, international jurisdictional law of universal application, and such questions are generally a matter of conflict of laws, particularly private international law. An example would be where the contents of a web site are legal in one country and illegal in another. In the absence of a uniform jurisdictional code, legal practitioners are generally left with a conflict of law issue.

Another major problem of cyberlaw lies in whether to treat the Internet as if it were physical space (and thus subject to a given jurisdiction's laws) or to act as if the Internet is a world unto itself (and therefore free of such restraints). Those who favor the latter view often feel that government should leave the Internet community to self-regulate. John Perry Barlow, for example, has addressed the governments of the world and stated, "Where there are real conflicts, where there are wrongs, we will identify them and address them by our means. We are forming our own Social Contract. This governance will arise according to the conditions of our world, not yours. Our world is different". A more balanced alternative is the Declaration of Cybersecession: "Human beings possess a mind, which they are absolutely free to inhabit with no legal constraints. Human civilization is developing its own (collective) mind. All we want is to be free to inhabit it with no legal constraints. Since you make sure we cannot harm you, you have no ethical right to intrude our lives. So stop intruding!" Other scholars argue for more of a compromise between the two notions, such as Lawrence Lessig's argument that "The problem for law is to work out how the norms of the two communities are to apply given that the subject to whom they apply may be in both places at once" (Lessig, Code 190).

With the internationalism of the Internet, jurisdiction is a much more tricky area than before, and courts in different countries have taken various views on whether they have jurisdiction over items published on the Internet, or business agreements entered into over the Internet. This can cover areas from contract law, trading standards and tax, through rules onunauthorized access, data privacy and spamming to more political areas such as freedom of speech, censorship, libel or sedition.

Certainly, the frontier idea that the law does not apply in "Cyberspace" is not true. In fact, conflicting laws from different jurisdictions may apply, simultaneously, to the same event. The Internet does not tend to make geographical and jurisdictional boundaries clear, but Internet users remain in physical jurisdictions and are subject to laws independent of their presence on the Internet. As such, a single transaction may involve the laws of at least three jurisdictions:

1. the laws of the state/nation in which the user resides,
2. the laws of the state/nation that apply where the server hosting the transaction is located, and
3. the laws of the state/nation which apply to the person or business with whom the transaction takes place.

So a user in one of the United States conducting a transaction with another user in Britain through a server in Canada could theoretically be subject to the laws of all three countries as they relate to the transaction at hand.

In practical terms, a user of the Internet is subject to the laws of the state or nation within which he or she goes online. Thus, in the U. S., Jake Baker faced criminal charges for his e-conduct, and numerous users of peer-to-peer file-sharingsoftware were subject to civil lawsuits for copyright infringement. This system runs into conflicts, however, when these suits are international in nature. Simply put, legal conduct in one nation may be decidedly illegal in another. In fact, even different standards concerning the burden of proof in a civil case can cause jurisdictional problems. For example, an American celebrity, claiming to be insulted by an online American magazine, faces a difficult task of winning a lawsuit against that magazine for libel. But if the celebrity has ties, economic or otherwise, to England, he or she can sue for libel in the British court system, where the standard of "libelous speech" is far lower.

Internet governance is a live issue in international fora such as the International Telecommunication Union (ITU), and the role of the current US-based co-ordinating body, the Internet Corporation for Assigned Names and Numbers (ICANN) was discussed in the UN-sponsored World Summit on the Information Society (WSIS) in December 2003

INTERNET LAW

The law that regulates the Internet must be considered in the context of the geographic scope of the Internet and political borders that are crossed in the process of sending data around the globe. The unique global structure of the Internet raises not only jurisdictional issues, that is, the authority to make and enforce laws affecting the Internet, but also questions concerning the nature of the laws themselves.

In their essay "Law and Borders — The Rise of Law in Cyberspace", David R. Johnson and David G. Post argue that it became necessary for the Internet to govern itself and instead of obeying the laws of a particular country, "Internet citizens" will obey the laws of electronic entities like service providers. Instead of identifying as a physical person, Internet citizens will be known by their usernames or email addresses (or, more recently, by their Facebook accounts). Over time, suggestions that the Internet can be self-regulated as being its own trans-national "nation" are being supplanted by a multitude of external and internal regulators and forces, both governmental and private, at many different levels. The nature of Internet law remains a legal paradigm shift, very much in the process of development.

Leaving aside the most obvious examples of governmental content monitoring and internet censorship in nations like China, Saudi Arabia, Iran, there are four primary forces or modes of regulation of the Internet derived from a socioeconomic theory referred to as Pathetic dot theory by Lawrence Lessig in his book, Code and Other Laws of Cyberspace:

1. **Law**: What Lessig calls "Standard East Coast Code," from laws enacted by government in Washington D. C. This is the most self-evident of the four modes of regulation. As the numerous United States statutes, codes, regulations, and evolving case law make clear, many actions on the Internet are already subject to conventional laws, both with regard to transactions conducted on the Internet and content posted. Areas like gambling, child pornography, and fraud are regulated in very similar ways online as off-line. While one of the most controversial and unclear areas of evolving laws is the determination of what forum has subject matter jurisdiction over activity (economic and other) conducted on the internet, particularly as cross border transactions affect local jurisdictions, it is certainly clear that substantial portions of internet activity are subject to traditional regulation, and that conduct that is unlawful off-line is

presumptively unlawful online, and subject to traditional enforcement of similar laws and regulations.

2. **Architecture**: What Lessig calls "West Coast Code," from the programming code of the Silicon Valley. These mechanisms concern the parameters of how information can and cannot be transmitted across the Internet. Everything from internet filtering software (which searches for keywords or specific URLs and blocks them before they can even appear on the computer requesting them), to encryption programs, to the very basic architecture of TCP/IP protocols and user interfaces falls within this category of mainly private regulation. It is arguable that all other modes of internet regulation either rely on, or are significantly affected by, West Coast Code.
3. **Norms**: As in all other modes of social interaction, conduct is regulated by social norms and conventions in significant ways. While certain activities or kinds of conduct online may not be specifically prohibited by the code architecture of the Internet, or expressly prohibited by traditional governmental law, nevertheless these activities or conduct are regulated by the standards of the community in which the activity takes place, in this case internet "users." Just as certain patterns of conduct will cause an individual to be ostracized from our real world society, so too certain actions will be censored or self-regulated by the norms of whatever community one chooses to associate with on the internet.
4. **Markets**: Closely allied with regulation by social norms, markets also regulate certain patterns of conduct on the Internet. While economic markets will have limited influence over non-commercial portions of the Internet, the Internet also creates a virtual marketplace for information, and such information affects everything from the comparative valuation of services to the traditional valuation of stocks. In addition, the increase in popularity of the Internet as a means for transacting all forms of commercial activity, and as a forum for advertisement, has brought the laws of supply and demand to cyberspace. Market forces of supply and demand also affect connectivity to the Internet, the cost of bandwidth, and the availability of software to facilitate the creation, posting, and use of internet content.

These forces or regulators of the Internet do not act independently of each other. For example, governmental laws may be influenced by greater societal norms, and markets affected by the nature and quality of the code that operates a particular system.

Net Neutrality

Another major area of interest is net neutrality, which affects the regulation of the infrastructure of the Internet. Though not obvious to most Internet users, every packet of data sent and received by every user on the Internet passes through routers and transmission infrastructure owned by a collection of private and public entities, including telecommunications companies, universities, and governments. This is turning into one of the most critical aspects of cyberlaw and has immediate jurisdictional implications, as laws in force in one jurisdiction have the potential to have dramatic effects in other jurisdictions when host servers or telecommunications companies are affected.

Free Speech on the Internet

Article 19 of the Universal Declaration of Human Rights calls for the protection of free expression in all media.

In comparison to traditional print-based media, the accessibility and relative anonymity of cyber space has torn down traditional barriers between an individual and his or her ability to publish. Any person with an internet connection has the potential to reach an audience of millions with little-to-no distribution costs. Yet this new form of highly accessible authorship in cyber space raises questions and perhaps magnifies legal complexities relating to the freedom and regulation of speech in cyberspace.

These complexities have taken many forms, three notable examples being the Jake Baker incident, in which the limits of obscene Internet postings were at issue, the controversial distribution of the DeCSS code, and Gutnick v Dow Jones, in which libel laws were considered in the context of online publishing. The last example was particularly significant because it epitomized the complexities inherent to applying one country's laws (nation-specific by definition) to the internet (international by nature). In 2003, Jonathan Zittrain considered this issue in his paper, "Be Careful What You Ask For: Reconciling a Global Internet and Local Law".

In the UK the case of Keith-Smith v Williams confirmed that existing libel laws applied to internet discussions.

In terms of the tort liability of ISPs and hosts of internet forums, Section 230(c) of the Communications Decency Act may provide immunity in the United States.

Internet Censorship

In many countries, speech through cyberspace has proven to be another means of communication which has been regulated by the government. The "Open Net Initiative", whose mission statement is "to investigate and challenge state filtration and surveillance practices" to "... generate a credible picture of these practices," has released numerous reports documenting the filtration of internet-speech in various countries. While China has thus far proven to be the most rigorous in its attempts to filter unwanted parts of the internet from its citizens, many other countries - including Singapore, Iran, Saudi Arabia, and Tunisia - have engaged in similar practices of Internet censorship. In one of the most vivid examples of information control, the Chinese government for a short time transparently forwarded requests to the Google search engine to its own, state-controlled search engines.

These examples of filtration bring to light many underlying questions concerning the freedom of speech. For example, does the government have a legitimate role in limiting access to information? And if so, what forms of regulation are acceptable? For example, some argue that the blocking of "blogspot" and other websites in India failed to reconcile the conflicting interests of speech and expression on the one hand and legitimate government concerns on the other hand.

The Creation of Privacy in U. S. Internet Law

Warren and Brandeis

At the close of the 19th Century, concerns about privacy captivated the general public, and led to the 1890 publication of Samuel Warren and Louis Brandeis: "The Right to Privacy". The vitality of this article can be seen today, when examining the USSC decision of Kyllo v. United States, 533 U. S. 27 (2001) where it is cited by the majority, those in concurrence, and even those in dissent.

The motivation of both authors to write such an article is heavily debated amongst scholars, however, two developments during this time give some insight to the reasons behind it. First, the sensationalistic press and the concurrent rise and use of "yellow journalism" to promote the sale of newspapers in the time following the Civil War brought privacy to the forefront of the public eye. The other reason that brought privacy to the forefront of public concern was the technological development of "instant photography". This article set the stage for all privacy legislation to follow during the 20 and 21st Centuries.

Reasonable Expectation of Privacy Test and emerging technology

In 1967, the United States Supreme Court decision in Katz v United States, 389 U. S. 347 (1967) established what is known as the Reasonable Expectation of Privacy Test to determine the applicability of the Fourth Amendment in a given situation. It should be noted that the test was not noted by the majority, but instead it was articulated by the concurring opinion of Justice Harlan. Under this test, 1) a person must exhibit an "actual (subjective) expectation of privacy" and 2) "the expectation [must] be one that society is prepared to recognize as 'reasonable.'"

Privacy Act of 1974

Inspired by the Watergate scandal, the United States Congress enacted the Privacy Act of 1974 just four months after the resignation of then President Richard Nixon. In passing this Act, Congress found that "the privacy of an individual is directly affected by the collection, maintenance, use, and dissemination of personal information by Federal agencies" and that "the increasing use of computers and sophisticated information technology, while essential to the efficient operations of the Government, has greatly magnified the harm to individual privacy that can occur from any collection, maintenance, use, or dissemination of personal information."

Foreign Intelligence Surveillance Act of 1978

Codified at 50 U. S. C. §§ 1801-1811, this act establishes standards and procedures for use of electronic surveillance to collect "foreign intelligence" within the United States. §1804(a)(7)(B). FISA overrides the Electronic Communications Privacy Act during investigations when foreign intelligence is "a significant purpose" of said investigation. 50 U. S. C. § 1804(a)(7)(B) and §1823(a)(7)(B). Another interesting result of FISA, is the creation of the Foreign Intelligence Surveillance Court (FISC). All FISA orders are reviewed by this special court of federal district judges. The FISC meets in secret, with all proceedings usually also held from both the public eye and those targets of the desired surveillance.

(1986) Electronic Communication Privacy Act

The ECPA represents an effort by the United States Congress to modernize federal wiretap law. The ECPA amended Title III and included two new acts in response to developing computer technology and communication networks. Thus the ECPA in the domestic venue into three parts: 1) Wiretap Act, 2) Stored Communications Act, and 3) The Pen Register Act.

- Types of Communication
- **Wire Communication:** Any communication containing the human voice that travels at some point across a wired medium such as radio, satellite or cable.
- Oral Communication:
- Electronic Communication

1. **The Wiretap Act:** For Information see Wiretap Act
2. **The Stored Communications Act:** For information see Stored Communications Act
3. **The Pen Register Act:** For information see Pen Register Act

(1994) Driver's Privacy Protection Act

The DPPA was passed in response to states selling motor vehicle records to private industry. These records contained personal information such as name, address, phone number, SSN, medical information, height, weight, gender, eye color, photograph and date of birth. In 1994, Congress passed the Driver's Privacy Protection (DPPA), 18 U. S. C. §§ 2721-2725, to cease this activity.

(1999) Gramm-Leach-Bliley Act

-This act authorizes widespread sharing of personal information by financial institutions such as banks, insurers, and investment companies. The GLBA permits sharing of personal information between companies joined together or affiliated as well as those companies unaffiliated. To protect privacy, the act requires a variety of agencies such as the SEC, FTC, etc. to establish "appropriate standards for the financial institutions subject to their jurisdiction" to "insure security and confidentiality of customer records and information" and "protect against unauthorized access" to this information. 15 U. S. C. § 6801

(2002) Homeland Security Act

Passed by Congress in 2002, the Homeland Security Act, 6 U. S. C. § 222, consolidated 22 federal agencies into what is commonly known today as the Department of Homeland Security (DHS). The HSA, also created a Privacy Office under the DoHS. The Secretary of Homeland Security must "appoint a senior official to assume primary responsibility for privacy policy." This privacy official's responsibilities include but are not limited to: ensuring compliance with the Privacy Act of 1974, evaluating "legislative and regulatory proposals involving the collection, use, and disclosure of personal information by the Federal Government", while also preparing an annual report to Congress.

(2004) Intelligence Reform and Terrorism Prevention Act

This Act mandates that intelligence be "provided in its most shareable form" that the heads of intelligence agencies and federal departments "promote a culture of information sharing." The IRTPA also sought to establish protection of privacy and civil liberties by setting up a five-member Privacy and Civil Liberties Oversight Board. This Board offers advice to both the President of the United States and the entire executive branch of the Federal Government concerning its actions to ensure that the branch's information sharing policies are adequately protecting privacy and civil liberties.

Legal enactments – examples

Great Britain

The Computer Misuse Act 1990 enacted by Great Britain on 29 June 1990, and which came into force on 29 August 1990, is an example of one of the earliest of such legal enactments. This Act was enacted with an express purpose of making "provision for securing computer material against unauthorized access or modification." Certain major provisions of the Computer Misuse Act 1990 relate to:

- "unauthorized access to computer materials",
- "unauthorized access with intent to commit or facilitate the commission of further offences", and
- "unauthorized modification of computer material."

The impact of the Computer Misuse Act 1990 has been limited and with the adoption of the Council of Europe adopts its Convention on Cyber-Crime, it has been indicated that amending legislation would be introduced in parliamentary session 2004–05 in order to rectify possible gaps in its coverage, which are many.

The CMA 1990 has many weaknesses; the most notable is its inability to cater for, or provide suitable protection against, a host of high tech attacks/crimes which have become more prevalent in the last decade. Certain attacks such as DDOS and BOTNET attacks can not be effectively brought to justice under the CMA. This act has been under review for a number of years. Computer crimes such as electronic theft are usually prosecuted in the UK under the legislation that caters for traditional theft (Theft Act 1968), because the CMA is so ineffective.

INDIA

An example of information technology law is India's Information Technology Act, 2000, which was substantially amended in 2008. The IT Act, 2000 came into force on 17 October 2000. This Act applies to whole of India, and its provisions also apply to any offense or contravention, committed even outside the territorial jurisdiction of Republic of India, by any person irrespective of his nationality. In order to attract provisions of this Act, such an offence or contravention should involve a computer, computer system, or computer network located in India. The IT Act 2000 provides an extraterritorial applicability to its provisions by virtue of section 1(2) read with section 75. This Act has 90 sections.

India's The Information Technology Act 2000 has tried to assimilate legal principles available in several such laws (relating to information technology) enacted earlier in several other countries, as also various guidelines pertaining to information technology law. The Act gives legal validity to electronic contracts, recognition of electronic signatures. This is a modern legislation which makes acts like hacking, data theft, spreading of virus, identity theft, defamation (sending offensive messages) pornography, child pornography, cyber terrorism, a criminal offence. The Act is supplemented by a number of rules which includes rules for, cyber cafes, electronic service delivery, data security, blocking of websites. It also has rules for observance of due diligence by internet intermediaries (ISP's, network service providers, cyber cafes, etc.). Any person affected by data theft, hacking, spreading of viruses can apply for compensation from Adjudicator appointed under Section 46 as well as file a criminal complaint. Appeal from adjudicator lies to Cyber Appellate Tribunal.

Digital evidence collection and cyber forensics remain at a very nascent stage in India with few experts and less than adequate infrastructure. In recent cases, Indian Judiciary has recognized that tampering with digital evidence is very easy.

Other

Many Asian and Middle Eastern nations use any number of combinations of code-based regulation (one of Lessig's four methods of net regulation) to block material that their governments have deemed inappropriate for their citizens to view. PRC, Saudi Arabia and Iran are three examples of nations that have achieved high degrees of success in regulating their citizens' access to the Internet.

Electronic signature laws

- Australia - *Electronic Transactions Act 1999* (Cth) (also note that there is State and Territory mirror legislation)
- Costa Rica - Digital Signature Law 8454 (2005)
- European Union - Electronic Signature Directive (1999/93/EC)
- Mexico - E-Commerce Act [2000]
- U. S. - Digital Signature And Electronic Authentication Law
- U. S. - Electronic Signatures in Global and National Commerce Act
- U. S. - Government Paperwork Elimination Act (GPEA)
- U. S. - Uniform Commercial Code (UCC)
- U. S. - Uniform Electronic Transactions Act - adopted by 46 states
- UK - s. 7 Electronic Communications Act 2000

Information technology law

1. Florida Electronic Security Act
2. Illinois Electronic Commerce Security Act
3. Texas Penal Code - Computer Crimes Statute
4. Maine Criminal Code - Computer Crimes
5. Singapore Electronic Transactions Act
6. Malaysia Computer Crimes Act
7. Malaysia Digital Signature Act
8. UNCITRAL Model Law on Electronic Commerce
9. Information Technology Act 2000 of India
10. Thailand Computer Crimes Act B. E. 2550

Information Technology Guidelines

1. ABA Digital Signature Guidelines
2. United States Office of Management and Budget

Enforcement agencies

The Information Technology Laws of various countries, and / or their criminal laws generally stipulate enforcement agencies, entrusted with the task of enforcing the legal provisions and requirements.

United States Federal Agencies

Many United States federal agencies oversee the use of information technology. Their regulations are promulgated in theCode of Federal Regulations of the United States.

Over 25 U. S. federal agencies have regulations concerning the use of digital and electronic signatures.

India

A live example of such an enforcement agency is Cyber Crime Police Station, Bangalore, India's first exclusive Cyber Crime enforcement agency.

- Other examples of such enforcement agencies include:
- Cyber Crime Investigation Cell of India's Mumbai Police.
- *Cyber Crime Police Station* of the state Government of Andhra Pradesh, India. This Police station has jurisdiction over the entire state of Andhra Pradesh, and functions from the Hyderabad city.
- In South India, the Crime Branch of Criminal Investigation Department, in Tamil Nadu, India, has a Cyber Crime Cell atChennai.
- In East India, Cyber Crime Cells have been set up by the Kolkata Police as well as the Criminal Investigation Department, West Bengal.

INFORMATION TECHNOLOGY LAWYER

An information technology attorney is a professional who handles a variety of legal matters related to IT. The attorney gets involved in drafting, negotiating, and interpreting agreements in the areas of software licensing and maintenance, IT consulting, e-commerce, web site hosting and development, and telecommunications agreements, as well as handling dispute resolution and assisting with the client's Internet domain name portfolio. An information technology attorney works with engineering, IT, and other business units and ensures that customer information gathered by company is collected, stored and used in compliance with privacy policies and applicable laws.

Duties also include providing high quality, specialized and practical advice in business-to-business and business-to-consumer arrangements and advising on issues like IT outsourcing arrangements, software and hardware supply and implementation agreements. An information technology attorney contracts for web site developers and consultants in relation to on-line projects. Provides support and maintains confidentiality/know how agreements. Contracts for Internet service providers and data protection advice. An information technology attorney should have a JD degree or an LL. M degree with admission to the local state bar.

Quotations

- "In Cyberspace, the First Amendment is a local ordinance."

  — John Perry Barlow, quoted by Mitchell Kapor in the foreword to *The Big Dummy's Guide to the Internet*
- "National borders aren't even speed bumps on the information superhighway."

  — Tim May, *signature*, from 1996

Digital signature

A digital signature is a mathematical scheme for demonstrating the authenticity of a digital message or document. A valid digital signature gives a recipient reason to believe that the message was created by a known sender, that the sender cannot deny having sent the message (authentication and non-repudiation), and that the message was not altered in transit (integrity). Digital signatures are commonly used for software distribution, financial transactions, and in other cases where it is important to detect forgery or tampering.

ETHICAL AND LEGAL IMPLICATIONS OF THE RISKS OF MEDICAL TOURISM FOR PATIENTS

Medical tourism involves patients' intentional travel to privately obtain medical care in another country Outflows of patients are reported to be increasing as they seek more accessible, affordable or unrestricted care elsewhere., Patients are travelling to a growing list of international destinations to obtain an array of procedures, ranging from those with low-to-high risk of complication or other negative outcomes. While there are few quantitative studies of complication rates associated with this practice, researchers examining outbound medical tourism from Oman found that 15% of 45 surveyed medical tourists experienced complications following treatment abroad, while a survey of the British Association of Plastic, Reconstructive and Aesthetic Surgery found that 37% of members had seen patients with complications resulting from medical tourism. Complications are only one type of health and safety risk to which medical tourists may be exposed.

Various forms of risk are commonly associated with medical tourism. Medical tourists who fly abroad are thought to be at heightened risk for deep vein thrombosis or pulmonary embolism owing to long-distance air travel following surgery. There is also concern that medical tourists are at risk of exposure to blood-borne infection due to inadequate blood collection, screening and storage protocols in destination countries. Individuals travelling for organ transplantation in particular may experience higher rates of severe infectious complications because of inadequate screening protocols abroad. Concern has also been raised that medical tourists may transmit infections to their home countries, demonstrated through the spread of New Delhi metallo-beta-lactamase 1 (NDM 1) to the home countries of patients who had been treated abroad.

Numerous researchers express concern about the quality of medical care available in some medical tourism facilities, though evidence to support many of these concerns is lacking. Although some facilities are accredited by such organisations as Joint Commission International and Accreditation Canada, much uncertainty exists regarding the value of accreditation as an indicator of high-quality care. Additional concern exists about the facilities' abilities to meet widely acknowledged quality indicators. For example, medical tourism can disrupt continuity of care and result in gaps in documentation of patients' medical history. As a result, medical tourists may lack adequate access to follow-up once back home owing to documentation gaps and resulting liability concerns held by physicians. Another area of quality concern pertains to the capacity of medical tourists to make informed decisions in the face of limited information about hospital quality, surgical outcomes and risks and complications.

Research about medical tourism is nascent. Empirical evidence regarding health and safety risks facing medical tourists is limited. To date, consideration of this issue in the literature is dominated by speculation and reports of individual cases and small case series and lacks meaningful input from clinicians and others with specific expertise in issues of patient health and safety. Much of what is known about the risks potentially faced by medical tourists comes from news media reports. For example, a Canadian newspaper series described infections resulting from medical tourists' pursuit of plastic surgery abroad, and an American newspaper report noted the corrective treatment required by a patient who obtained plastic surgery abroad. Turner reviewed 26 news reports which focused on the deaths of patients following cosmetic or bariatric surgery abroad. Among other important findings, it was discovered that medical tourists' postoperative deaths occurred across high-income, middle-income and low-income destination nations, and not only in countries commonly thought to have lax safety standards.

Canadian patients are known to travel to a range of medical tourism destinations, both for procedures that are covered in the public Medicare system (eg, orthopaedic surgeries) and those that are not (eg, dental care)., Recent research shows that they are often motivated to seek medical care abroad out of a desire to save costs on procedures not covered by Medicare, access care faster than if they were assigned to a domestic wait-list and obtain procedures that are not commonly available or not available at all in Canada. Acknowledging this outbound patient flow, we held a focus group among safety experts in the province of British Columbia (BC) to explore their views concerning risks that patients from the province may be exposed to by engaging in medical tourism. This constitutes the first scholarly attempt to consult with this stakeholder group about medical tourism. Herein, we report on focus group findings, linking these empirical insights to existing ethical and legal issues associated with medical tourism. We examine ethical and legal implications associated with the findings for two reasons. First, there is a growing body of ethical and legal scholarship about medical tourism to draw upon when addressing the practical implications of this practice., Second, while participants specifically commented on the use of medical tourism by patients from BC, Canada, engagement with the wider ethics and legal literatures assists with 'scaling up' the findings and demonstrating their transferability to other home countries for medical tourists.

METHODS

The purpose of this study was to gain the first empirical insights into health and safety professionals' perspectives on the risks of outbound medical tourism by Canadians, with a focus on the province of BC, and to begin considering appropriate interventions to secure these patients' health and safety. Our research team was made up of health services, ethics and legal scholars with established research interests in medical tourism, as well as an independent patient health and safety professional from BC who served as a knowledge end-user collaborator on the study. To accomplish our purpose, we held a focus group in September 2011 in Vancouver, BC with professionals representing distinct domains of expertise. Prior to undertaking this research, approval for the study was received from the Office of Research Ethics at Simon Fraser University.

Recruitment

We aimed to have 6–10 representatives participate. We use the term 'representatives' to indicate that participants were invited to share their own perspectives and those of the organisations and agencies where they worked. As such, we sought out high-level representatives (eg, directors, managers, etc) to participate or recommend individuals from their respective organisations and agencies who would be well suited to attend the focus group. To begin recruiting, we first identified distinct domains of expertise that we wanted to be represented in the focus group based on a review of the health and safety issues commonly raised in medical tourism and the related domains of professional practice, relying heavily on the expertise of our knowledge end-user collaborator. We then conducted online searches to identify organisations and agencies relevant to these domains, identifying specific people who worked within them and sharing the outcomes of these searches with our knowledge end-user collaborator for input as well as confirmation of the relative importance of potential organisations and agencies. We next sent these individuals invitations to participate. If unable to attend, they were asked to recommend others with similar expertise whom we could invite. It was explained in the invitation that participants were not required to have extensive existing knowledge about medical tourism.

Twenty-nine representatives were invited to participate. Fifteen were unavailable or did not wish to participate. Five did not respond to our invitation. Nine representatives accepted our invitation. Of this cohort, two withdrew prior to the focus group owing to changes in availability. The domains of expertise represented by the seven participants were tissue banking, blood safety, health records, organ transplantation, dental care, clinical ethics and infection control.

Data collection

The focus group ran for 4 h. Two facilitators guided the conversation while a note-taker recorded observations. It began with introductions followed by an overview of the goals. A discussion followed, guided by the questions: what is medical tourism and what do you think are some of the main patient health and safety issues associated with medical tourism. The facilitators then gave a brief overview of the key issues discussed in the medical tourism literature to ensure that participants were working from a common understanding of key issues. Participants next discussed what they understood to be the implications of the health and safety risks they had previously identified. The facilitators then gave another brief overview, this time focused on published case reports of negative health outcomes stemming from medical tourism. A final discussion ensued, which focused on identifying interventions for addressing health and safety risks.

Analysis

A digital recording of the focus group was transcribed and thematic analysis was applied. Thematic analysis involves identifying trends and identifying linkages between these trends and issues identified in the existing literature. In undertaking analysis, we first undertook an independent transcript review. Following this, a team discussion was held to identify the dominant health and safety risks identified. After reaching consensus on these risks and their scope, the data relating to each were extracted into separate word processing files for further review. The extracted data were then used to shape the structure of the results section and inform our discussion of the links between the findings and the existing knowledge on medical tourism, with a particular focus on the ethical and legal implications.

Results

Five dominant health and safety risks for outbound medical tourists from BC were identified: (1) complications; (2) specific concerns regarding organ transplantation; (3) transmission of antibiotic-resistant organisms; (4) (dis) continuity of medical documentation and (5) (un)informed decision-making. In this section, we discuss each of them separately. Verbatim quotations from participants are italicised.

Complications

Recognising that patients can face complications when obtaining medical care at home, participants had particular concerns about complication risk as a result of medical procedures obtained abroad. One participant who had seen many severe complications following medical tourism explained that 'when it goes wrong it really goes wrong'. The risk of complications was thought to be dependent on the procedure obtained and the patient's existing health status. For example, several participants discussed the risks particular to patients managing chronic disease with complex medical histories or pharmacological regimes. It was thought that, in these cases, there could be a greater risk of complications: "given the demographic... many [medical tourists]...have some chronic disease management that they're dealing with...and it's like oh my God [the risks they could face]."

Participants were concerned about the demands the BC healthcare system faced as a result of treating complications incurred through medical tourism. They expressed uncertainty over "the support for them (medical tourists) on their return and...is our health care system then responsible for the sequelae of them undergoing the procedure somewhere else if they develop a complication?" Many participants had concerns over the potential demands on clinicians and health and safety professionals for providing such care. It was also noted that medical tourists experiencing complications could be embarrassed about their situation. As a result, they might be reluctant to seek care upon return home, increasing their risk for continued negative health outcomes. "Yeah they might be feeling really bad and they've got an infection...and they're feeling really stupid [for going abroad] and it's like 'oh it might go away, I'll...try home remedies' or something and by the time they get to the medical care then it's out of control." Participants expressed concern that delays in treating complications might require additional resources from the BC health system.

Specific concerns regarding organ transplantation

Concerns emerged regarding transmission of infectious disease via transplantation, which was raised as an issue distinct from complications associated with other surgeries. Many participants expressed uncertainty regarding the safe acquisition of organs abroad and selection criteria for donors, indicating that non-industry-based information is lacking. It was noted that "occasionally we can know that they're [a medical tourist is] doing this [planning to go abroad] 'cause they announce it in advance, and…they're required to get vaccinated, the whole Hepatitis range and all these things and that's because they're not screening the donors [abroad]." However, in most cases, there is no warning of a patient's intent to go abroad for transplantation and so there is no opportunity to encourage vaccination before departure.

Because of the unclear organ screening standards and a lack of information about organ provenance and infection rates at facilities, individuals going abroad for transplant are at risk of exposure to infectious diseases. Participants were particularly concerned about the impacts of organ transplant patients' acquired infections on the BC health system upon return home, and the potential public health implications of infection spread. They pondered policy formulation in this area, recognising that "how we deal with…patients who may be coming back into our hospitals with infections and…what the precautions are" are key concerns that need to be addressed when creating domestic protocols for addressing this issue.

Transmission of antibiotic-resistant organisms

Participants were aware that some medical tourists from BC had indeed been exposed to antibiotic-resistant organisms while abroad. This poses a risk to public health upon return home. One participant noted that she had "become aware of as an issue of…patients returning from foreign countries… carrying some really interesting bugs." Treating patients with 'really interesting bugs' is challenging, wherein health and safety officials need to identify unusual strains of organism that they might not have previously encountered, which can delay treatment.

Participants discussed the challenges of policy formulation to address the risk of the spread of antibiotic-resistant organisms locally from outbound medical tourism. They focused on the costs of screening, isolation and testing for antibiotic-resistant organisms after medical tourists sought treatment upon return home. A participant noted that "if you write a policy that says anybody who's been admitted to a hospital abroad needs to be isolated when they're brought into your hospital, that has huge implications, and/ or if you would say 'well I'm going to do a screening swab on every single one of these patients whose been hospitalized abroad before I admit them to my hospital', huge lab costs." Agreeing that effective policy responses will be difficult to create, participants stressed the important role played by hospital infection control protocols in BC, such as hand washing, to limit organism spread.

(Dis)continuity of medical documentation

Participants learnt from clinicians and other front-line providers that patients returning from medical care abroad often bring back incomplete medical records or no documentation of the care they received. Although some clinicians have requested results and records from international medical providers, destination facilities were often uncooperative. "One letter [about a patient's treatment abroad]...was sent to me blacked out... from a Mexican clinic and they just said 'how dare you ask me for this'."" Participants suggested that limited medical documentation provided to medical tourists could reflect a low standard of care abroad, masking shortcomings.

Participants agreed that patients typically understand it is their right to request records to bring home with them when engaging in medical tourism. However, they indicated that patients rarely do so, even though it would be reasonable for them to insist: "I want to see my chart, I want to see... I'm going back to wherever I live, I want to take my stuff with me in case something goes wrong." Participants also did not believe patients had enough health literacy to question why a destination facility would not take their medical histories, something they reported was common. Meanwhile, failure by clinicians to obtain this information can result in complications or other negative outcomes. In effect, "the procedure [becomes] compromised... because they [were not asked for] a health history... So it kind of goes back to that health literacy point."

(Un)informed decision-making

Participants discussed at length issues of informed decision-making. They generally felt medical tourists were uninformed about risks they may face abroad, as well as factors they should consider when selecting a facility. Participants characterised uninformed decision-making as a significant problem among medical tourists, particularly among those who obtained dental or cosmetic procedures. They posited that for some patients, the decision to obtain a procedure abroad is made with minimal thought. "We...are really concerned that there's a lack of understanding [by patients] and...it's driven by [the appeal of low] cost." It was also reported that patients' decisions to go abroad were sometimes made hastily. Participants characterised such decision-making as risky, in part because patients' satisfaction is evaluated retroactively based on outcomes. "It's interesting because their criteria for saying 'it was a dumb decision [to have medical care abroad]' is only based on the consequences."

Participants suggested that if medical tourists do not fully understand the risks of the procedure they plan to purchase, it is questionable whether they are in a position to give informed consent. A participant noted that "sixty percent of Canadians have a hard time meeting one of the components of consent, understanding... And so a certain assumption around their capacity to understand [is made]..." It was suggested that patients may not know the right questions to ask to ensure that a facility implements the correct safety controls. "Do [patients] actually ask things like infection rates at these facilities?... We have best practice guidelines in processing medical devices, [but] what's the standard in these countries?" Participants were also concerned that patients' decision-making capacities may have begun to lessen in the face of *upsell* messages used by facilities abroad, encouraging them to purchase additional procedures.

Discussion

The findings reveal that the representatives we spoke with have a number of concerns regarding the risks that can confront outbound medical tourists from BC. Many of the risks they identified are discussed in the existing literature. This is an important empirical finding as it demonstrates that those with expertise in infection control, blood safety, clinical ethics and other fields associated with patient health and safety confirm the relevance of risks previously hypothesised about in the medical tourism literature.

Some issues did not receive as much attention in the focus group as we may have expected relative to their coverage in the medical tourism literature. First, there was limited discussion about the experimental procedures (eg, stem cell therapies) pursued abroad and their associated risks despite significant coverage in the popular and academic literatures., This may reflect the participants' limited exposure to medical tourists who have obtained such procedures. Second, although legal liability is often discussed in relation to risks inherent in medical tourism, , , it received relatively little consideration by the participants. Although there was no health law representative, we expected more explicit discussion of this issue given the centrality of legal liability to debates around medical tourism. Third, although concern about the quality of care received abroad was discussed, this topic received minimal attention relative to others. This may have been because health and safety issues are thought to be implicitly about care quality. Fourth, although health and safety risks are sometimes couched around larger health equity concerns and, in particular, in destination nations, , these concerns did not emerge in participants' discussions. This may reflect participants' lack of awareness of the health equity debates that surround medical tourism.

The findings offer new insights into current debates concerning the health and safety risks in medical tourism. One of these pertains to participants' identification of health system limitations to addressing concerns. For example, the lack of existing protocols for treating patients treated abroad and the prohibitively high costs of and legal barriers to putting patients into isolation who had acquired antibiotic-resistant organisms were identified as limitations. Another new insight is participants' concern that the general lack of health literacy will lead to outbound medical tourists ultimately experiencing health and safety risks, a point that broadens existing concern about medical tourists' lack of reliable access to third-party information about facilities and surgeons abroad.

Ethical and legal implications

Some issues raised by participants' parallel legal and bioethics scholars' concerns with addressing the health system and public health effects of individual medical tourists' decisions., The concern, established in tort law, pertains to whether or not patients must assume the full costs of their decisions so that the repercussions are not unfairly borne by others. Such concerns are heightened in a universal healthcare system like Canada's where provincial/territorial budgets are fixed and health resources are shared by all. This egalitarian approach to access raises the issue of fairness in relation to addressing complications or the outcomes of other risks experienced owing to medical tourism. This is because Canadian citizens will be burdened by these collectively imposed costs without accessing the individual benefits of engaging in medical tourism. This same ethico-legal concern has been raised in other home countries for medical tourists with public healthcare systems, including the UK., Demonstrating an awareness of this concern, participants questioned the extent of their responsibility for addressing negative outcomes experienced by outbound medical tourists, given these patients' individual decisions to access care abroad.

The potential for collective effects emerging from individual patients' decisions to go abroad for private medical care emerged from participants' discussions of the risks of infection spread due to medical tourism. Complications stemming from treating infections may pose costs for the domestic healthcare system and could take the form of a low-probability, but high-impact, event that would require isolating many patients or even quarantining a hospital. Participants expressed frustration at the lack of good solutions to these problems at the hospital level and, in particular, their inability to quarantine, test or even identify all medical tourism patients. The solutions they offered focused on infection control measures, such as hand-washing procedures, which are not specific to addressing the health and safety risks posed by medical tourism in particular. They did, however, hint at system-level reforms such as limiting coverage for unauthorised transplant tourism or better regulation of medical tourism facilitators (eg, licensing, standardised training), both of which have analogues in the legal and bioethics literatures.,

Patient autonomy, including through informed consent, is a cornerstone of bioethics, and health law has been flagged as a concern for medical tourists., In the context of medical tourism, informed consent can be disrupted by misleading or incomplete information on websites, difficulties in obtaining information about success rates and the quality and standard of care in destination facilities., Participants echoed these existing concerns, adding that the limited health literacy among Canadians, coupled with inadequate access to accurate information, could heighten patients' inabilities to make an*informed* decision about medical tourism and ultimately to accept the risks of going abroad.

While obtaining informed consent for medical procedures is difficult under optimal considerations, the international dimension of medical tourism raises special concerns. Participants expressed that patients may not be aware of the risks of infectious diseases contracted abroad or that they will be unable to obtain medical records for foreign care; more generally, it was thought that medical tourists do not know what questions to ask to better understand their risks or, owing to well-recognised cognitive biases, fail to adequately appreciate these risks. Participants also expressed concern that obtaining information about the risks of specific treatments in particular facilities would be very difficult. This opacity is problematic because information on whether internationally accepted safety protocols are being followed is typically unavailable and patients may not be aware of the need to ask about these protocols or feel empowered to do so. Because of the multiple jurisdictions involved and lack of clarity in terms of which the jurisdiction's law applies in circumstances of medical tourism, effective legal solutions to these problems are difficult to establish, thereby placing pressure on patients' home healthcare systems, including health and safety professionals, to address them in an ad hoc fashion.

Recommendations

First, there is a need for more research about health and safety risks in medical tourism, including: quantifying risk occurrence and determining which negative outcomes are attributable to medical tourism. Second, protocols are needed to identify patients that have engaged in medical tourism, to treat these patients, as well as to enable infection control and containment procedures. Similarly, increased familiarity with destination country protocols is needed. Third, information about the risks of engaging in medical tourism needs to be effectively transmitted to potential medical tourists. As suggested by the participants, this can be achieved both by providing materials on the risks of medical tourism and improving the public's overall health literacy. Finally, action needs to be taken to address participants' and others' (eg, 25) concerns about discontinuities in medical documentation for medical tourists. For example, consideration could be given to developing a template that destination country physicians complete as a precondition of treatment.

Study limitations

First, a limitation of focus groups is that particular individuals may dominate. Although we encouraged all participants to engage in talk, two spoke most often. Second, we are aware that some health and safety domains were not represented. For example, there was no care quality representative or individual from the province's Ministry of Health despite efforts to recruit both. Third, reliance on a single focus group with participants in BC limits generalisability. However, as this is a qualitative study, generalisability is not a goal. Instead, we seek transferability, accomplishing this by providing details others need to assess the relevance of the findings to their specific contexts.

Conclusion

We spoke with seven BC-based participants with considerable expertise in key patient health and safety domains. Participants identified five main health and safety risks associated with outbound medical tourism by BC patients. Concern was expressed that medical tourism might have unintended and undesired effects upon provincial/territorial healthcare systems. In particular, participants noted that individual choices of medical tourists could have significant public consequences if domestic healthcare facilities must expend resources treating postoperative complications of medical tourists. They also expressed concern that medical tourists returning home with infections, particularly antibiotic-resistant infections, could place healthcare providers such as themselves and other patients at risk of exposure to infections that are refractory to standard treatment regimens and pose significant risks. There was considerable uncertainty over how such risks should be addressed and mitigated. This uncertainty suggests that clinicians, patients, healthcare administrators and other involved parties are likely to gain from a public dialogue about developing policy responses to both the risks and benefits associated with medical tourism, not only within Canada but in all countries facing outflows of medical tourists.

Bibliography

- Abitzsch, Sven (1996). "Prospects of Space Tourism". Presented at the 9th European Aerospace Congress, Berlin. Hosted at Space Futures.
- Beaver, Allan (2002). *A Dictionary of Travel and Tourism Terminology*. Wallingford: CAB International. p. 313.
- China -the new number one tourism source market in the world".
- Griffiths, Ralph; Griffiths, G. E. (1772). "Pennant's Tour in Scotland in 1769". *The Monthly Review, Or, Literary Journal*(London: Printed for R. Griffiths) 46: 150. Retrieved 23 December 2011.
- Harper, Douglas. "tour (n.)". *Online Etymology Dictionary*. Retrieved 23 December 2011.
- Houlot, Arthur. (1961). Le Turisme et La Biblie. Revue l´Académie Internationale du Turisme. Monaco.
- Hunziker, W; Krapf, K (1942). *Grundriß Der Allgemeinen Fremdenverkehrslehre* (in German). Zurich: Polygr. Verl.OCLC 180109383.
- International Association of Scientific Experts in Tourism."The AIEST, its character and aims".
- International tourism challenged by deteriorating global economy". *UNWTO World Tourism Barometer* (World Tourism Organization) 7 (1). January 2009.
- International tourism receipts surpass US$ 1 trillion in 2011" (Press release). UNWTO. 7 May 2012.
- Jonathan Mitchel (2009). "Value chain analysis and poverty reduction at scale". Overseas Development Institute.
- Korstanje, M. 2007 The Origin and meaning of Tourism: Etymological study.E Review of Tourism Research. Vol 5 (5): 100-108. Texas A&M University, US
- Leiper, Neil (1983). An Etimology of Tourism. Annals of Tourism Research (2). New York: Pergamon Press. Volume 10
- Manber, Jeffrey (2009). *Selling Peace: Inside the Soviet Conspiracy that Transformed the U.S. Space Program*. Burlington, Ont.: Apogee.
- Theobald, William F. (1998). *Global Tourism* (2nd ed.). Oxford [England]: Butterworth–Heinemann. pp. 6–7.
- UNWTO World Tourism Barometer Interim Update". *UNWTO World Tourism Barometer* (World Tourism Organization). August 2010. Retrieved 17 November 2011.

- UNWTO World Tourism Barometer". *UNWTO World Tourism Barometer* (World Tourism Organization) 11 (1). January 2013. Retrieved 2013-04-09.
- World's top destinations by international tourism receipts". *World Tourism Barometer.* UNWTO. May 2012. Retrieved 16 June 2012.
- Ahmed, Saqib Iqbal (27 October 2009)."GSI Commerce to buy Retail Convergence for $180 mln". Reuters. Retrieved 6 April2013.
- Amazon buys Diapers. com parent in $545 mln deal. MarketWatch. Retrieved 21 December 2012.
- Amazon Buys Zappos; The Price is $928m, not $847m. TechCrunch. 22 July 2009. Retrieved 21 December 2012.
- AppWrapper Volume 1 Issue 3 Ships (press release).
- Benckendorff, Pierre J.; Sheldon, P. J.; Fesenmaier, D. R. (2014). *Tourism Information Technology (Second Edition).* Wallingford, UK: CABI. ISBN 978-1-7806-4185-0.
- Cantoni, Lorenzo; Xiang, Zheng (2013). *Information and Communication Technologies in Tourism 2013. Berlin – Heidelberg: Springer. ISBN 978-3-642-36309-2.*
- *Caperna A., Integrating ICT into Sustainable Local Policies. ISBN 9781615209293*
- *Diane Wang: Rounding up the "Ant" Heroes. Sino Foreign Management. Retrieved 3 September 2011.*
- *eBay acquires PayPal. Investor. eBay. Retrieved 21 December 2012.*
- *Egger, Roman (2005). Grundlagen Des Etourism: Informations- Und Kommunikationstechnologien Im Tourismus (in German). Aachen: Shaker. ISBN 978-3-8322-3663-2.*
- *Egger, Roman; Buhalis, Dimitrios (2008). Etourism Case Studies: Management and Marketing Issues. Amsterdam [etc.]: Butterworth-Heinemann. ISBN 978-0-7506-8667-9.*
- *FIrst Electronic Stamps Being Put to Test. Sunday Business. 6 April 1998. Retrieved 16 July 2013.*
- *Good Practice in Information and Communication Technology for Education. Asian Development Bank, 2009.*

Index